DATE DUE

DE 23 '94			
NO 27'00			
FE 11 '10			

DEMCO 38-296

Sugar's Secrets

Race and the
Erotics of Cuban
Nationalism

Sugar's Secrets

Race and the

Erotics of Cuban

Nationalism

Vera M. Kutzinski

A. James Arnold, Series Editor
New World Studies

UNIVERSITY PRESS
OF VIRGINIA

Charlottesville and London

THE UNIVERSITY PRESS OF VIRGINIA
Copyright © 1993 by the Rector and Visitors
of the University of Virginia

First published 1993

Library of Congress Cataloging-in-Publication Data

Kutzinski, Vera M., 1956-
  Sugar's secrets : race and the erotics of Cuban nationalism / Vera
M. Kutzinski.
     p.   cm. — (New world studies)
  Includes bibliographical references and index.
  ISBN 0-8139-1466-3. — ISBN 0-8139-1467-1 (pbk.)
  1. Cuban literature—20th century—History and criticism.
  2. Pluralism (Social sciences) in literature.   3. Racially mixed people in literature.
  4. Nationalism—Cuba.   5. Cuba—Popular culture.   6. Pluralism (Social sciences)—Cuba.   7. National characteristics, Cuban.   I. Title.   II. Series.
  PQ7378.K87   1993
  860.9'355—dc20   93-7644
                                                                        CIP

Publication of this volume was made possible in part
with the assistance of the Frederick Hilles Publication
Fund of Yale University.

Printed in the United States of America

for Jenny, Joan, and bine

Toi, mon poète d'avenir, et toi mon amant de demain, et toi mon ami des révoltes futures, qu'as-tu fait de nous femmes dans tes gestes et tes paroles d'aujourd'hui? Où sont les femmes dans ton *Bois d'ébène,* Roumain? Où sont-elles dans ton *West Indies,* Guillén? Que faison-nous Damas dans tes *Pigments?*

You, my poet of the future, and you, my lover of tomorrow, and you my friend of future revolts, what have you done with us women in your words and gestures today? Where are the women in your *Bois d'ébène* (Ebony wood), Roumain? Where are they in your *West Indies, Ltd.,* Guillén? What do we do, Damas, in your *Pigments?*

—Daniel Maximin, *L'Isolé soleil* (*Lone Sun*)

SIN AZUCAR NO HAY PAIS

Without sugar there is no country

—Nicolás Guillén, *El diario que a diario* (*The Daily Daily*)

Contents

Illustrations

Preface

What sparked my interest in Cuba some years ago when I was still a graduate student was a fascination with Afro-Antilleanism's cross-racial poetics and, moreover, with the racial diversity of those who rendered their "Cubanness" in literary form, mostly poetry. For, with the exception of very few individuals, those who wrote most of this *poesía de lo negro*—which loosely translates as "poetry of blackness"—were not, as it were, of color. To a white African-Americanist like myself, one who is also a European (though, for better or worse, a rather Americanized one at this point), this literary practice was attractive: The idea of cultural *mestizaje*, or transculturation, seemed to offer a way of legitimating my own critical enterprise and of justifying my intellectual and emotional investments in difference and otherness. Here, then, was an opportunity for me to remove, conceptually at least, the stigma of being a cultural outsider. Or so, at least, I thought.

I quickly became aware, however, that it was deemed either naive or politically improper in Afro-Hispanist circles to take seriously the kind of crossing of racial-cultural boundaries that most Afro-Antillean poetry represents. According to some, anyone trying to see *mestizaje* more benignly as a process of cross-cultural exchange would participate, however unwittingly, in the liquidation of "blackness." With most of my critical paradigms heavily invested in what Wilson Harris has termed "the cross-cultural imagination," I found myself once again between ideological positions. While there is nothing particularly glamorous about such in-betweenness, it has certain benefits in the end. It made me realize that identity, including my own, is always compromised. It is at best an open question, something to be negotiated and renegotiated across all kinds of divides on an almost-daily basis. There are no safety zones of comfortable assumptions to which one might retreat in times of crisis, not even for those who enjoy relative social and economic privileges.

This book grew out of a very personal need to take a long, hard second look at the cross-cultural paradigms that had so intrigued me, not in order to dismiss them summarily but to understand exactly how they function in specific contexts. My critical practice has changed accordingly, as have the questions I ask of myself. One of those questions is: In what concrete ways does the encounter with other cultures alter the ways in which I think of myself and the ways in which I have been trained to construct an identity in different personal and professional settings? What follows is implicitly an attempt at engaging this question and similar ones.

There are countless ways in which the writing of this book has benefitted from the efforts of a great many people—colleagues, friends, and family on both sides of the Atlantic—at times unbeknownst to them. I especially thank Roberto González Echevarría, Enrique Pupo Walker, Antonio Benítez Rojo, Gustavo Pérez Firmat, Jay and Lois Wright, A. James Arnold, Benjamin Bennett, Kimberly Benston, Kathleen Balutansky, David Dabydeen, Hazel V. Carby, Christopher Miller, Gerald D. Jaynes, Rudolph P. Byrd, Jacqueline Goldsby, Bill Lowe, Robert von Hallberg, Alan and Julia Thomas, Günter Lenz, Klaus Milich, Reinhard Doerries, and, last but not least, my editor Cathie Brettschneider for encouragement and sustenance offered in so many different shapes and forms, from specific criticisms and suggestions to pep talks. Whatever my particular disagreements with the Latin Americanists among them, I remain deeply grateful for all their inspiration and support. Bill Johnson González cheerfully proofread the entire manuscript with considerably more concentration than I could have mustered at that stage of the game. Any residual errors are of course solely my own responsibility.

I may never have reached that stage had it not been for the generous support of the National Endowment for the Humanities, which provided a Summer Fellowship that allowed me to complete my research on the Afro-Antillean movement. The Mellon Foundation, the Whitney Humanities Center at Yale, and Yale's Morse

Junior Faculty Fellowship gave me the time I needed to make this book what I wanted it to be. A John F. Enders Faculty Research Assistance Grant from the Yale Graduate School aided in the preparation of the illustrations for publication.

My most profound gratitude goes to Shamoon Zamir, who read every single draft of the manuscript with an admirable degree of patience and rigor. The spirited debates that ensued from those readings, though at times rather aggravating to me, were among the most challenging of intellectual exchanges I can remember in recent years. Another, very special kind of debt I owe to Joan Korenman, Sabine Bröck, and Jennifer Alleyne-Johnson, who kept reminding me, gently but firmly, of my responsibilities as a woman in academia. I trust that they will continue to do so. Finally, I salute my brother Kai and his wife, Sonja, for stripping me, in one fell swoop, of any illusions I may have had about my "Germanness" by marking my place at their wedding banquet with a card that read, plainly, "American sister."

V.M.K.
New Haven, Conn.

Acknowledgments

From *Poesía completa y prosa selecta* by Luis Palés Matos. Copyright (c) 1978 by Bibliotéca Ayacucho, Caracas. Reprinted by permission.

From *Tuntún de pasa y grifería: Poemas afroantillanos* by Luis Palés Matos. Copyright (c) 1937 by Bibliotéca de Autores Puertorriqueños. Reprinted by permission.

From *Obra poética*, Vol. 1, by Nicolás Guillén. Copyright (c)1974 by Nicolás Guillén and the Instituto Cubano del Libro, Editorial Arte y Litertura. Reprinted by permission of Angel Augier and the Fundación Nicolás Guillén.

From *Orbita de la poesía afrocubana* by Ramón Guirao, Copyright (c) 1983 by Ucar, García y Cía. Reprinted by permission of CENDA, The Cuban National Center for Authors' Rights.

From *La zafra* by Agustín Acosta. Copyright (c) 1926 by Editorial Minerva. Reprinted by permission of CENDA, The Cuban National Center for Authors' Rights.

From *Cuaderno de poesía negra* by Emilio Ballagas. Copyright (c) 1934 by Imprenta La Nueva, Santa Clara. Reprinted by permission of CENDA, The Cuban National Center for Authors' Rights.

From *Canción negra sin color* by Marcelino Arozarena. Copyright (c) 1966 by Contemporáneos. Reprinted by permission of CENDA, The Cuban National Center for Authors' Rights.

From *Poesía afroantillana y negrista* by Jorge Luis Morales. Copyright (c) 1976 by the University of Puerto Rico. Reprinted by permission.

From "Unseasonal Flowers: Nature and History in Plácido and Jean Toomer" by Vera M. Kutzinski. Copyright (c) 1990 by

Vera M. Kutzinski and the *Yale Journal of Criticism*. Reprinted by permission.

From the translation of "Majestad negra" by Luis Palés Matos in *Callaloo* 10, no. 2 (c) 1987 by Aníbal González Pérez and the Johns Hopkins University Press. Reprinted by permission.

From the translation of "Mujer nueva" and "El abuelo" by Nicolás Guillén in *Callaloo* 10, no. 2. Copyright (c) 1987 by Vera M. Kutzinski and the Johns Hopkins University Press. Reprinted by permission.

From Alfonso Camín, *Maracas y otros poemas*. Mexico: La Impresora Azteca, 1952. While every effort has been made to locate possible copyright owners of this text, we have been unable to do so.

Sirviente tratando de besar un busto by Víctor Patricio Landaluze. Reprinted from Adelaida de Juan, *Pintura cubana: temas y variaciones*. (c) 1980 by the Universidad Nacional Autónoma de México. Reprinted by permission.

Ingenio Buenavista by Eduardo Laplante, from *Los ingenios: Colección de vistas principales de azúcar de la Isla de Cuba,* 1857. Courtesy of the Library of Congress.

La mulata by Víctor Patricio Landaluze. Reprinted from Adelaida de Juan, *Pintura cubana: temas y variaciones*. Copyright (c) 1978 by UNEAC. Reprinted by permission of CENDA, The Cuban National Center for Authors' Rights.

From *Cuba en las marquillas cigarreras del siglo XIX* by Antonio Núñez Jiménez. Copyright (c) Antonio Núñez Jiménez and Ediciones Turísticas de Cuba, 1985. Reprinted by permission of CENDA, The Cuban National Center for Authors' Rights.

Sugar's Secrets

Race and the
Erotics of Cuban
Nationalism

Introduction

Cuban Color

El espíritu de Cuba es mestizo. Y del espíritu hacia la piel nos vendrá el color definitivo. Algún día se dirá, "color cubano."

Cuba's soul is a half-breed. And it is from the soul not the skin that we derive our definitive color. Some day it will be called "Cuban color."

—Nicolás Guillén, *Sóngoro cosongo*

> Pero si no puedo ser
> Negra, ni tampoco blanca,
> Entonces, alguna cosa
> Soy por el cruce de razas.
> Soy, por la mezcla de sangre,
> Un nuevo tipo: Mulata,
> Cincuenta por ciento negra,
> Cincuenta por ciento blanca.
>
> But if I can neither be
> Black nor white,
> Then I am something
> Because of the crossing of races.
> I am, because of my mixed blood,
> A new type: Mulata,
> Fifty percent black,
> Fifty percent white.

—Fortunato Vizcarrondo, "La mulata"

1

I

One of the turning points in Alejo Carpentier's *The Lost Steps* (*Los pasos perdidos*) (1953) is the narrator's encounter with the mestiza Rosario. As the bus carries the travelers ever deeper into the South American interior, the diarist's attention shifts from his exasperated efforts at remembering the opening paragraph of the *Quijote* to the physical appearance of the woman who will soon become his lover and muse.

From where I sat I could see a little less than half her face, with its high cheekbone under an eye slanting toward the temple and hidden under the emphatic arch of the eyebrow. It was a pure profile from brow to nose, but suddenly, below these proud, impassive features, the mouth turned full and sensual, with lean cheeks rising toward the ear, the strongly modeled lineaments set in a frame of thick black hair held in place, here and there, by celluloid combs. Several races had met in this woman: Indian in the hair and cheekbones, Mediterranean in brow and nose, Negro in the heavy shoulders and the breadth of hips. . . . There was no question but that this living sum of races had an aristocracy [*raza*] of her own.[1]

The initial withholding of Rosario's name underscores her symbolic function in a novel obsessed with cultural origins. For the narrator, as for Carpentier, she embodies the mixing of "the great races of the world, the most widely separated, the most divergent, those which for centuries had ignored the fact that they inhabited the same planet" (82 [148]). This allusion to the European discovery and conquest of America, appropriate to the novel's setting and to its diary form, clearly establishes the terms on which the narrator's ensuing romance with Rosario will be premised. Despite her mixed ancestry and the history of violence it implies, Rosario is systematically cast in the mythic role of native Other. The narrative makes every effort to erase history by identifying her with a landscape sentimentally privileged in its presumed lack of temporality. Significant in this regard is that Rosario's entrance into the novel is marked as a rebirth facilitated by the narrator himself: "The woman suddenly seemed to come to herself; she gave a scream, clutched me, and, almost inarticulate, begged us not to let her die again" (79 [145]). This symbolic act of fashioning a racial and sexual Other quite literally out of thin mountain air removes whatever historical particulars might have stood in the way of the narrator's identifying Rosario both with the landscape and with its native inhabitants: "she took on an ancestral silhouette that brought her much closer to these [the native Indian] women than to those whose blood, in generations past, had lightened her skin. I understood why this woman who was mine now had given me such a sense of *race* [*raza*] that day beside a mountain road when I saw her return from death" (173 [234]). As the novel's quest for origins progresses, Rosario "became more authentic, more real. . . Relationships became established between her flesh and the ground we were treading" (106–7 [171]). But exactly what those relationships are remains nebulous.

The subsequent death of Rosario's father functions as a further strategic divestment of historical bonds. It prefaces the first, frenzied sexual encounter between Rosario and the narrator. Although an obvious replay of the acts of violence, sexual and otherwise, associated with colonialism, their "rapid and brutal embrace, without caresses, more a struggle to crush, to overpower, than a pleasure-giving union" (152 [212]), is also, at least provisionally, validated as "natural," as belonging to an interior space undisturbed by historical power relations. The sole odious reminder of an exterior world is the Medusa-like head of a half-crazed, delirious (and presumably lesbian) Mouche, a synecdoche dangling grotesquely over the lovers who "were two, in another world" (152–53 [212]).

Given the narrator's highly ironic, yet self-assured, recasting of their frantic coupling in terms of conquest and domination—"I had sown myself beneath the down I had stroked with the hand of the master" (153 [212])—it is hardly surprising that Rosario would emerge from his embrace as "the woman who 'serves' the man in the noblest sense of the word" (154 [213]). This supposedly natural, native woman "without complications," who, the narrator believes, "would always be within the reach of [his] desire" (199 [260]), is so familiar a product of the colonial imagination that further detailing of the text's bluntly sexist and racist pronouncements, only occasionally qualified by a spurious rhetoric of mutuality, would amount to belaboring the obvious. But while nothing is gained, ultimately, from charging either Carpentier or his narrator (or both) with misogyny and racism, one cannot ignore or cavalierly dismiss such biased content as irrelevant to the novel's seemingly more universal concern with the predicament of the modern artist. Paul Julian Smith's remarks on the study of gender and sexuality, which are equally relevant to the study of racial representations, speak eloquently to this point.

I take it for granted that to adopt a thematic approach (the supposedly empirical analysis of "content") is inappropriate where sexuality is concerned. . . I am concerned less with the specificity of Spanish or Latin American "experience" of sex, than with the enabling conditions of sexual difference itself. The role of theory is to investigate those conditions and not simply reproduce them in the guise of manifest content. In the realm of gender study content analysis goes hand in hand with the search for "positive images": the literary text is to be judged against a set of preexisting standards against which it is invariably found wanting. . . it seems unhelpful simply to dismiss male writers who exhibit signs of sexism, but far more productive to examine those "negative images" for the contradictions they bear within them, to reveal that any such content is an ideological construct.[2]

Of the negative images *The Lost Steps* projects, and there are many when it comes to the novel's representations of women, that of Rosario proves most revealing as an ideological construct embedded within the specific cultural, political, and economic history of Cuba and, by extension, other parts of the Hispanic Caribbean. While the geography in which the novel locates Rosario is important to the extent that it allows the narrative to set aboriginal features above the European and especially the African contributions to her mixed lineage, that geography is less relevant to the choices Carpentier made in his construction of Rosario. Far from being idiosyncratic, those choices and their attendant biases are in fact very much part of a highly sexualized and racialized discourse on national culture that began to acquire currency in Cuba during the early nineteenth century. By the opening decades of the twentieth century, that discourse, known as *mestizaje,* was well established.

Mestizaje can variably be translated as miscegenation, racial amalgamation (as in *blanqueamiento*, whitening), creolization, racial mixing, inter- or transculturation.[3] It is perhaps best described as a peculiar form of multiculturalism—one that has circulated in the Caribbean and in Hispanic America, most notoriously in Brazil, as a series of discursive formations tied to nationalist interests and ideologies.[4] This multiculturalism acknowledges, indeed celebrates, racial diversity while at the same time disavowing divisive social realities. In Cuba,[5] it evolved as social practices such as interracial sex and critical voices of reformist abolitionists were putting increasing pressure on colonial ideologies and economic developments. Its historical beginnings in the island that was at the time the commercial and cultural center of the Caribbean can be traced back to the fear of slave insurrections that pervaded the first half of the nineteenth century as a result of the successful Haitian Revolution (1791–1803) and to the negrophobic "Africanization of Cuba" scare brought on by ever-increasing demands for slave labor that accompanied the rapid expansion of Cuba's sugar industry. Specific reference points are the Aponte Conspiracy of 1812 and the conspiracy of La Escalera (The Ladder) of 1844.[6] Since the abolition of slavery in 1886 this fear has resurfaced at various points in Cuban history as an anxiety about ethnic, particularly black, enclaves that could (and did) threaten the cause of Cuban national unity in the face of both Spanish colonialism and, after 1898, U.S. economic and political imperialism.[7] Among such enclaves were the secret religious organization of the ñáñigos (banned by the government of José Miguel Gómez in 1903), the Comité de Veteranos de la Raza de Color formed in 1902, and the so-called Negro Protest Movement that had been active particularly in Cuba's eastern provinces since the early 1900s and led to the founding of the Partido Independiente de Color (PIC) in response to the 1908 elections.[8]

While cross-cultural situations, real and imaginary, are hardly unique to a Cuban or even a Caribbean setting,[9] the discourse of *mestizaje* has had a peculiar currency in Cuba. Since the 1890s, when José Martí began to popularize the idea of "our half-breed America" (*nuestra América mestiza*),[10] *mestizaje* has been perhaps the principal signifier of Cuba's national cultural identity. Martí writes in "Our America" ("Nuestra América") in 1891 that

The native-born half-breed [*el mestizo autóctono*], has vanquished the exotic Creole. . . . There can be no racial hate, because there are no races. The rachitic thinkers and theorists juggle and warm over the library-shelf races [*razas de librería*], which the open-minded traveler and well-disposed observer seek in vain in Nature's justice, where the universal identity of man leaps forth from triumphant love and the turbulent lust for life. The soul emanates, equal and eternal, from bodies distinct in shape and color. Whoever foments and propagates antagonism and hate between races, sins against Humanity.[11]

These are high-minded, well-intentioned words, designed to soften the racial differences and conflicts that threatened to divide Cuba and other budding Hispanic American nations at a crucial stage in their respective histories. Still, to invoke "Nature's justice" in a country where slavery had not been officially abolished until 1886 is at best problematic, at worst hypocritical. Besides, Martí's insistent refrain in "My Race" ("Mi raza") (1893), that "there will never be a war between the races in Cuba," was proved rather a false prophecy in 1912.[12] To point this out is not so much to question Martí's moral integrity, which would be both inappropriate and fruitless, as to call attention to the evasive maneuvers his writings perform particularly around racial issues. This evasiveness, which, as we shall see, implicitly extends to issues of gender and sexuality, is constitutive of what I term the discourse of *mestizaje* that nourishes Cuban nationalism in both the nineteenth and twentieth centuries.

What concerns me in this book, then, is how the new, "half-breed" race, of which Carpentier's Rosario is but a slightly displaced representative, has been discursively engendered in Cuba since the early 1800s. I am particularly interested in the roles or places the Rosarios have historically been assigned within the discourse of *mestizaje* as it manifests itself in Cuban literature, ethnography, and popular culture. My focus on Cuba, with some brief excursions into other parts of the Hispanic Caribbean, notably Puerto Rico, makes this book a case study of sorts. As such, it is also a point of departure for exploring larger questions and debates about Caribbean cultural production that I will pursue at some later point.

Of particularly importance about the sexual and racial stereotype of the mestiza or mulata,[13] which makes its official entrance into Cuban literature in the form of the Rosario Alarcón in Cirilo Villaverde's short story "Cecilia Valdés" and in his acclaimed abolitionist novel of the same title (1837 and 1882), are its intricate and contradictory ties to the ideological construction of that imagined community called Cuba.[14] And this community encodes its national identity in the iconic figure of a mulata—that of the Virgen de la Caridad del Cobre, the coppery Virgin of Charity who is Cuba's patron saint—not to mention in the countless images of mulatas that have been circulated in the island's literature and popular culture for roughly the past two centuries. In fact, by the early twentieth century, terms such as *cubanidad* and *cubanía* (which designate different versions of, or approaches to, Cubanness[15]) were, for all intents and purposes, synonymous to *mestizaje*. Most saliently contradictory about such discursive entanglements is the symbolic privileging of a socially underprivileged group defined by its mixed race or phenotype, its gender, and its imputed licentious sexuality. In the case of the mulata, high symbolic or cultural visibility contrasts sharply with social invisibility.[16] The opening chapter of *Graveyard of the Angels* (1987), Reinaldo Arenas's "recreation" of Villaverde's novel, makes that point with precision.

Rosario doesn't speak. She closes her eyes and seems to sleep. With her eyes closed she is better able to contemplate the entire course of her life: granddaughter of a slave grandmother and an unknown white man; daughter of a dark mulatta and an unknown white man; mulatta herself, lover of a white man who is abandoning her, and mother of a baby girl who will also never know her father. Now she understands that she was only an object of pleasure for the man who is taking her child away from her, and that misery, disdain, and helplessness are her only wordly possessions. *And she understands more: She understands that in the world which she inhabits there is no place for her, not even in oblivion.*[17]

This amounts to saying that there is no place for the mulata in the culture and the society that so consistently represents itself through her. The iconic mulata, then, is a symbolic container for all the tricky questions about how race, gender, and sexuality inflect the power relations that obtain in colonial and postcolonial Cuba.

Arenas's point, clearly, is that it is not the mulata who is out of order but Cuban society itself.

To raise such questions is all the more important because of certain discursive injunctions, or what I have previously referred to as strategic evasiveness. Carpentier's narrator, for one, insists that Rosario "was fulfilling a destiny that it was better not to analyze too much, for it was governed by 'big things' whose workings were obscure and, besides, were beyond man's [sic] understanding. That is what she meant when she said that 'it is not good to think about certain things'" (180 [241]). This bias against analyzing things too much, which here is curiously attributed to Rosario herself, resonates loudly with Martí's invective against "rachitic thinkers and theorists" with their "library-shelf races" who are, like Carpentier's figure of the artist at the end of "Sisyphus' vacation (278 [330])," exiled from an Emersonian realm of Nature whose mysterious workings are supposedly beyond human grasp. But if, according to *The Lost Steps,* such exile is inevitable, so is critical analysis, especially of a discourse that seeks to conceal its premises by naturalizing them. Once we treat Nature as a culturally invented space where social differences of whatever kind can simply be transcended rather than engaged or negotiated, it also becomes clear that the construction of that space has a firm basis in material history.[18]

II

The kinds of questions with which I began this study were fairly straightforward ones: How have Cuban writers and institutions since the early nineteenth century represented their own society? From what cultural resources or local codes have they constructed those representations? And, more pointedly, exactly what role have race, gender, and sexuality historically played in the formulations of Cuba's national identity?

Despite the literary bias evident in my selection of texts, what most concerns me in this book is not the kind of genealogical continuity that might be narrated in the form of a literary tradition but *iconographies*, sets or patterns of images, discursive effects in both literature and popular culture that, at different points during the nineteenth and twentieth centuries, seek to articulate Cubanness. Clearly, discursive formations such as Cubanness (and Caribbeanness) are not produced by authorial subjects, not even by a group of authors arranged as a literary tradition. While my historical interests compel me provisonally to retain the concept of the author, I do not regard the individual texts I discuss as the results mainly of personal idiosyncracies. Rather, they are modulations of discourses that are historically tied to specific economic and political group interests. The most pervasive of those interests in Cuba since the early nineteenth century have been those of the tobacco and sugar industries that fostered, directly or indirectly, a number of important political and cultural institutions, among them La Sociedad Económica de Amigos del País (The Economic Society of Friends of the Country), *tertulias* (or literary salons), print shops, and presses. Those institutions, among others, disseminated the images that encoded Cuba's evolving national self-definition.

At various points in Cuban history, the discourse of *mestizaje* intersects and interweaves in subtle ways with the discourse of sugar.[19] Though Cuba's almost monocultural sugar economy[20] no doubt created the conditions that bred racial injustice and racial strife, it would be far too simple to position *mestizaje* as counterdiscursive in relation to sugar's cultural and political hegemony. Rather, the discursive field of Cuban nationalism is significantly constituted by *historically shifting* alignments of, and alliances between, the different economic, social, and cultural interests that vie for polititical and representational power. While the texts and visual images I discuss in the following chapters do not equally revolve around the figure of the mulata, they are all located, at times precariously, at intersections that mark historically specific instances in the formation and consolidation of Cuba's nationalist cultural ideology. That ideology can be traced from nineteenth-century iconographies of the mulata to twentieth-century notions such as José Vasconcelos's Whitmanian "raza cósmica" (cosmic race) and the Antillean practice of *poesía negra* or *poesía mulata*.[21] It extends well into the present. What interests me are the ways in which that evolving ideology en-gendered and deracialized Cuba, thus further entrenching racially and sexually determined social hierarchies.

Due to its dual investment in literary and theoretical issues and in as much of a materially situated historicism as a deconstructionist can muster, my approach is almost inevitably characterized by a persistent (and, I hope, productive) tension between close textual readings of, and more far-flung historical commentaries on a variety of different authors, texts, and political landscapes. While such tension may not always make for a smooth narrative surface, it also does not produce the illusion of theoretically tidy scenarios where historically none exist. The narrative surface of this book is additionally troubled by frequently bilingual citations. While I have tried (at my editor's request) not to overburden the book with dual quotations, I nevertheless found it important to offer both Spanish and English texts in many places, especially when I comment on texts that have never been translated into English. In most instances where I cite the English version only, I have provided page references to a Spanish edition for those who may wish to consult it and in order to maintain at least some consistency in my use of sources. Unless I indicate otherwise, I use my own translations.

Chapter 1, "Imperfect Bodies," explores some early constructions of the mulata stereotype at a critical time in Cuban history; the first half of the nineteenth century, which was a time of unprecedented economic expansion, the rise of abolitionism, and ideological censorship. While antislavery narratives proliferated in the 1830s and 1840s, the censors saw to it that none of these texts were published in Cuba until much later, in some instances not until the early twentieth century. These literary accounts of the drama of slavery are, in many respects, the cornerstones of Cuba's literary tradition. But at the time, they were accessible only to a very small group of writers and intellectuals. My specific interests lie more with texts that were actually published during those years, such as the first part of Villaverde's *Cecilia Valdés* and two little-known popular poems from the 1840s by Francisco Múnoz del Monte and Bartolomé José Crespo y Borbón (a.k.a. Creto Gangá), respectively. Perhaps needless to say, none of these texts express abolitionist sentiments. But they do comment in a variety of ways on race relations in a country that was increasingly preoccupied with national independence and a separate cultural identity. The figure of the mulata in each of these texts is made up of the multifarious anxieties, contradictions, and imperfections in the Cuban body politic.

In these early literary representations of what is clearly a society in transition, economically and culturally, sugar and tobacco put in only cameo appearances. Their discursive entanglements, at once antagonistic and complicitous at a time when sugar plantations became an altogether too familiar part of Cuba's landscape, are much more in evidence in the lithographs and paintings to which I devote chapter 2, "Caramel Candy For Sale" (a line from *Cecilia Valdés* inspired this title[22]). The opening foci of this chapter are Eduardo Laplante's famous engravings of Cuban sugar estates and Víctor Patricio Landaluze's popular lithographs and paintings of Cuban types from the 1850s and 1860s. But the most widely disseminated images within Cuba were those on the exquisitely crafted labels or wrappers, known as *marquillas,* with which the numerous tobacco manufacturers advertised their products for the domestic market. These *marquillas* depicted a wide variety of images, including Laplante's sugar mills and of course mulatas and other racial stereotypes. The emergence of these visual artifacts tells much, on the one hand, about how technology impacted Cuban culture and society, and, on the other, about the ways in which Cuba's two major industries, sugar and tobacco, represented their fledgling nation both at home and abroad.

Chapter 3, "Plácido's Pastoral," is one of two chapters devoted to a single author, indeed to a single text: in this case, Plácido (Gabriel de la Concepción Valdés), nineteenth-century Cuba's Great Mulatto Poet, and his poem "La flor de la caña" (The sugarcane blossom). Against the claims of those who have sought to depoliticize Plácido's poetry while at the same time making him a martyr for national liberation, I read this poem as an attempt at reconfiguring the discourse of sugar and its particular ideological construction of a Cuban national identity from the viewpoint of a nonwhite writer. My reading also, implicitly, takes issue with a tendency in African-American and, more recently, in Afro-Hispanic criticism to dismiss and devalue texts, in this case by nonwhite writers, on the grounds that their politics of representation do not conform to liberal late-twentieth-century expectations. For the same reasons, I take exception to critical projections of the desire for a "black aesthetic" onto Cuban, as well as onto other Hispanic-American, literatures, so that the history of Afro-Hispanic American literature can be narrativized as a journey toward a thematics of blackness that would compensate for prior elisions of racial issues.[23] To castigate nineteenth-century nonwhite writers such as Plácido and the slave poet Juan Francisco Manzano, whose work I also discuss briefly, for their presumed lack of racial awareness, or at any rate for their failure "adequately" to render that awareness in their poetry, invalidates any other concerns their writings may (and do) articulate. There is ample evidence in the writings of both Plácido and Manzano that race and even gender were issues of which these poets were very much aware. This does not mean that their writing is not, for various reasons, imbricated with the conventions of hegemonic discourses, at times even complicitous with them. But such imbrications are extremely complex affairs, not just uncritical embraces of white values.[24] This chapter seeks to attend to such complexities.

A similarly troubling text is Martín Morúa Delgado's *Sofía*, a rather neglected late-nineteenth-century novel to which I devote chapter 4, "Filomena's Law." One of Cuba's most distinguished nonwhite politicians by the turn of the century, Morúa was an ardent critic of Villaverde's and conceived of *Sofía* as a rewriting of *Cecilia Valdés*. What I find most fascinating about Morúa's literary efforts is the precision with which *Sofía* attends to the sociosexual construction of race in nineteenth-century Cuba and the consistency with which the novel links those issues to slavery and sugar production.

From these nineteenth-century discursive entwinements the mulata emerges as a product of mostly white and distinctly masculine desire. But it is not until the rise of Afro-Cubanism in the mid-1920s that the homosocial dimensions of the desire for multicultural models in aesthetics and politics become more explicit. At that point, the Cuban mulata, reconfigured as *poesía mulata*, becomes *the* site where men of European and of African ancestry rhetorically reconcile their differences and, in the process, give birth to the paternalistic political fiction of a national multiculture in the face of a social system that resisted any real structural pluralism. Chapter 5, "Antidotes to Wall Street," which takes its title from Carpentier's first novel, *¡Ecue Yamba-O!* (1933), contextualizes this reconfiguration within the momentous shifts in economic and political power during the early decades of the first Cuban republic. The historical emergence of *poesía mulata* and of nationalistic concepts such as *cubanía* and *mestizaje* cannot be separated from the conflictual U.S.-Cuban relations during the early twentieth century, which had a tremendous impact on the island's quite disastrous racial politics.

Chapter 6, "Sublime Masculinity," narrows the focus to select poetic representation of the mulata by, among others, Felipe Pichardo Moya, Emilio Ballagas, Ramón Guirao, Marcelino Arozarena, Luis Palés Matos, and above all Nicolás Guillén. I briefly return to Carpentier's *The Lost Steps* to play off the novel's structural homoeroticism against my comments above on its heterosexual plot. In addition to considering the theoretical implications of a homoerotically and interracially inflected nationalist paradigm, I trace these masculinist poetics back to the quite overtly homosocial structures in a number of Guillén's early Afro-Cuban poems. While my return in this final chapter to Guillén's poetry is clearly inevitable given his poetry's overall significance to the Afro-Antillean movement, it is also an implicitly self-critical move, as my previous work on Guillén completely neglects the sexual and erotic dimensions of *mestizaje* exemplified by some of his major poems.[25] Rather than trying to cover up or explain away the different ideological investments of my earlier work, I have taken this book as an occasion for engaging with them by attempting to unravel their premises.

While nothing could be further from my mind in these two Afro-Cuban chapters than to adopt the role of apologist for the racial politics of so-called *negrista* texts, for instance Palés Matos's *Tuntún de pasa y grifería* (1937), I find it equally inappropriate to brush aside the *poemas negros/mulatos* written by whites as at best "inauthentic" and at worst racist instances of what Guillén once called "circumstantial tourism."[26] To distinguish between *poesía negrista* (negroid or fake black poetry, poetry in blackface) and *poesía negra* ("real" or authentic black poetry) is a fruitless endeavor that resorts to racial essentialism instead of scrutinizing the social constructedness of race and historicizing its discursive effects. I will use Stuart Hall's concept of "inferential racism" to argue that the majority of Afro-Antillean poems have "racist premises and propositions inscribed in them as a set of unquestioned assumptions" that continue to "enable racist statements to be formulated without ever bringing into awareness the racist predicates on which the statements are grounded."[27] One does not raise such predicates to the level of awareness by bringing indiscriminate charges of racism against all whites who write about African-American cultures, and by censoring black writers whose texts, for whatever reason, stray from what are construed as politically correct thematics and acceptable modes of representation at any given time.[28]

My point throughout is that it will not do either to uncritically hail *mestizaje* as the achievement or promise of a diverse culture that Hispanic America forever holds out to or against the United States, the land of unreconstructed racism, or, conversely, to demonize *mestizaje* as "ethnic lynching,"[29] not even in the face of abundant evidence to counter the purported existence of raceless utopias in Cuba and elsewhere in Hispanic America.[30] The recent flourishing of African-American and postcolonial theory notwithstanding, many Afro-Hispanists appear content to limit their critical enterprise to identifying positive representations of race in literary texts, while negative, even ambiguous, images are generally labeled racial stereotypes. This thematic bias of most current approaches to Afro-Hispanic American writing has had the effect of discouraging inquiries into *how* such stereotypical representations are constructed in the first place and *how* they function in specific historical settings.[31] At the same time, such approaches have disregarded the disruptive theoretical and political potential latent within stereotypes such as that of the mulata.[32]

III

To the extent that this book attempts to resist the strategic self-effacement of masculinity—which is frequently, though not exclusively, white—it is also an implicit statement about the corollary erasure of the female subject from the critical discourses on Cuban and other Hispanic-American cultures. In this sense, these chapters, which I see as "disloyal" readings[33] on a number of different levels, are contributions to Hispanic-American and Caribbean feminist studies. Though I do not regard Cuba, past or present, as representative of the whole of Hispanic America or, for that matter, the entire Caribbean, I suspect that similar patterns of racialization and genderization are operative elsewhere. As far as Cuba is concerned, there is little doubt in my mind that the conspicuous scarcity of women writers, especially nonwhite women writers, in a country that has produced so many of Hispanic America's foremost male writers, bears a troubling relation to the dissemination of a racialized national discourse that is prominently masculinist and frequently misogynistic. If this speculation is even remotely accurate, then a historical-critical assessment of the race-sex-gender dynamics of this discursive practice is necessary and indeed overdue.[34]

It is, to my mind, symptomatic of particular masculine biases in the literary and critical discourses on Cubanness, Caribbeanness, and Hispanic-Americanness that gender, even more often than class,[35] has rarely been considered a legitimate or even an appropriate topic for discussion, except of course in the context of women's writing.[36] But critical interest in the work of Caribbean and mostly white Hispanic American women writers, sponsored in some measure by the fairly recent and not-so-unproblematic impact Western European and Euroamerican feminisms have had on curricula and research agendas in various parts of the Americas, is still, in many ways, in its infancy stage.[37] Gender differences and sexuality as topics within Hispanic American and Caribbean literatures have received far less, and certainly far-less-serious, attention than race, and theoretical approaches to the race/gender/sexuality nexus are even fewer.[38] This lack of critical attention may well have been a function of the relative dearth of literary writings by nonwhite women[39] from those geographic areas, especially when compared to the impact of black feminism/womanism on the academic establishment in the United States during the past two decades and its profitable relations with the publishing industry.[40] But not-so-benign neglect of the production of women writers by a male-dominated literary establishment further consolidated during the years of the so-called boom of the Latin American novel is hardly the only problem, and possibly not even the most serious one. It appears that, at least in Cuba, women in general and nonwhite women in particular have had no standing as self-conscious subjects in the national discourses on culture, of which *mestizaje* is one of the most pervasive.[41] There are, of course, exceptions, but how many published nonwhite women writers are there in today's Cuba in addition to Nancy Morejón?[42] How many were there before her? For instance, the only woman associated with Afro-Cubanism was the immensely popular *recitadora* Eusebia Cosme whose participation, however, was limited to lending her voice to the poetry of her male compatriots.

This raises of course the fundamental question of a discursive site that might be occupied by the nonwhite female writer in a country such as Cuba, a question that also declares the limits of my present inquiry. For the moment, I am taking a cue from Sylvia Wynter's suggestion that "rather than only voicing the 'native' woman's hitherto silenced effect we shall ask: What is the *systemic function* of her own silencing both as woman and, more totally, as 'native' woman?"[43] In order to examine this systemic function, I focus on the constructions of interracial masculinity that hide behind racially mixed femininity and that have the concrete effect of legitimating *male* social, economic, and political power in the specific historical settings of nineteenth- and twentieth-century Cuba. Edward Said (and, more recently, Toni Morrison) has warned that to dismiss "incorrect" representations of racial and other differences as mere "lies or myths which, were the truth about them be told, would simply blow way," is seriously to underestimate how well such ambivalent modes of knowledge serve the powers-that-be.[44] It is those kinds of discursive alliances, and the possibilities for challenging their claims to representational authority in the realms of culture and politics, that this book endeavors to explore.

1

Imperfect Bodies

Yo soy la reina de las mujeres
en esta tierra de promisión;
yo soy de azúcar, yo soy de fuego,
yo soy la llave del corazón.

I am the queen of all the women
in this promised land;
I am made of sugar and of fire,
I am the key to the heart's desire.

I

Two events ambiguously frame the so-called *período negro* in Cuban literary and social history: the 1821 publication of slave-poet Manzano's first volume of poetry, *Poesías líricas: Cantos a Lesbia* (Lyric poesies: Songs for Lesbia), and the execution of Cuba's Great Mulatto Poet Plácido in 1844 for his supposed spearheading of the infamous Escalera Conspiracy (more on this in chapter 3).[1] The Cuban government responded to the rise of abolitionism by tightening ideological screws to the point of outright violence. The unflinching brutality with which the O'Donnell regime crushed La Escalera, and with it the evolving free black artisan class, shows that the widespread fear of slave insurrections on Cuban soil bordered on public hysteria. Reports in 1838 of a slave uprising in neighboring Trinidad rekindled memories of the Haitian Revolution almost to the point of panic at a time when African slaves were being brought to Cuba in ever-increasing numbers. For Haiti's legacy was twofold: While the first black republic offered a dangerous model to Cuba's own slave and free black populations, Haiti's economic downfall made Cuba the single largest producer of sugar in the Caribbean and opened the doors to virtually unlimited expansion. Attaching steam engines to the traditional sugar mill and building a railroad system facilitated rapid growth, but mechanization neither improved the slaves' working conditions nor decreased the demand for cheap labor—on the contrary.[2] Slave imports reached staggering proportions, despite Spain's 1817 treaty with Britain to ban the transatlantic slave trade by 1820. Between 1821 and 1860 more than 350,000 *bozales,* African slaves who had not been "seasoned" elsewhere, were illegally shipped to Cuba, frequently with U.S. assistance.[3] At certain points in the 1840s, slaves and free blacks together actually outnumbered Cuba's white residents.

Proportionate to the production of sugar in this largest of the Antilles grew the desire for economic and political self-determination. While the majority of Cuba's criollo elite would agree in principle that slavery was incompatible with the cause of national independence, economic considerations superseded moral concerns until well into the second half of the nineteenth century. But if the nationalist strivings were fundamentally at odds with the demands of a sugar economy that continued to depend heavily upon slave labor, the possibility of slave emancipation posed other problems. What role the island's sizable African population, once freed, might play in a fledgling republic was indeed a hotly debated issue. Some, like José Antonio Saco, saw "whitening" as a solution and proposed that all blacks, foreign-and native-born, be shipped back to Africa.[4] Others, notably Domingo Del Monte, a retired sugar baron turned reformer and patron of the arts, hoped for gradual changes in race relations.[5] Del Monte and his coterie placed their faith in literature, especially in antislavery narratives, as an instrument of such change.

The earliest examples of the "romantic abolitionism"[6] that the Del Monte group has come to represent appeared in poetry, notably José María Heredia's "Himno del desterrado" (Hymn of the uprooted) (1825), Del Monte's own "La patria" (The fatherland) from *Romances cubanos* (1833), José Jacinto Milanés's "El negro alzado" (The runaway black) (1836), and Manzanos's famous "Mis treinta años" (My thirty years) (1839). But the antislavery narratives and novels—the majority of which were associated with the famed Matanzas-Havana *tertulias* Del Monte organized—were much more remarkable on the whole than these poems, and of much greater significance to later generations of Cubans, who have returned to the drama of slavery with some frequency. Part of that drama was that not a single antislavery narrative passed the censor until 1875, when Antonio Zambrana's *El Negro Francisco* was printed in Cuba. Only Gertrudis Gómez de Avellaneda's novel *Sab* (1841) and Manzano's *Autobiography* (1840) escaped that fate by being published outside of Cuba, in Spain and in England, respectively.[7] The original text of Manzano's *Autobiografía*—the only known Cuban slave narrative—which was completed in 1838, did not see print until a nearly a century later, in 1937, and the second part of this work, if indeed it ever existed, remains lost.[8] The manuscript, however, was clandestinely circulated among the Del Monte group. Similarly, Félix Tanco y Bosmoniel's *Petrona y Rosalia,* the only surviving portion of his projected series, "Escenas de la vida privada en la isla de Cuba" (Scenes of private life on the island of Cuba),[9] was not published until 1925. Anselmo Suárez y Romero's *Francisco,*—like Manzano's narrative commissioned in the 1830s by Del Monte, who insisted on adding the subtitle *El ingenio, o Las delicias del campo* (The sugar mill, or the delights of the countryside)[10]—was published posthumously in 1880. The author's attempt to include portions of the novel in his 1859 *Colección de artículos* failed. The full version of *Cecilia Valdés,* more a panoramic novel of Cuban manners and mores than an antislavery narrative proper, did not see print until 1882.[11]

Literary censorship and military action were not the only forms of sociopolitical control the Cuban government exercised in those days. In 1805 civil legislation was introduced to regulate interracial marriages, specifically marriages between persons of known nobility and/or known *limpieza de sangre* (purity of blood) with blacks or mulato/as—the emphasis here is on *known,* as some persons of Euro-African descent were of lighter complexions than

many supposedly pure-blooded Spaniards.[12] This caused obvious
confusion and problems in a society in which "phenotype was . .
ideologically collapsed with genotype and social status," though
economic factors could sometimes intervene in both directions.[13]
Despite the rampant "Africanization of Cuba" scare, few interracial couples were denied marriage licenses prior to 1864. That year,
however, marked the beginning of a period of total prohibition,
certainly a blow to those who had placed their hopes in the gradual
biological assimilation of Cuba's nonwhite population. The new
restrictions on interracial marriages were a direct response to the
threat that slave emancipation in the United States implicitly posed
to the island's "tranquility," which was of course based on "the
links of obedience and respect which the coloured race should en-
tertain for the white."[14] Yet, royal decrees and local edicts could
hardly contain the spread of racial mixing. After all, concubinage
and casual sex were practiced much more frequently than interracial matrimony, especially, though not exclusively, among white
Cuban men belonging to the middle and especially to the upper
classes.[15]

Socially ambitious light-skinned mulatas, also known as *amar-
illas,* or high yellows, and prized for their exotic beauty, were fair
game for sexual liaisons with white men. The majority of these
affairs did not lead to marriage, either in historical reality or in
fictional accounts. The destiny of most of the racially mixed characters, male and female, in the novels of reformist abolitionism in
Cuba and elsewhere is predictably tragic.[16] Even though *Cecilia
Valdés* modifies the "tragic" formula by keeping its protagonist
alive, the three generations of mulatas Villaverde chronicles are
each locked in a cycle of sexual exploitation, abandonment, and
despair that is maintained by the women's unwitting complicitous-
ness in perpetuating the conditions of their abuse. So the darker-
complexioned Josefa instructs her granddaughter that "Tú [Ce-
cilia] . . eres casi blanca y puedes aspirar a casarte con un blanco.
¿Por qué no? . . Y has de saber que blanco, aunque pobre, sirve
para marido; negro o mulato ni el buey de oro" (You . . are almost
white and can therefore aspire to marrying a white man. And why
not? . . And you must keep in mind that a white man, even a poor
one, will be the better candidate for a husband; you don't marry a

black or a mulato even if he has all the money in the world).[17] Even
if Villaverde's admittedly remarkable novel does not (according to
Jill Netchinsky, whose study privileges earlier narratives) embody
what Netchinsky perceives as "the foundation myth of Cuban literary culture," that is, antislavery poetics,[18] *Cecilia Valdés* can be
taken as representative of a racialized and sexualized cultural iconography that offers an alternate mythic foundation: the Cuban
cult of the mulata.

In his attempt to "reenchant the Cuban cult of the *mulata* besides (but not too far away from) its erotic and sexist cant," Eduardo González notes that Villaverde's "*mulata* protagonist and her
rich iconography play a marginal and controlled role" in most
readings of *Cecilia Valdés* as the founding text of Cuban realism.
This point is well taken, but González pushes his argument too far
by adding that "to appreciate a writer like Villaverde within and
without his national boundaries, we ought to imagine him at least
in part as a woman writer."[19] The fact that Villaverde, in addition
to lending Cecilia both his initials and his birth date, dedicated his
novel to "Cuban women" (which ones?) hardly makes him a
woman writer, even if one extended the definition of that term to
include men addressing a specifically female readership, which Villaverde does not.[20] In fact, he writes from a distinctly masculine
vantage point, a salient feature of costumbrista realism and its "authentic" constructions of Cuban life to which I will return in the
following chapter.

II

No matter how masculine the political and commercial activities
were that controlled colonial Cuban society in the nineteenth century, the images that dominate the literary and popular imagination at the time were both female and, in the broadest sense of the
term, black. Much like North American writers of the ante- and
postbellum periods, Cuban novelists were particularly fascinated
by women of ambiguous racial origin.[21] However, whereas the
tragic-mulatta stereotype in U.S. fiction conformed to the ideal of
the Southern lady and "possessed none of the lasciviousness asso-

ciated in the popular imagination with her race,"[22] some Cuban writers, including Villaverde, created a rather different female type. Villaverde's portrait of Cecilia Valdés, for example, does not subscribe to nineteenth-century conceptions of pure and noble womanhood (by definition white and embodied in the novel by the "delicate" and "supernatural" but rather nondescript Isabel Ilincheta) to the same extent than other literary constructions of more classically tragic mulatas do, notably Tanco's Rosalia and Suárez y Romero's Dorotea. Cecilia's femininity, by contrast, is a dangerous combination of beauty and malice. Villaverde's painstakingly detailed description of the character who shares his initials is revealing in a number of ways.

Although "her type was that of the virgins depicted by the most famous painters," Cecilia is not altogether perfect: "sus facciones muy regulares, su frente alta, y su nariz recta . . . formaban un conjunto bello, que para ser perfecto sólo faltaba que la expresión fuese menos maliciosa, si no maligna" (her very regular features, high forehead and straight nose constituted a beautiful whole, and the only thing she lacked in order to be perfect was for her facial expression to be less malicious, even if it was not evil).[23] *Sólo* of course is the operative word in this passage. The understated lack is indeed the single most significant qualifier of Cecilia's innocently white appearance (more on this in chapter 2). If Hortensia Ruiz del Vizo's claim that *Cecilia Valdés* established the mulata as the ideal of feminine beauty in nineteenth-century Cuba is correct,[24] then it is important to attend carefully to the imperfections that are a crucial part of that construct's design.

The above lines are included in the first part of *Cecilia Valdés*, which was published in 1839, and modulations of its themes and images abound in nineteenth-century Cuban literary and popular culture.[25] Francisco Muñoz del Monte's poem "La mulata," published anonymously in Havana in 1845 and one of the earliest detailed portraits of the mulata, caricatures her as the kind of vampirish monster that was absent from North American literature until the notorious trilogy (1902–7) by Thomas Dixon, Jr.[26] Muñoz's mulata may have been in part inspired by Villaverde's "little bronze virgin," whose unwittingly incestuous desire for Leonardo Gamboa poses an overt threat to an already weakened patriarchy.[27] But it is quite fruitless to attempt to trace specific influence relations, since Villaverde's images of mulatas were hardly unfamiliar to his contemporaries. Unlike Villaverde's well-tempered realist constructs, Muñoz's caricature draws liberally on all the "filthy materiality" and unbridled feminine sexuality archetypically associated with witches, freaks, prostitutes, and, since the early nineteenth century, with black women.[28] All this is quite obvious even in the most cursory reading of this poem, especially from its sensationalistic fourth section, which alone comprises no less than fifteen of the thirty-five stanzas. What I would like to explore, then, are some of the more subtle procedures of this long poem, not in order to rescue it from the banality of the clichés it deploys with such gusto, but to point to areas of ambiguity and contradiction representative of nineteenth-century Cuban attitudes toward race and sexuality.[29] Here are the two opening stanzas.

> ¡Mulata! ¿Será tu nombre
> injuria, oprobio o refrán?
> ¡No sé! Sólo sé que al hombre
> tu nombre es un talismán.
>
> Tu nombre es tu vanagloria
> en vez de ser tu baldón;
> que ser mulata es tu gloria,
> ser mulata es tu blasón.
>
> Mulata! Could your name be
> injury, opprobrium or legend?
> I don't know! I know only that for a man
> your name is a talisman.
>
> Your name is your vainglory,
> instead of being your offense;
> being a mulata is your glory,
> being a mulata is your coat-of-arms.[30]

That no individual woman is being addressed here is already clear from the poem's title, which invokes a generic type, one of Víctor Patricio Landaluze's famous Cuban types, whom I shall introduce in the next chapter. What most characterizes this female type, hardly a traditional muse, is her lack of a stable (that is, a legal) identity: a name. This lack of a discursive position also implies the lack of a social position. Telling in this respect is the structural analogy between the two exclamations in the first stanza— "¡Mulata!" at once invocation and curse, and "¡No sé!"—which introduces an uncomfortable note of uncertainty whose grammatical equivalent is the question that extends across the first and second lines. In order for the mulata to be represented as something other than an open question, she has to be somehow *positioned,* socially and discursively. The poet's task, then, is to name a new and different species and to place it within the social, sexual, and racial hierarchies of colonial Cuba. The nouns "injury," "opprobrium," "vainglory," and "offense" are all, in a sense, names that identify the mulata as a transgressor and situate her on the nether side of social (and lyric) convention. The heavy-handed rhyming of "baldón" with "blasón" may not exactly add to these stanzas' lyricism, but it proves an effective mockery of the very idea of social status and female honor in the case of the mulata: her sole coat of arms is her complexion, which most certainly has a heraldic function. The mulata's liminality signals both excess, the existence of something that would offend and possibly injure the representational and social economies of this poem, and the need for containing it. What functions as containment is the talisman metaphor that locates social and racial differences in the "proverbially" mysterious and perilous realm of female sexuality, while at the same time invoking the equally mysterious but benevolent powers of Cuba's dusky Virgin of Charity. The mulata thus inscribed becomes a paradoxical mythic embodiment of both secretive sexuality and protective virginity.

Claudette May William's point, in one of the few commentaries on this poem, that "because the mulata defies the racist logic of [Cuban] colonial society . . mythification is an expression [of] the speaker's unwillingness to modify his ideological position in the face of conflicting reality," is well taken, even if it contradicts one of her earlier statements.[31] Within the mythic, as opposed to the sociohistorical, realm, everything can be brought under control, and the poem hurries on to another, this time entirely rhetorical, question: "¿su almo encanto la mulata / lo debe acaso a su tez?"

(Does the mulata perhaps owe / her heavenly charm to the color of her skin?). Needless to say, only "foolish people doubt it" (Dúdanlo las gentes necias), but the poet knows better. Even if "la canela" (cinnamon) was regarded as socially superior to "el carbón" (coal)—though economically the latter was more valuable—skin color, that "most visible of fetishes" according to Homi Bhabha, was nonetheless the visible stain of slavery. In social terms, its attraction could be nothing less than fatal.[32]

But slavery, it appears, is not an appropriate topic for this poem. Much like the mulata's subjectivity and her actual sexuality, slavery is consistently displaced by references to Christian and Greek mythologies that would have been more palatable both to Muñoz's readership and to the Cuban censors.

> Es la mulata la fatal manzana
> que al suelo arroja la infernal discordia;
> nueva Elena, la guerra la acompaña;
> todo hombre es Paris, toda casa es Troya.

> Venus de bronce, como el bronce mismo,
> que dos metales diferentes forman,
> dos seres antipáticos la engendran,
> dos principios distintos la coloran.

> The mulata is the deadly apple
> that infernal discord dropped on the ground;
> the new Helen, war accompanies her;
> each man is Paris, each house is Troy.

> Venus of bronze, like bronze itself,
> made from two different metals,
> two opposed beings engender her,
> two different principles color her.

The attributes of Muñoz's bronze Venus who, instead of "a girdle of myrtle and roses," wears "a burning circle of fire / that consumes the careless one who touches it," are quite similar to those with which Villaverde invests his Cecilia: "because of her light bronze color she might well have passed for the Venus of the hybrid Ethiopian-Caucasian race"—note Villaverde's use of the conditional tense here. In keeping with this, Leonardo Gamboa describes Cecilia as "toda pasión y fuego, es mi tentadora, un diablito en figura de mujer, la Venus de las mula . . " (all passion and fire, she is my temptress, a little devil in the shape of a woman, the Venus of the mula . .).[33] Stanzas 8–11 readily confirm these iconographic similarities by identifying the different "principles" or "beings" (species?) that engender this Venus/Vesuvius as "razas," races. On the other hand, Muñoz appears much more eager than Villaverde to supply his readers with easy moral judgments: The contrast between "Circassian grace" and "African sparks," that is, lust, between "Norman blood" and "hot Ethiopian veins," is instantly replayed as the moral struggle between "barbarism" and civilization.

> Punto de transición entre dos razas
> discordes, implacables, rencorosas,
> el Cáucaso por suya la reclama,
> como suya el desierto la pregona.
>
> Y la barbarie y la cultura luchan
> en su frente tostada y majestuosa,
> como en la frente de Luzbel un día
> lucharon bien y mal en la gloria.
>
> De blanco y negro inexplicable engendro,
> sublime, cuando quiere se enamora,
> insaciable en sus iras como el tigre,
> apacible en su amor como paloma.
>
> Antítesis viviente de dos mundos,
> cambiante anfibio, esfinge misteriosa,
> que el enigma propone a los pasantes,
> y al que no lo descifra lo devora.

> Point of transition between two
> discordant, implacable, opposed races,
> on the one side, the Caucasus claims her,
> and the desert proclaims her its own.
>
> And barbarism and culture struggle
> in her tawny and majestic forehead,

as one day in the forehead of Lucifer
good and evil met in glorious battle.

Inexplicably engendered by white and black,
sublime, she falls in love as she likes,
insatiable in her wrath like a tiger,
peaceful in her love like a dove.

Living antithesis of two worlds,
ever-changing amphibian, mysterious sphinx,
who poses a riddle to the passersby,
and devours those who cannot solve it.

The erasure of Cuba's history of colonialism and slavery, which the poem reduces to a glorious mythic battle between good and evil, culminates in the adverb "inexplicably," which, like the Sphinx's riddle, endorses the mystery in which interracial heterosexual rape was (and continues to be) shrouded. The poem's faint allusion to Oedipus, encoded in that riddle, introduces the specter of incest as a much-dreaded result of confused, and thus probably "contaminated," genealogies, for which women are usually held responsible.[34] Cuban writing, from the antislavery narratives to *Cecilia Valdés* and to Morúa Delgado's *Sofía,* was obsessed with incest situations resulting from interracial rape and concubinage. Muñoz's veiled reference to incest by way of the Oedipus myth reinsinuates the poem's initial anxieties about racial mixing as a threat to a political order dependent on physiognomy as reliable index of class differences. The mulata, then, measures the extent to which what appeared to be previously fixed sexual, social, and racial hierarchies within that political order are no longer stable— no longer reliably (that is, physiognomically) marked. In "La mulata," however, the tabooized desire is no longer exclusively, or even primarily, female. This point is of considerable importance, and I will return to it shortly. But for the moment, the poem's focus remains on the mulata, that "ever-changing amphibian" whom the poet still seeks to control.

At the beginning of section three, the poetic voice bursts forth from its temporary omniscient anonymity in another lyric address so as to put the mulata in her "proper" place. That place is a negative (offensive) social and conceptual space specifically defined and delimited by promiscuous female sexuality.[35]

> Tú no eres blanca, mulata,
> ni es oro puro tu pelo,
> ni tu garganta es de plata,
> ni en tus ojos se retrata
> el divino azul del cielo.

> You are not white, mulata,
> nor is your hair pure gold,
> nor is your throat made of silver,
> nor do your eyes reflect
> the heavenly blue of the sky.

This stanza resolves the representational conflicts and moral ambivalences chronicled previously in the poem by inverting the ideal of white femininity. In so doing, Muñoz absolves upper-class white men in particular from the sociopolitical consequences of their sexual desire. As in later variations on this theme, including Guillén's, the question of white men's responsibility for their past and present actions is circumvented. Whatever threat the mulata poses in her deviation from the neoclassic ideal of feminine beauty and her transgression of Cuban society's racial and class boundaries is safely contained in the poem's Manichaean and deeply misogynist allegory. As the mulata is decisively classified as "not white," the proverbial lava that previously only boiled in her bosom suddenly erupts, and carnality is unleashed upon the world of the poem in images of burning pupils, dark purple lips, and, Muñoz's favorite, globes of quivering flesh. That the poet's reminder to the mulata is an act of symbolic violence, a violence readily transferred onto *her* actions, is entirely swept away by this soft-pornographic imagery. If, three stanzas later, the imagery shifts briefly to sunbathed meadows and gracefully swaying palm trees, this brief pastoral interlude serves only to set the scene for a trite recasting of the Edenic myth in which the by-now unambiguously blackened, yet definitely American, mulata is assigned the role of serpentine seductress.

Y en tus brazos locamente
el hombre cae sin sentido,
como cae en fauce hirviente
de americana serpiente
el pájaro desde el nido.

And into your arms the man falls
madly, deprived of his senses,
like a bird that falls from its nest
into the boiling mouth of
an American serpent.

What follows in the remaining stanzas extends the earlier allegory of the struggle between savagery and civilization, now no longer carried out behind the mulata's "tawny . . forehead," but externalized as violent sexual intercourse. This sacrificial ritual amounts to an apocalyptic castration fantasy in which the voluptuous female serpent, whose body moves to the heavy beat of a large eastern drum, literally swallows the helpless male bird.[36] Muñoz's language in this final section of the poem betrays a common masculine fear of the *vagina dentata*, "a cultural femininity which is envisioned as a greedy mouth, never satisfied."[37]

El hombre es suyo.
el blanco le obedece servilmente;
en la boca fatal de la serpiente
el encumbrado pájaro cayó.

Vereísle entonces. En flexible roscas
sus brazos lo encadenan y lo oprimen,
lo enlazan, lo entrelazan, lo comprimen,
lo aprisionan, lo apremian sin piedad.

. . . . .

Elástica culebra, hambriente boa,
la mulata a su víctima sujeta,
lo oprime, estrecha, estruja, enreda, aprieta,
y chupa y lame y muerde su furor.

. . . . .

Y crece, y crece, la embriaguez en tanto,
y crece el suspirar y la lid crece,

> y la víctima muerde y se estremece,
> y agoniza y sin duda va a expirar.
>
> The man is hers.
> The white man obeys her like a servant;
> the lofty bird has fallen
> into the serpent's deadly mouth.
>
> Look at him/her then. Her arms, in flexible twists,
> enchain him and squeeze him,
> entwine him, intertwine him, compress him,
> imprison him, urge him on without pity.
>
> . . . . .
>
> Elastic snake, hungry boa,
> the mulata grabs her victim,
> squeezes, stretches, wrings him, wraps herself around
>   him, grips
> him tightly, and sucks and licks and bites furiously.
>
> . . . . .
>
> And the intoxication grows stronger and stronger yet,
> the sighs increase and the struggle mounts,
> and the victim bites and shudders,
> and agonizes and will no doubt die soon.

No detailed reading of these and similar stanzas is necessary to elicit the predatory qualities with which Muñoz blatantly invests black female sexuality. However, to speak of *black* female sexuality here is somewhat redundant since the body of the dark-complexioned woman appears to be the only available site of female sexuality in nineteenth-century Cuban literature. White women, that is, those of *known* "purity of blood" and hence of social standing, were, almost by definition, exempt from such sexualization. Leonardo Gamboa's description of his future bride, Isabel, in *Cecilia Valdés* exemplifies this attitude: Her lean body, he claims, shows no trace of feminine plumpness and sensuality; she is "de mármol por lo rígida y por lo fría, inspira respeto, admiración, cariño tal vez, no amor loco, no una pasión volcánica" (she is made of marble, stiff and cold; she inspires respect, admiration, affection perhaps, but not mad love, not volcanic passion.[38] Women like Isabel Ilincheta were confined, literally and figuratively, to the combined spheres of the domestic and the maternal, from which the mulata in this poem has already been excluded through her association with images of sterility such as the desert and the dry sirocco. The mulata's function is to provide sexuality without reproductive complications. Her womb is a tomb.

To distance himself from the "vanquished athlete" ("vencido atleta") whose orgiastic demise is imminent, the poet in these final sections has once again retreated to omniscient, seemingly genderless safety. From the secure disengagement of this position, one in which the poet has clearly subdued his own carnal appetites in the interest of *disseminating* information,[39] the brunt of his irony is leveled not so much at the mulata, who supposedly just cannot help herself, as at her victim—that bird of social distinction who falls, foolishly and senselessly, from his high nest. The hyperbole here is directed at Cuban upper-class criollos, the group among which concubinage was most frequent and whose members were least likely to contract interracial marriages. Even though prominent spokesmen of the sugar oligarchy, such as Arango y Parreño, favored racial mixing as a solution to Cuba's "Africanization," they hardly thought of recruiting their own families to the cause of "whitening." The overriding concern on the part of these men would have been to protect their social standing. Villaverde's Leonardo Gamboa is a case in point. According to the symbolic logic of "La mulata," the practice of interracial (hetero)sex, legalized or not, would amount to nothing less than the social death of this particular class. While Muñoz casts the mulata in the role of aggressor in his allegorized power struggle for the maintenance of a particular kind of sociosexual order, the poet's pitiless disengagement from the hapless, passive male in his poem betrays an awareness that the colorful seductress represents only a symptom of a class-specific "madness."[40] If within the narrative of the poem the mulata emerges as triumphant, her victory is also immediately qualified by the reminder that she is "nothing more than a being of bronze" ("No hay más que un ser de bronce: la mulata"). At the end of the poem, when the callous mulata lights her cigar and awaits her next victim ("la cruel mulata su cigarro enciende,/y a inmolar va otro hombre a su placer"), that talismanic object assumes the absurd shape of a cigar-smoking serpent. This outlandish but, in some respects, rather hilarious caricature confounds what might otherwise appear to be a coherent symbolic system.

The poem clearly does not aspire to literary realism but constructs a fetish to be possessed vicariously. A conventional framing device, the metatrope of the statue is also a variation on the earlier image of the Sphinx. It functions to distance both the poet *and* his presumably white, possibly male readership from the scene of the crime, as it were, in order to make that scene itself the site of voyeuristic pleasure. From this vantage point, the poem's ultimate purpose might appear to manage and reorder transgressive white, male desire by relegating sexual pleasure to the realm of voyeuristic fantasies while at the same time warning against indulging those fantasies in the social realm. Even though the poem is ostensibly about the mulata, its overriding concern is the threat she poses to white, male power, whose proper transfer is guaranteed only within the legal perimeters of marriage. The violent death of Leonardo Gamboa on his wedding day tells much the same tale. Leonardo's murder at the jealous hands of José Dolores Pimienta signifies the necessary fictional sacrifice of disruptive male desire (his own and his father's) to the material and racial self-preservation of an already weakened colonial patriarchy. Leonardo's death, like that of the white bird in Muñoz's poem, can be read as an ironic attempt at defending whatever is left of patriarchal privilege.

But what is also, perhaps primarily, being played out in this poem are class resentments among whites, for Muñoz specifically lampoons the sexual practices and fantasies of Cuba's male aristocracy. The real locus of licentious sexuality here is not only the mulata herself but also the no-good men of the leisured classes who become her all-too-willing "slaves." To the extent that "La mulata" ridicules this kind of irrational masculinity, it undercuts the stereotypes Muñoz deploys with such relish. The source of vicarious pleasure, then, is not simply the titillating combination of sex, race, and violence to which Muñoz admittedly devotes a great deal of energy, but the opportunity his poem afforded white readers, male and female, to adopt a position of moral superiority both toward the mulata *and* toward those who courted her fatal charms. For in its ambiguous gender, the earlier "Vereísle" ("look at him/her") does not permit the object of the poet's and the reader's gaze to be construed as exclusively, even primarily, female. The reader is invited, then, not only to look *at*, and thus to eroticize, but to look *down upon* the men who are implicated in the mulata's "offense." The pleasure derived from looking either at or down upon this spectacle, or both, is a function of the moral self-righteousness with which the reader is encouraged to compensate for lesser socioeconomic status, sexual frustration, or, again, both. What initially appears to be a representational crisis occasioned by the disruptive figure of the mulata turns out in fact also to be a political crisis within Cuba's non-so-homogenous white "community." But even as it satirizes the decadence of privileged males, "La mulata" actually thwarts a broader critique of sexuality in the context of Cuban race relations. For Muñoz's uses intraracial divisions to shield his own and his projected white reader's racial and sexual biases from scrutiny. The force of the poem's moral judgments depends on how well it masks a discursive position inflected with both whiteness and masulinity but, it seems, without class privilege.

III

Bartolomé José Crespo y Borbón's "La mulata," published in 1847, appears to share little more with Muñoz del Monte's poem than its title. While little else is known about Muñoz other than that he was a lawyer born in Santo Domingo who came to Cuba as a child and remained there for the rest of his life, Crespo's literary biography is much more extensive and a matter of public record. Particularly relevant to a reading of his "La mulata" is the fact that throughout his career as a satirist he created a number of different authorial personae for himself. The most popular of those was that of Creto Gangá, "escritor bozal" (African writer). Creto's distinctively "African" voice sounded almost weekly from the pages of *El Diario de La Habana, Noticioso y Lucero, El Faro Industrial, El Diario de la Marina, El Plantel,* and especially *La Prensa,* in the form of letters such as "Cata que yo lo criba a la groria a mi mugé

Pancha Lucumí" (Letter I wrote in praise of my woman Pancha Lucumí), part of a series in *La Prensa* in 1848.[41] In the following year, there was even an exchange of letters between Creto Gangá and one Siriaco Mandinga, carried out in *La Prensa* and *El Faro Industrial*.[42] In addition, Creto's *sainetes*, Cubanized versions of Francisco Covarrubias's immensely popular comedies, had been staged regularly in Havana since 1847, the year that inaugurated Creto's spectacular career as a popular playwright with the publication and performance of the burlesque comedy *Un ajiaco, o la boda de Pancha Jutía y Canuto Raspadura* (A Cuban stew; or, the wedding of Pancha Jutía and Canuto Raspadura). It is in this role as a "black" (or, better, blackface) writer that Crespo y Borbón has been hailed as a precursor of Afro-Cuban poetry.[43]

Crespo's emphasis on "lo negro," things black or blackness in an abstract sense, as an integral part of Cuba's national culture has been compared in importance to Víctor Patricio Landaluze's paintings and engravings.[44] Like many of Landaluze's paintings and engravings, Crespo's literary masquerades were a part of the costumbrista realism exemplified by *Cecilia Valdés*. Another significant document of this popular trend was *Los cubanos pintados por sí mismos: Colección de tipos cubanos* (Cubans painted by themselves: Collection of Cuban types) (1852), which Landaluze illustrated. But it was not until two years later that Landaluze actually began to include nonwhites among the ten Cuban "types" he contributed to Crespo's volume *Fiestas con motivo de la llegada del Excmo. Don José de la Concha* (Celebrations on the occasion of the arrival of His Excellency, Don José de la Concha) (1854). By that time, Creto/Crespo's *costumbrismo caricaturista* (caricature realism) was already well known in Havana, in part due to Crespo's *Las habaneras pintadas por sí mismas, en miniatura* (Havana's women painted by themselves, in miniature), a volume of *romances* (ballads) that appeared in the same year as Creto's *Un ajiaco*. One remarkable thing about *Las habaneras*, which, like the later *Los cubanos*, is written entirely in what Creto Gangá would call "lengua branca" (white language), is that it made a point of including types such as "La mulata." Here is what I take to be the first section of that poem, which is not visually divided into stanzas.

Es un compuesto de todo,
es entre hereje y cristiana,
es como su misma piel,
entre negra y entre blanca;
es lo mismo que la trucha
que fluctúa entre dos aguas;
pulga que quieta atormenta,
y pacifica si salta;
pimiento que visto, gusta,
y que comido da rabia;
licor que olido conforta,
y que bebido emborracha;
cantárida que da vida
unas veces, y otras mata.

She is a compound of everything,
she is between heretic and Christian,
she is like her skin itself,
between black and between white;
she is the same as the trout
that fluctuates between two waters;
as the flea that torments when still
and consoles when it jumps;
as the pepper that looks appealing
and when eaten lights a fire;
as liquor whose smell comforts,
but that intoxicates when consumed;
as the cantharis that at times gives life
and at others kills.[45]

Situated in the context of Creto/Crespo's socioliterary caricatures, this poem inevitably takes on certain comical features.[46] While this is hardly a portrait of the mulata painted, as it were, "po se memo" (by herself), Crespo nevertheless succeeds in calling attention to the inadequacy and inappropriateness of the paratactic catalog of similes the poem initially heaps upon this figure. The indeterminate reference to the mulata's skin color as being somewhere between black and white is as close as it gets to a physical description, and even though "hereje" and "cristiana" are quite predictably associated with "negra" and "blanca" respectively, this poem, unlike Muñoz del Monte's, does not translate these associations into moral terms. In fact, any inclination the reader may have toward such conventional valorization is undermined, even trivialized, by the comparisons that accumulate in orderly parallel progression. But upon closer scrutiny, the sense of order these grammatically parallel constructions create turns out to be rather deceptive. The various images called upon to represent the mulata's "in-betweenness" do not really add up to much. If anything, they testify to the unreliability of a formalized symbolic system that would allow readers consistently to invest each of these binary oppositions with moral correspondences. The poem's initial Manichaean thrust dissolves its own clichéd categories by pushing them well beyond their conceptual limits and beyond seriousness.

The disjunctive "pero" that opens the poem's next sentence (and section) abruptly halts the procession of similes to introduce unexpected changes in perspective and imagery that provisonally liberate the poem and the figure of the mulata from previous structural and conceptual constraints.

> Pero como hemos de verla
> no es en estado de esclava,
> sino cuando libremente
> y por sus respetos anda.
> Esa en fin, a quien parece
> muy poca toda la acera
> por donde pasa, y con cuyos
> contoneos de caderas
> hace agitar por do marcha
> cortinas, toldos y muestras.

> But we must see her
> not as a slave,
> but walking freely and
> as she pleases.
> As one, finally,
> to whom the sidewalk
> on which she strolls
> seems too narrow,
> and whose swinging hips upset
> curtains, awnings, and shop signs.

After further discrediting the conflation of racial with moral categories by implicitly designating such practice a condition of slavery, Crespo proceeds to reconstruct the mulata as a figure for political, sexual, and poetic freedom. As already anticipated in the first section of the poem, such freedom supposedly results from the disruption of (at least grammatical) order. At the textual level, such a disruption is achieved by including in the poem what would appear to be a rather quotidian scene: an ordinary, anonymous mulata walking along one of Havana's narrow streets. She is undistinguished except for the movement of her swaying hips, on which the poem focuses and whose spectacularly disastrous effects it comically exaggerates. Compare the following lines from a contemporaneous popular song.

> No hay mulata más hermosa.
> más pilla y más sandunguera,
> ni que tenga en la cadera
> más azúcar que mi Rosa.

> There is no mulata more beautiful,
> more cunning and more graceful,
> nor one who has more sugar
> in her hips than my Rosa.[47]

The mulata walks in a certain way—"libremente" or, as it were, with "sugar in her hips"—that superficially agitates both the material environment represented in the poem and the representational process itself. Freedom (from slavery? from social convention?) is represented as a particular kind of rhythmic movement, whose sexual connotations can hardly be missed. It is as if the mulata's gait, ordinary though it may seem, eluded the social and representational economies of slavery. But just how liberating is this eminently sexist and racist image, and for whom? If anything can be said in favor of Crespo's poem, which clearly does not grant the mulata any measure of (self-)consciousness, it is that its final catalog of metonymic substitutions comically deflates whatever symbolic possibilities one may be tempted to see in her "performance."

Que más que mujer parece
por lo que se contonea,
una barquilla azotada
por el viento y la marea;
empinando papalote
cambiado con ligereza;
majá que ondulante sigue
con velocidad su presa,
caña brava remecida
por remolinos, bandera
o gallardete a quien vientos
siempre encontrados flamean;
paloma de cola alzada
que alegre se pavonea;
molinillo de batir
chocolate en mano diestra.

She seems more than a woman
because of her swaying,
a boat rocked
by wind and tide;
a soaring kite
transformed by swiftness;
a winding snake in speedy
pursuit of its prey,
bamboo tossed to and fro
by whirlwinds, a banner,
or pennant fluttering in
the ever-present winds;
 a dove with a raised tail,
strutting merrily like a peacock;
a chocolate beater
in the experienced hand.

There is nothing either particularly alluring or disconcerting about these lines that, despite their triteness, have the advantage of making little sensationalistic investment in female sexuality. Even the fleeting comparison of the mulata's gyrations to the winding of a snake is hardly sufficient for the kind of sociosexual allegory Muñoz sets up. On the whole, these rather unremarkable, even hackneyed images mock and preempt any reading of the mulata as a symbolically overdetermined figure. Such restraint could be construed as liberating if it were not for the fact that the joke in this poetic satire is not just on an audience fearful of the kind of racial mixing the mulata represents but also on the mulata herself. Almost predictably, the poem's final image of mixing or blending, which refers back to the poem's opening and thus closes the frame, has recourse to a familiar terrain of racial and sexual signifiers to ridicule the mulata's delusions of social grandeur based on her appearance: She may think that she is a proud peacock, but she is really nothing more than a puffed-up little dove with oversized hips. While the very incongruity of the chocolate beater with which Crespo supplements this deflation recalls Muñoz's caricature of the mulata as a cigar-smoking serpent, there is something else that links these peculiar, almost surreal, fabrications: the respective, and seemingly forced, associations of the mulata with sugar and tobacco.

Given Crespo's own penchant for public masquerades, it is appropriate to ask which discursive position he adopts to poke fun both at the mulata's pretensions and at his readership's racial phobias. The opening line of the poem's middle section is particularly telling in this regard: Who exactly is the "we" in "Pero . . hemos de verla" (But we must see her)? The authorial voice here is part of an anonymous collectivity that distances itself from the mulata in the very process of "seeing" her ("we must see her" could also be read as "we must define or read her"), and it would not be amiss to identify the "we" as a masculine pronoun. The significance of this distance between "we" and "her," mediated by the verb *to see,* is that it suggests the existence of a stable, centered (collective) self that sees without itself being seen. The mulata, though at the center of this poem, is clearly not part of that collectivity. But if, at the level of gender, the oppositional categories of self and other are fully maintained, which already renders suspect the idea of freedom the poem seeks to advance, what about racial differences within the collective masculine "we"? After all, the mulata's supposed theatrics were a cause of concern not only among whites. This is clear from a scene in *Cecilia Valdés* that anticipates Nicolás Guillén's poem "Mulata." In this scene a haughty Cecilia's refusal to dance with the black Dionisio prompts the sarcastic rebuke, "Si a otros puede engañar, a mí no" (You may be able to deceive others with your white skin, but not me).[48]

I am suggesting the existence of a double, indeed a duplicitous, perspective in this poem, an ambivalence that may be read as the rhetorical equivalent of Crespo's multiple authorial disguises. The earliest of these masks is that of "el Anfibio," the Amphibian, from *El látigo del Anfibio, o sea, Colección de sus poesías satíricas a los estravagantes* (The Amphibian's lash, or, Collection of his satirical poetry for eccentrics) (1839–40), Crespo's first volume of poetry, which he published under the name of Luis de Borbón and which, according to Cruz, already contains the seeds of his later *bozal* writings as Creto Gangá.[49] Government censorship can certainly be cited as a compelling reason for Crespo's extravagant simulation, but there is more to it than such an explanation would admit. Surrounded by "el Anfibio," Luis de Borbón, Creto Gangá, and other fictions of the author—possibly even Siriaco Mandinga—Bartolomé José Crespo y Borbón, the name he continued to use along with all these others, becomes itself a convenient fiction. It is convenient precisely because it separates the author from the person and thus frees him from social accountability, and not just to the censor. Even if "Bartolomé José Crespo y Borbón" does not designate a stable self or guarantee the existence of an integral authorial consciousness that subsumes all other masks, even if it is but one of the eccentric satirist's many faces, the easy exchangeability of these masks—some black, some white—implies relations of equality between radically different social positions where historically no such equality existed.

If, in other instances, the linguistic identities of Crespo and Creto are more clearly separable, their poetic voices being so radically different that it would be impossible to mistake one for the other,[50] "La mulata" is situated on an uncertain middle ground where the figure of the mulata itself represents the possibility of confusing Crespo with Creto, both of whom are part of the distant "we." "La mulata" may well be called an example of playful textual confusions of identity that appear to break down the representational conventions that uphold the rigid stratification of mid-nineteenth-century Cuban society. But while this breakdown is imminent within the masculine authorial perspective(s) of this poem, it is also superficial and very temporary, not to mention the fact that it obscures the real conditions of social oppression.[51] And, most importantly perhaps, it has nothing to do with the mulata, who merely provides the textual playground. It is also telling in this regard that Crespo would claim for himself one of the disconcerting characteristics Muñoz attributes to the mulata: he himself slips into the role of that "ever-changing amphibian." The difference is that, for him, it is only a discursive position whose indeterminacy comes without social and political burdens. Whatever freedom this mix-up may represent, it is a distinctly white (though perhaps not exclusively male) prerogative.

It has been argued, and for good reasons, that for a writer like Crespo y Borbón, the "Africanized" persona of Creto Gangá with his distinct *bozal* accent afforded an opportunity to satirize Cuban slave society and voice abolitionist sentiments in the only way that would pass the censor—in blackface.[52] More direct pronouncement of such criticisms, among them Alfredo Torroella's play *El mulato,* were invariably silenced and forced into exile.[53] In the same breath, however, as acknowledging that even those simply suspected of promoting the abolition of slavery risked fates worse than exile, especially in the years following the fiasco of La Escalera, it is perhaps necessary to point out that abolitionist sentiment was not incompatible with racial bias. Morúa Delgado, as we shall see, cites *Cecilia Valdés* as the most salient example of that compatibility in Cuba, but that novel was by no means an isolated instance. In the case of Crespo y Borbón, it is possible, and to my mind plausible, to argue that the mask of Creto Gangá not only allowed him to articulate unpalatable, even perilous, social criticisms but also, at the same time, to respect the clauses of the same political (and aesthetic) contract he appeared to be violating. What appear to be violations or transgressions, then, are but temporary investments in the relative power of particular discursive positions that contract made available. Crespo's dramatized duplicitousness—fake black, genuine white?—is in fact what establishes his authorial control over his material at the very point where he appears to relinquish it. The textual situations created by these shifting positions are comical precisely because they are ideologically safe. In this respect, the writings of Creto Gangá are comparable to that of North American minstrelsy to the extent that they provided nineteenth-century Cuban audiences with a kind of safety zone where ambivalent feelings about slavery and race could be indulged without having to be confronted directly.[54] Minstrelsy, comments Berndt Ostendorf,

anticipated on stage what many Americans deeply feared: the blackening of America. Minstrelsy did in fact create a symbolic language and a comic iconography for "intermingling" culturally with the African Caliban while at the same time "isolating" him socially. In blackening his face the white minstrel acculturated voluntarily to his "comic" vision of blackness, thus anticipating in jest what he feared in earnest. By intermingling with a self-created symbolic Ethiopian he meant to forestall actual assimilation. Yet, however caricatured this vision of blackness may have been it began the translation of black music, black song, and black dance into the mainstream of American popular culture. However, this was a slow process. Initially, it was not the genuine black folklore which appeared on the minstrel stage, but the white man's version of it. But then a feedback pattern emerged and black folklore entered the stage surreptitiously under cover of a white-imposed stereotype.[55]

In the case of Crespo's "La mulata," ideological safety is maintained in a different way. As racial and, for that matter, class differences between men are textually blurred by implying, quite wrongly, that all men have access to the same masculine system of signification,[56] the nonwhite female body becomes the exclusive signifier of race and sexuality. It also becomes a site—in fact *the* site—of Cubans' struggle over cultural meaning and political authority.

2

Caramel Candy for Sale

Yo soy la causa de que los hombres
a las blanquitas no den amor,
porque se mueren por mis pedazos
y los derrito con mi calor.

I am the reason why men
don't make love to the whitegirls,
because they die for parts of my body,
and I melt them with my heat.

I

The popular comedies Bartolomé José Crespo y Borbón wrote
as Creto Gangá, from *Un ajiaco* (A Cuban stew)[1] to *Debajo del
tamarindo* (Under the tamarind tree, 1864), ought not to be confused with the *teatro bufo,* a form that did not reach Cuba until the
late 1860s.[2] In this later category belong plays such as Francisco
Fernández's enormously successful *Los negros catedráticos* (The
black professors), *El bautizo* (The baptism), and *El negro cheche*
(The black braggart) from the 1860s. Unlike Creto's burlesques,
these vaudeville plays did not usually feature *bozales* ("unsea-
soned" Africans) or *negros de nación* (blacks who belonged to specific African cultural communities), but focused instead on ridiculing the social pretensions of the ultrarefined, citified *catedráticos*
and the *curros,*[3] who were much closer to certain North-American

minstrel types such as the "black dandy" than were Creto's caricatures. At the same time, then, that antislavery writings, literary or
not, were vigorously suppressed by the colonial governor-
generalship's censors, black and mulato stereotypes flourished in
Cuban popular theater and in the visual arts, most notably in lithography. In this chapter I focus on another no-less-public but not
so well-known stage for cross-cultural performances: the tobacco
marquillas, decorative 12 × 8.5 centimeter lithographs that were
used as wrappers and labels by Havana's cigar and cigarette manufacturers at least since the 1840s. My main sources are two albums
edited by Antonio Núñez Jiménez: *Cuba en las marquillas cigarreras del siglo XIX* (Cuba as portrayed in nineteenth-century cigarette lithographs) (1985) and *Marquillas cigarreras cubanas* (Cuban cigarette lithographs) (1989). Both are based on the collection
of 3,932 *marquillas* in the José Martí National Library in Havana,
from which 125 items are reproduced in the 1985 volume and 245
in the 1989 edition.[4]

   Lithography, like other technologies such as railroads, was introduced to Cuba before it came to Spain. Like other significant
cultural and technological imports, it arrived, in this case from
France, by way of Santiago de Cuba where, in 1824, the Dominican Juan de Mata y Tejada founded the island's first *litografía.*[5]
Three years later, Luis Caire established the Imprenta Litográfica
Habanera, and in 1839 two other Havana presses followed: that
of Francisco Cosnier, which printed the illustrations for the first
version of *Cecilia Valdés* (the novel itself was published by Lino
Valdés's Imprenta Literaria in 1839[6]) and, beginning in 1840,
worked regularly for the *tabaquerías,* the tobacco factories; and
that of Fernando Costa which, among other things, did illustrations for *El Plantel.* Others followed as the demand for lithographs
increased both from recently launched periodicals such as *La
Charanga, La Revista de La Habana, La Caricatura, Don Junípero, Juan Palomo,* and *El Correo Habanero,* as well as from the
thriving tobacco industry.[7] Núñez Jiménez points out that in 1848
there were 232 *fábricas de tabaco* and 180 *fábricas de cigarros* in
Cuba, each of which needed to make itself distinctive (63).[8] To
do so, they designed unique *emblemas,* or brand labels: a band of
musicians for the Charanga de Villergas division of Llaguna and

Company; a peasant girl picking flowers for the Para Usted brand of Eduardo Guilló's Royal Cigar Factory; a buxom figure of Justice for Luis Susini's La Honradez.[9] The *cigarrerías* also ran serial lithographs (*escenas*) for collectors, ranging from prophetic almanacs and portrait galleries of kings, artists, and mythological figures, to zoological alphabets, Cuban fruits, and, most frequently, cartoonlike scenes of contemporary life that included, of course, many depictions of blacks and mulatos.[10]

II

In 1857, ten years after the successful debut in Havana of Creto Gangá's *Un ajiaco,* the Havana *litografía* of Luis Marquier, founded in 1847, published *Los ingenios: Colleción de vistas de los principales ingenios de azúcar de la isla de Cuba* (The sugar mills: Collection of views of the major sugar plantations on the island of Cuba). This collector's edition of twenty-eight exquisitely crafted lithographs by the French painter and engraver Eduardo Laplante depicted scenes of the most important sugar mills in nineteenth-century Cuba.[11] The mixture of the scientific and the picturesque, as well as the emphasis on accuracy of observation and measurement in *Los ingenios* is characteristic of the many illustrated books and albums that followed the 1810 publication of the *Atlas pittoresque* (Paris), the most popular of the thirty volumes documenting the Latin American travels (1799–1804) of Alexander von Humboldt and the French botanist Aimé Bonpland.[12] Other works within this visual genre were Claudio Gay's two-volume *Atlas de la historia física y política de Chile* (Paris, 1854), C. Nebel's *Voyage pittoresque et archéologique dans la partie le plus interéssante du Méxique* (Paris, 1836), Ramón de la Sagra's *Atlas physique, politique, et naturelle de Cuba* (Paris, n.d.), and, most importantly for my purposes, the albums by the Frenchman Federico Mialhe and the Basque Víctor Patricio Landaluze. Mialhe is best known for his *Isla de Cuba pintoresca*—which was published in Havana by the Litografía de la Real Sociedad Patriótica, probably in 1838 or 1839),[13] and was reprinted by José María Andueza in Madrid in 1841 as *Isla de Cuba pintoresca, historica, política, literaria, mer-*

cantil, e industrial—as well as for *Isla de Cuba,* printed by Luis Marquier's press probably in the late 1840s or early 1850s, and for *Album pintoresco de la isla de Cuba* published in Berlin around the same time. Landaluze's most popular album was the 1881 *Tipos y costumbres de la isla de Cuba,* printed in Havana.

Núñez Jiménez's two editions can be regarded as the most recent examples of, or throwbacks to, that tradition of costumbrista realism. Like their nineteenth-century predecessors, they offer "typical" representations of Cuban culture designed for largely non-Cuban audiences. *Cuba en las marquillas cigarreras del siglo XIX,* for instance, is an oversized paperback, a beautiful coffee-table book published by Cuba's tourism office. Featuring texts in three languages—Spanish, French, and English—it is reminiscent of Mialhe's *Isla de Cuba pintoresca. Marquillas cigarreras cubanas,* on the other hand, is a rather expensively produced hardcover volume published under the auspices of the Spanish State Commission for the Fifth Centennial of the Discovery of America and the Cuban Commission for the Half Millennium of the Meeting of Two Worlds, in collaboration with the Cuban tobacco industry. Like the *marquillas* themselves and certainly like *Los ingenios,* these two books advertise Cuban culture, and of course Cuban products, abroad.[14]

The extent to which *Marquillas cigarreras cubanas* in particular serves specific advertising purposes while officially posing as mere historicocultural documentation is clear not only from the long section on the traditional medicinal uses of tobacco but also, more overtly even, from the mention of a host of historical personalities, ranging from Balzac, Newton, Lord Byron, Kipling, and Longfellow to Ernesto "Che" Guevara, who testify to the pleasures of smoking. This kind of veiled advertising, presented as a form of consumer information, is of particular interest at a time of controversies, in the United States and Europe, about the use of tobacco and concerted attempts to limit the advertising of tobacco products even further. The volume's eulogy of the *vegueros,* Cuba's agrarian petit bourgeoisie, and the tobacco workers as the group that was most progressive and zealous in its desire for national independence is, of course, an advertisement of a different kind: it ideologically legitimates the tobacco industry by testifying to its historical commitment to the Cuban cause. In addition, both volumes are interesting in the context of Cuba's more recent efforts to promote tourism, which have increased significantly since the radical political changes in Eastern Europe and in the former Soviet Union have placed the island in an exceedingly precarious political and economic position.[15]

But let me return to the nineteenth century and to *Los ingenios*. As if to refute Fernando Ortiz's claim that "tobacco is a seeker after art; sugar avoids it," this little book, with its precious illustrations and the accompanying texts by Cuban landowner Justo Germán Cantero, offers a remarkable display of what Benítez Rojo has called a "strong will . . to set itself up in terms of myth, of origin, of truth, of power, legitimate power, inexhaustible power which is the very foundation of law and nationhood."[16] Though *Los ingenios* was sold only to a handful of subscribers, its portentous message was disseminated much more broadly, and at a fraction of the book's cost, when shortly afterwards, the Havana *tabaquería* La Honradez, owned by Luis Susini and Son, reproduced most of Laplante's engravings on its *marquillas*.[17] Not only do these *marquillas* testify to the pervasiveness in nineteenth-century Cuba of the discourse of sugar. They in fact open a new chapter in the complicated history of sugar's competitive entanglement with tobacco. The discursive intersection of the two economical-cultural sectors that this particular series of *marquillas* represents is fraught with fascinating ironies, since the tobacco industry suddenly depicts on its own advertisements their most aggressive rival: the sugar plantation.

At the end of the eighteenth century, the Cuban tobacco planters and the nascent Havana sugar barons clashed over the sugar industry's insatiable demand for fertile land in close proximity to the port of Havana. This clash resulted in the relocation of the tobacco plantations from Güines to Vuelta Abajo. Tobacco fields were destroyed at the same time that world sugar prices soared to spectacular heights. It was sugar that held the promise of enormous expansion and profits, whereas the tobacco trade had been controlled by Spain since the founding of the Real Compañía del Comercio de La Habana in 1739.[18] To claim, then—as Fernando Ortiz would more than a decade later in his influential *Contrapun-*

teo cubano del tabaco y el azúcar (*Cuban Counterpoint: Tobacco and Sugar*) (1940)—that "tobacco has always been more Cuban than sugar," that it spelled liberty instead of slavery, and "that in the history of Cuba sugar represents Spanish absolutism; tobacco, the native liberators," would appear to be a nostalgic mystification of historical developments.[19]

Clearly, sugar and tobacco were not "all contrast," even if one is "a scientific gift of civilization" and the other "the magic gift of the savage world."[20] Nor did Ortiz conceive of *Cuban Counterpoint* as a historical study in any positivistic sense but, rather, as a "type of dialogued composition that carries the dramatic dialectic of life into the realm of art"—Pérez Firmat comments dryly that Ortiz "was never a very good scientist." According to Benítez Rojo, *Cuban Counterpoint* is a text that "does not seek its legitimation within the discourse of the social sciences, but rather within those of literature, of fiction. That is, it puts itself forward from the outset as a bastard text [*como un texto bastardo*]," a fable of sorts whose own mode of existence is as "promiscuous" as its origins.[21] Evidence of this discursive promiscuity is readily available throughout Ortiz's text, but I am particularly interested here in the shared features of Ortiz's two fabulous protagonists, "the dark tobacco" (*el moreno tabaco*) and "the whitened sugar" (*la blanconaza azúcar*), and their defiance of dichotomy. We are told, for instance, that sugar "was mulatto from the start." It is "a miscegenation of flavors," Ortiz contends, at the same time as he compares cigars to "luscious cinnamon skin" and the color of different types of tobacco to the "intermediary and mixed pigmentation" of Cuban women.[22] The classification of nonwhite women in terms of different grades of refined sugar is most striking in the *marquilla* series entitled "Muestras de azúcar de mi ingenio" (Sugar samples from my plantation), run by Eduardo Guilló's Para Usted brand and reproduced in both of Núñez Jiménez's volumes.[23] Some salient captions from this series are: "Quebrado de primera" (First-rate—from the centrifuge) and "Blanco de segunda (trén comun)" (Second-rate white—common train), both of which refer to light mulatas, while "Quebrado de segunda" (Second-rate) features a brown-skinned woman with "negroid" features. This series, clearly, marks another discursive intersection of tobacco and sugar, not in visual but in linguistic terms: all the captions here draw on the elaborate repertoire of scientific terms associated with sugar production.

The economic and cultural relationship between sugar and tobacco in nineteenth-century Cuba, then, is characterized by promiscuity of a very specific kind. The appearance of Laplante's engravings on La Honradez's *marquillas* testifies at once to the ever-increasing importance of sugar as an economic power *and* a hegemonic cultural discourse, as well as to the tobacco industry's inevitable complicity with it, lest tobacco, like everything else in the proximity of these "precocious case[s] of industrialization," be reduced to a position of utter insignificance.[24] What is awesome about *Los ingenios* as a whole is the stark visibility of the institutions and apparatuses of power.[25] From these lithographs, the sugar plantation emerges as nothing less than a teleological force; it *is* the Law, and as such, it is self-evident and self-explanatory. The tall, pristinely white chimneys of the *casas de calderas,* or boiler houses, towering over the red-tiled roofs of the lower buildings of the *purga,* or refinery, the open sheds in which the bagasse was stored and the clay was mixed for the purification of the sugar, and the *barracones,* or slave quarters, confidently take their place right next to the indigenous Royal Palms, and their ever-present gauze ribbons of smoke mingle innocently with the clouds. Laplante's engravings communicate the same "feeling of pride" with which Leonardo Gamboa points out the sugar mill La Tinaja in *Cecilia Valdés.*

Para ello había motivo sobrado, no ya sólo por el valor en dinero que representaba la finca, y por las consideraciones sociales que se les guardaban a sus dueños, mas también por el cuadro bello y pintoresco del conjunto, contemplado a buena distancia; *encubridora eficaz de los lunares y manchas inherentes a casi todas las obras, así humanas como divinas.*

He had reason enough to be proud, not only because of the property's monetary value, and because of the social prestige it afforded its owners, but also because of the beautiful and picturesque view of the whole place from a distance; *it effectively/efficiently covered up the*

Figure 1. *Ingenio Buenavista,* 1857, lithograph by Eduardo Laplante (courtesy of the Library of Congress)

spots or blemishes inherent in almost any work, human as well as divine.[26]

Laplante's pictorial image of the Buena Vista Sugar Mill (fig. 1), owned by none other than Justo Cantero himself, comes closest to the descriptions of La Tinaja in Villaverde's novel. Both are perfect examples of the very process of distancing that blots out the "blemishes" or "stains" of human, especially slave, labor. The only kind of human activity represented in the above quotation is that of contemplation, of looking. The visual equivalent of this in the original lithograph of *Ingenio Buenavista* are the small figures of three caballeros placed in the foreground at the picture's visual center, the owner's elegant residence, or *casa de vivienda,* atop a distant hill. These male figures appear to be engaged in leisurely activities; one of them seems to be in the process of inscribing something on a tree, perhaps a self-referential gesture on the lithographer's part. In the background below we see a solitary black slave who appears to be fishing, and farther back, a group of slaves on their way to work in the cane fields. These already-minute black

Figure 2. *Ingenio Buena Vista,* n.d., cigarette lithograph, La Honradez (reprinted with the permission of CENDA)

figures have been completely erased from La Honradez's reproduction of *Ingenio Buena Vista* (fig. 2), where the only visible human presence are two (not three) white men contemplating the scenery. The entire scene has now been turned into the leisured space of a Cuban pastoral. This takes even further Laplante's own practice, in most of his engravings of sugar plantations, of keeping human representations to a bare minimum. Slaves in particular become mere specks of dust that spoil the pleasant view, the harmonious and nonexploitative representation of power. At the same time, however, their very insignificance underscores the overwhelming, literally de-humanizing presence of the sugar mill and its technological prowess.[27] The following passage, again from *Cecilia Valdés,* is a precise illustration of that technological prowess.

Bajo más de un concepto era una finca soberbia el ingenio de *La Tinaja,* calificativo que tenía bien merecido por sus dilatados y lozanos campos de caña-miel, por los trescientos o más brazos para cultivarlos, por su gran boyada, su numeroso material móvil, su máquina de vapor con hasta veinticinco caballos de fuerza, recién importada de la América del Norte, al costo de veinte y tantos mil pesos, sin contar el trapiche horizontal, también nuevo y que armado allí había costado la mitad de aquella suma.

In more ways than one the sugar mill *La Tinaja* was a superb outfit, an adjective it well deserved because of its vast and luxuriant fields of sugarcane, the more than three hundred hands that cultivated them, its large herd of oxen, its excellent equipment, including a steam engine of up to twenty-five horsepower, which had recently been imported from the United States at a cost of more than $20,000, not counting the horizontal mill [Jamaica train] installed on the premises, which was also new and had cost half of that sum.[28]

It would not be inappropriate to read the fleeting metonym "brazos"—hands or arms; instead of *braceros,* field hands—as a euphemism for slaves. It is overdetermined in that it represents not only human labor but, more specifically, the very process of psychological and physical deformation that reduces human beings to one of many items in this inventory of technical equipment and natural resources that constitutes the sugar plantation's questionable, yet unquestioned, merit. It is perhaps in this context that one should place Ortiz's remark that the cultures of the African slaves were "destroyed and crushed under the weight of the cultures in existence here, like sugarcane ground in the rollers of the mill."[29] Ortiz's concise analogy confirms the naturalization of slave labor and slave culture, which legitimates their exploitation and dehumanization—what is more benignly called cultivation.[30]

The way in which Laplante's engravings have been reproduced on the *marquillas* adds another dimension to the legitimation of economic, political, and cultural power already inscribed in the lithographs themselves and discussed at some length by Benítez Rojo. I am referring to the elaborate, two-inch visual frames that partially envelop the actual reproductions of the various sugar plantations as decorative borders (*orlas*). Their purpose and function, however, exceeds the purely ornamental. In these particular frames, unlike in those used in other *marquilla* series, nature motifs predominate, preferably arcadian landscapes whose psychological function is that of providing an "uninvolved compensatory context" that induces release from social and political tensions.[31] In the left-hand margins colorful Audubon-like close-ups of exotic birds, plants, and other natural specimens, among them extinct—hence, peaceful—Indians, usually alternate with neoclassical portraits of mostly aristocratic-looking young women. What ensures the "naturalness," that is, the innocence, of those female portraits that are occasionally nudes and incorporates them into this catalog of natural-history motifs is the almost invariable passivity of their postures. Their glances are always chastely cast down; they never directly confront the viewer.[32] In addition, the majority of them are variations on the Virgin Mary icon, complete with one exposed breast.[33] The space to the right, always reserved for each tobacco factory's pictorial blazon, is in the case of figure 2 occupied by yet another neoclassical image, a representation of Justice in a gilded oval frame. Part of that frame is the inscription on the arch above the figure's head: "Los hechos me justificarán" (The facts will justify me), which, in the context of these particular *marquillas*, has clearly unintended ironic resonances. The end (product), it would seem, does indeed justify the means (slave labor). Together, all these purportedly ornamental symbolic images constitute what I call, with Barthes in mind, an authenticating iconography.[34]

Figure 2 works somewhat differently than the majority of these *marquillas*. Sporting the motif of the bird and serpent already familiar from the somewhat different context of Muñoz del Monte's "La mulata," it replaces the Audubon-like arcadia with an image of Darwinian Nature-as-conflict—note the absence of any human beings in the frame. La Honradez's emblematic figure of Justice, a mythic representation of human civilization, offers an appropriate contrast to Nature's savagery. The centered image of the sugar plantation, then, articulates the relationship between these two spaces; it mediates between the two equally mythic states. Rather than a naturalization of technology, then, the sugar mill represents the triumph of Reason over Nature. This is indeed what Clive Bush has called "the dream of reason."

The question that comes to mind at this point, given my earlier comments on the *formal* existence of the sugar plantation both in *Los ingenios* and in these *marquillas,* is why something that is

supposedly self-evident would require authentication or legitimation in the first place. Clearly because it is, after all, not self-evident
or self-explanatory, and this is precisely what the abundant, even
excessive, representations of Nature signify, even in those instances
where they have been reduced to abstract and seemingly nonrepresentational floral ornaments. Technology in the shape of the sugar
plantation becomes part of Nature even as it, as instrument of civilizing Reason, dominates, destroys, and eventually replaces it.
Within the process of representation, the sugar plantation's impos-
ing presence is paradoxically established both as natural and as
aesthetically pleasing in its formal unity and symmetry. While this
process of composition is already part of the original engravings
of *Los ingenios*, its underlying principles become more readily accessible in the visual context of the *marquillas's* baroque iconography and its distinct formal hierarchies. This two-dimensional iconography, in which ancient myths stand by new ones, is structured
according to the double tradition of epic and pastoral. It enacts
the classical dialectics of war and peace, recast either in terms of
Technology and Nature or Reason and Nature, as it achieves elegant, *harmonious* resolutions. These images of refined harmony
confer a sense of invariable reality constituted by what may well
be called a "corporate social viewpoint."[35]

III

It is conspicuous that the various close-ups in the frames of the
above *marquillas* do not feature blacks and mulatos, not even as
noble savages. This, however, does not mean that so-called persons
of color were rarely represented on these wrappers. On the contrary, racial stereotypes proliferated on the cigarette *marquillas*.
They indirectly perpetuated the hegemonic discourse of sugar in
which they were conceived either as absences or as mere dots or
"spots." Given the widespread use of *marquillas* as a marketing
tool among Cuban cigarette manufacturers approximately since
the 1840s, as well as the popularity these stereotypes enjoyed at
that time, it would have been impossible to exclude them from the
"theater" of representative life that formed an important part of

Figure 3. "Los diablos coronados castigarán tus pecados" (The crowned devils will punish your sins), 1866, cigarette lithograph, La Honradez (reprinted with the permission of CENDA)

these lithographs' standard repertoire. These genrelike scenes, set in human-sized environments carved out from within totality[36]— the sugar plantation or, much more frequently, the city—are populated by crude caricatures of half-clad *bozales* uninhibitedly performing their wild "pagan" dances on the traditional "Día de Reyes" (Day of Kings), January 6, their contorted bodies bearing little resemblance to those in Federico Mialhe's famous engraving *El Día de Reyes*. Núñez Jiménez includes two such prints, complete with often derogatory captions and framed with the usual ornate borders: one from La Honradez's "Prophetic Almanac for the Year 1866" (fig. 3), the other from Eduardo Guilló. Their respective captions read, "Los diablos coronados castigarán tus pecados" (The crowned devils will punish your sins) and "Samba la culebra, si siñó" (Shake a leg, yessir).[37] Other prints have more of a predilection for situation comedy, which occasionally involves a

Figure 4. "¿Come ñame uté? Fransico pa servi a uté" (What is your name? / Are you eating yams? Francisco at your service), n.d., cigarette lithograph, Para Usted (reprinted with the permission of CENDA)

play on the discrepancy between visual and verbal representation. This is the case, for example, in one of the Guilló prints (fig. 4), which features two black men sitting at a table outside a *bohio,* as those crude, palm-thatched huts were called. One of them is eating yams. The caption, a representation of their vernacular dialogue, reads, "¿Come ñame uté? Fransico pa servi a uté." The simple-minded humor of this sketch depends entirely on the fact that the question can be understood in two ways: either as "Are you eating yams?" or as "What is your name?" The answer, "Francisco, at your service," of course results from a misunderstanding based on the homophony of *ñame* and *llame* on the one hand and of *come* and *como* on the other. That this possibility for confusion was by no means peculiar to Afro-Cuban speech would have mattered little to an audience accustomed to associating "incorrectly" pronounced Spanish with the members of an inferior caste.

But this kind of humor is positively benign when compared to

Figure 5. "¡¡¡Vengan a ver esto!!!" (Come look at this!), n.d., cigarette lithograph, Para Usted (reprinted with the permission of CENDA)

that of other *marquillas* from Guilló's Para Usted label, which are
vicious caricatures of blacks imitating Cuba's white bourgeoisie in
both dress and demeanor—one is reminded of Crespo y Borbón's
strutting mulata here. One (fig. 5) shows two fashionably dressed
black couples dancing a minuet in a rather pastoral setting, while
the other (fig. 6) features even more stylishly outfitted *curros* or
catedráticos, probably on their way to a "colored" dance. The captions sarcastically and condescendingly identify these images as a
social outrage and an aberration: "¡¡¡Vengan a ver esto!!!" (Come
look at this!) and "¡¡¡Ave María gallo!!!" (Holy cow). These sentiments are quite reminiscent of some of Villaverde's disparaging
narrative comments on the dances of the "gente de color" (persons
of color) in 1830 Havana: "A fair number of black and mulato
women had arrived, for the most part overdressed in gaudy clothing of the worst taste. The men of the same class . . displayed no
better taste."[38] In the second of these prints, the verbal outrage
over such poor taste is visually underscored by a stunned little dog

Figure 6. "¡Ave María gallo!" (Holy cow!), n.d., cigarette lithograph, Para Usted (reprinted with the permission of CENDA)

to the left and the dwarfish figure of a black *calesero* (coachman) to the right, whose broad, knowing smile and crossed arms remind the viewer of the "proper" place of these uppity black socialites, seemingly oblivious to the significance of their skin color. More malicious yet is one of La Honradez's prints advertising, as it were, "Agua florida para blanquear la piel" (Flower water for whitening the skin). It consists of before and after profiles of a *negro bembón*, a thick-lipped, broad-nosed black dandy whose presumably hilarious offense is to have taken the idea of whitening far too literally (fig. 7). While it may be possible to suggest that such cartoonlike caricatures also indirectly mock the members of Cuba's native aristocracy and their own preoccupation with social status, such an argument seems strained. It is impossible to ignore that these prints had the effects of embedding racial stereotypes in the popular imagination. One might add that these and other caricatures that appear on the *marquillas* were not so much inspired by Cuban folklore, as Fernando Ortiz has it, but, much like the minstrel

Figure 7. "Agua florida para blanquear la piel" (Flower water for whitening the skin), n.d., cigarette lithograph, La Honradez (reprinted with the permission of CENDA)

shows, were substitutes for folklore that developed specifically in urban settings.[39]

Of special interest in this context are three *marquilla* series: "Vida y muerte de la mulata" (Life and death of the mulata) by the Charanga de Villergas division of Llaguna and Company (fifteen prints); "Historia de la mulata" (History of the mulata) by Eduardo Guilló's Para Usted label (seven prints); and "La vida de la mulata" (The life of the mulata) by the already-familiar La Honradez (four prints), all issued during the mid-to-late nineteenth century.[40] Throughout the nineteenth century, the mulata, a social by-product of the sugar-and-slave economy, is most frequently associated not with the rural setting of the sugar plantation but with the kind of urban environment that Ortiz would label "hampa afrocubana," the Afro-Cuban underworld, in his book of the same title (1906). As we have already seen in Crespo y Borbón's "La mulata," her domain are the streets of Havana and other centers of commercial activity, and her movements represent the saucy rhythms of common life. In fact, she comes to embody certain exchanges deemed characteristic of the city, most notably the illicit sexuality of a streetwalker.[41] The fact that such a public existence could readily be interpreted as a pathological condition—nineteenth-century medicine regarded all manifestations of female sexuality as pathological—made the mulata a prime target for the tobacco factories' mass-produced serial lithographs and their not-infrequent use of sexual innuendo, facilitated by the underlying association of smoking with burning desire. But before discussing these three *marquilla* series in more detail, I would first like to situate them within the context of nineteenth-century Cuban visual arts, specifically by relating them to earlier and contemporaneous images of blacks and women in painting and engraving.[42]

Cuban painters, for most of the nineteenth century, were far too steeped in neoclassical themes and conventions even to acknowledge the existence of blacks in their work.[43] Consistent with the fact that in Cuba, as in the United States, "the most popular medium for 'genre' about the mid-[nineteenth] century was not the oil painting but the lithograph,"[44] images of blacks appeared almost exclusively in engravings, whose practicioners favored representative national types over pastoral panoramas and idealized portraits of Cuba's native aristocracy. The first, though barely visible, images of blacks are found in an engraving of Havana's Plaza del Mercado by Elias Durnford, aide-de-camp to the earl of Albemarle, who headed the British invasion of the city. This engraving is one of Durnford's *Six Views of the City, Harbour, and Country of Havana* (1764/65). As parts of the island's exotic local color (pun intended), nonwhites captured the imagination of foreign visitors to a far greater extent than they did the interest of Cuba's native visual artists.[45] It is not surprising, then, that the most distinctive and most detailed early depictions of Cuban blacks and mulata/os should have been part of the work of three Frenchmen, Hipolito Garneray, Mialhe, and of course Laplante. But, above all, there was Landaluze.[46]

Landaluze arrived in Cuba in the 1850s. By 1881, the year in which his famous lithograph collection *Tipos y costumbres de la isla de Cuba* was published, he had emerged as the most talented and prolific chronicler of the island's nonwhite population. What is usually deemed most remarkable about Landaluze's work is the painstakingly detailed, almost photographic, realism that characterizes his representations of popular Cuban types such as the black *calesero* and of the festive garb worn during ritual celebrations by Cuba's *negros de nación* (he lived in Guanabacoa, whose population included members of numerous ñáñigo and *abakuá* religious groups). Many of his engravings, as well as his paintings, are instances of sentimental anecdote and domestic comedy.[47] They are like blowups of the tiny representations of human drama that characterized the conceit of spontaneity in costumbrista painting, as opposed, for instance, to the distancing, the self-conscious sense of artifice in the work of Sawkins and Laplante.[48] Fernando Ortiz's description of *Tipos y costumbres* as "an ethnographic museum " is quite appropriate.[49] Landaluze's brand of realism, his emphasis on the visual authenticity of his Cuban types, is thoroughly infused with the "rigor (mortis)" of nineteenth-century natural science, its classificatory zeal and concurrent faith in amassing visual facts.[50] Bush comments that, during the eighteenth and nineteenth centuries, "Linnaeus's classification of species gives a model of scientific stability as important and with as far-reaching effects as the popular conception of Newton's cosmology."[51] In other words, the acclaimed realism of Landaluze's fixed character types is quite comparable to that of representative specimens exhibited in natural-history museums. The scientific stability these institutions represented became an implicit model for social stability. The values of use and control, previously applied specifically in relation to nature, are thus transferred to the social arena. This is most striking in Landaluze's magnificent lithograph entitled *La mulata* (fig. 8).

Perhaps most intriguing about Landaluze's full-length depiction of a mulata in the company of an older black woman, who could be either her mother or her grandmother, is the relation between these two figures and the male artist-viewer inscribed in the women's bodily postures and the expressions on their faces. Carol Armstrong's reading of Degas's *The Interior* (1868), which is also known as *The Rape,* is useful here: "*The Interior* thematizes the

Figure 8. *La mulata*, n.d., lithograph by Víctor Patricio Landaluze (reprinted with the permission of CENDA)

visual relationship between male and female that informs the genre of the female nude. For it is not quite right to say that there is no gesture here, no action: the male figure in *The Interior* gestures and acts through his gaze."[52] Though located outside of the picture, the absent, invisible artist in Landaluze's lithograph nevertheless acts on the two women, whose leisurely stroll he appears to have interrupted, through his gaze. Even though *La mulata,* unlike Degas's painting, does not visually thematize (and certainly does not problematize) this male-female relationship, its distinct traces create something akin to a narrative situation.

The lithograph captures precisely the moment of interruption when the two women pause to react to an intrusive presence; both turn their heads to look over their shoulders and back at the artist-viewer. As striking as the contrast in age and attire is the difference in their responses: The splendid mulata, stylishly coiffured and sporting an elegant gown with a tight bodice and a lavish train, is half smiling, her head bent down ever so slightly in a coquettish greeting, a gesture of recognition not of an individual but of a particular, familiar situation. As the (male) viewer's glance travels down her slender but shapely figure, he notices that the suggestive allure of her nod is reflected in, and emphasized by, the way in which she holds her open fan, which no longer hides her face but has been lowered and is perpendicular to her body.[53] Her bodily syntax and facial expression indicate an internalization of the male gaze. The expression of the mulata's chaperone, on the other hand, seems openly to deflect that gaze: her head held high, the older woman casts a distant, disdainful look of suspicion at the artist-viewer. She is still holding the mulata's left arm and seems to urge her more reckless (or submissive) companion to keep on walking. Unlike her fashionable (grand)daughter, she wears a simple, shapeless dress, with a nondescript plaid shawl chastely covering her head and shoulders. Her hair is tightly wrapped in a coil or bandanna that reaches down to her eyebrows, leaving exposed only an almost masculine visage hardened, one assumes, by age and grief.[54]

This lithograph is typical of Landaluze, whose "realistic" mulatas "are always young and pretty women; they are never engaged in hard labor: they are objects for the pleasure of men," that is, for erotic appropriation and delectation.[55] At the same time, it belongs to a broader discourse on female sexuality and race, traceable in visual conventions that connect this engraving with other nineteenth-century representations of women, especially constructions of the sexualized female in European painting.[56] The most obvious of these conventions is the fact that *La mulata* depicts *two* women, not one, as the title, which makes no mention of the black matron, would indicate. This kind of doubling recalls paintings like Manet's *Olympia,* in which a white female figure is paired with a black figure, by the nineteenth century usually of the same gender, so as to imply their sexual similarity.[57] While the older black woman in this case is not a servant but probably a relative, and even though she is portrayed in the most unfeminine and thus asexual way possible—masculinized facial features, almost completely flattened physique without even a hint of feminine curves—her iconographic function is nevertheless similar to that of black servants in eighteenth- and nineteenth-century French painting; her role is to sexualize her companion. In *La mulata,* however, this iconographic strategy is somewhat redundant, since the mulata herself is already thoroughly sexualized by her coquettish pose, by her explicit identification as being of mixed blood in the print's title, and, more subtly, by details such as her full, voluptuous lips, very curly black hair, and slightly-too-broad nose—racialized features that "spoil" the aesthetic ideal of harmony and symmetry. For purposes of comparison, I interject a description of Cecilia Valdés.

La complexión podía pasar por saludable, la encarnación viva, hablando en el sentido en que los pintores toman esta palabra, *aunque a poco que se fijaba la atención,* se advertía en el color del rostro, que sin dejar de ser sanguíneo había demasiado ocre en su composición, y no resultaba diáfano ni libre. ¿A qué raza, pues, pertenecía esta muchacha? Difícil es decirlo. Sin embargo, *a un ojo conocedor no podía esconderse* que sus labios rojos tenían un borde o filete oscuro, y que la iluminación del rostro terminaba en una especie de penumbra hacia el nacimiento del cabello. Su sangre no era pura y bien podía asegurarse que allá en la tercera o cuatra generación estaba mezclada con la etíope.

Her complexion might have passed for healthy, the coloring was vivid, in the sense that painters use that word, *although if one examined it carefully,* one would detect in the color of her face, notwithstanding its ruddy glow, that it had too much ocher in its composition, which detracted from its clear and free quality. To what race, then, did this girl belong? Difficult to say. But *to the knowing eye could not remain hidden* the dark band or border of her red lips, nor that the brightness of her face ended in a sort of shadow at the hairline. Her blood was not pure, and one could be certain that back in the third or fourth generation it had been mixed with Ethiopia.[58]

Villaverde's painterly technique and vocabulary attends to detail in the same way that Landaluze's does—detail, that is, as empirical evidence of essential impurity, in both the racial and the sexual sense (note the flagrant contradiction inherent in this approach to realism).[59] The conflation of race with female sexuality is particularly pronounced in an earlier passage that comments on Cecilia's "small" mouth whose "full lips" nevertheless indicate "más voluptuosidad que firmeza de carácter" (more voluptuousness or sensuality than strength of character).[60] In Landaluze's *La mulata,* female sensuality and sexuality are foregrounded by yet another external detail: a luxurious silk manta or *pañolón,* that is, a large square shawl, which is draped in loose folds over the mulata's delicate back and arms in a way that draws the viewer's eye to her buttocks. Much more significant than Gilman's contention that buttocks were one of the primary nineteenth-century European icons of atavistic (and anomalous) female sexuality is that the richly textured fabric of the shawl, which actually distracts from the mulata's curves more than it reveals them, is itself a signifier of the kind of theatrical artificiality associated with the idea of the "fallen" woman, whose prototype is the actress.[61] Female sexuality, as it is externalized and encoded in specific details of *both* skin and dress, can then be valorized, on the basis of visual evidence, as moral degeneracy—Villaverde's equation of voluptuousness with presumed lack of moral fortitude is a case in point. In Landaluze's print, sexual excess and its concurrent lack of morality is encoded in yet another icon, the mulata's so-called Darwin's ear, no less pronounced here than it is in Manet's *Nana.*[62] This particular icon pretends to offer additional sociobiological evidence of the mulata's immorality that is as subtle as her slightly, but suggestively, raised dress.

A different, yet closely related, example of Gilman's overall claim that, in the nineteenth century, the sexual becomes a central structuring feature of systems that relate difference to pathology is *La mulata: Estudio fisiológico, social y jurídico* (Madrid, 1878) by the Puerto Rican Eduardo Ezponda. This pseudo-social-scientific study, a forerunner of Fernando Ortiz's famous criminological-ethnographic treatise *Los negros brujos: Hampa afrocubana* (1906), relates racial and sexual difference to social pathology even more explicitly than do Landaluze's engraving and Villaverde's novel.[63] Clearly in accord with religioscientific credos that "hybridism is heinous," that racial impurity is "against the law of nature," espoused with remarkable vociferousness both in the antebellum and postbellum United States,[64] Ezponda, also known as author of the abolitionist story "Doña Laura de Contreras" (1882), confidently attributes the mulata's alleged moral degradation to her color: she inherits "the degradation of the slave race with her skin." This inheritance, in other words, accounts for what he calls her "confused notions about good and evil" and her depraved materialism, qualities that, so the reasoning goes, inevitably predestine her to an existence of delinquency.[65] The chaperone in Landaluze's picture personifies that fate. The older woman's masculinized grimace, a supposed characteristic of aging prostitutes, is by far the most explicit visualization of moral debasement due to gender and race (as "species"), both constructed on the "empirical" basis of physiognomy. An embodiment of the "dark shadow" of racial difference that the "knowing eye" of Villaverde's narrator detects on Cecilia's high forehead, the matron's image functions as a warning to less discerning readers, who might otherwise be deceived by the mulata's generally pleasing appearance, "la regularidad de sus facciones y simetría de sus formas" (the regularity of her features and symmetry of her bodily shape).[66] Like Josefa, whom Villaverde represents in similar terms, and to a lesser extent Rosario, Cecilia's "mad" mother, Landaluze's aged chaperone is a conflation of the mulata's past and future, a representation of that infamous skeleton in many Caribbean closets: the black (grand)mother who is hidden when company comes.

Landaluze's work, Adelaida de Juan argues, catered to Cuba's bourgeois colonial ideology in two ways: on the one hand, he projected images of idle servants and slaves, implying that slavery was a state of well-being; on the other, he fetishized women—mostly nonwhite women—as objects of male pleasure.[67] Clearly, *La mulata* fits both these categories. But what of the quite explicit constitution of the paintings's female subjects by the white artist-viewer's masculine gaze? Is it problematized (for us perhaps, but not necessarily for Landaluze's contemporaries) by the tension between the women's very different reactions? While this foregrounding of the representational process does make accessible ideological contradictions—primarily the fear of racial difference and the simultaneous attraction to it—it is also constitutive of the reality-effect of this print, which depends precisely on the decontextualized differential play between black and white, feminine and masculine. The absence of any background setting that would introduce an element of contingency ultimately ensures the "proper" distance between the viewer and his subjects, a distance that initially appears to have been abolished by the picture's implicit narrative of their suggested interaction. The lack of background makes the two women appear like specimens in a textbook.[68] The contrast between *La mulata* and one of Landaluze's paintings from the same period, *Sirviente tratando de besar un busto* (Servant trying to kiss a bust) (fig. 9), will help clarify this point.

At the center of this anecdotal drawing-room scene is a very dark-black manservant, a stereotypical *negro bembón*, who has evidently interrupted his house-cleaning tasks secretly to indulge his fascination with a female bust of white marble on an equally white pedestal. One is reminded here of Leonardo Gamboa's description of Isabel Ilincheta, which I quoted earlier, and of Villaverde's not-so-ironic comments on the slaves' "idolatrous" adulation of her. Even the colors of the ornately decorated drawing room, as well as the servant's own red vest, do not distract from the exaggerated Manichaean juxtaposition of disfigured blackness and pure, aestheticized whiteness that dominates this beauty-and-the-beast encounter. Still holding a feather duster, the servant, whose closed eyes indicate total obliviousness to his surroundings (above all, of course, to the masterly artist-viewer), cautiously and awkwardly leans forward, pursing his enormous lips to kiss those of the bust.[69] Landaluze's voyeuristic scenario both endorses his

Figure 9. *Sirviente tratando de besar un busto* (Servant trying to kiss a bust), n.d., oil painting by Víctor Patricio Landaluze (reprinted with the permission of the Universidad Nacional Autónoma de México)

colonial viewers' mythic fear of black male sexuality and safeguards white women's chastity. There is not even a hint of sexuality
in his representation of white femininity as a cold marble bust
without a body. At the same time, however, the painter feminizes
the black servant with his feather duster and house slippers, a form
of representational emasculation that renders these character's actions safely comical.[70] In iconographic terms, the expected punishment for the offense about to be committed has already been administered, which allows the spectators a comfortable emotional
distance from this controlled theatrical scene. One of Villaverde's
characters, the mulato José Dolores Pimienta, articulates the link
between representational and social constraints that underwrites
the different iconographies operative in both of Landaluze's prints
when he laments: "Y es muy duro, durísimo, insufrible, . . . , que
ellos [los blancos] nos arrebaten las de color, y nosotros no po-
damos ni mirar para las mujeres blancas" (And it's hard, very hard,
unbearable, . . . , that *they* [white men] take the colored women
away from us, and we can't even look at white women).[71] Need
one wonder about Villaverde's sympathies here?

The same thematics are almost obsessively reiterated in the
marquillas, among which Landaluze's caricature would by no
means have been out of place. In fact, he himself is immortalized
in one of the labels.[72] Of the three series I mentioned above, Llaguno and Company's "Vida y muerte de la mulata" is of special
interest, not only because it is the most detailed pictorial chronicle
of the mulata's social career but because its distinctive *orla* is itself
a miniature history of Cuban lithography (fig. 10). This frame,
which depicts five musicians in the midst of elaborate garlands of
gigantic flowers (a stylized version of the pastoral motifs discussed
earlier), is an extension of the firm's distinctive label, La Charanga
de Villergas (Villergas's Brass Band). That the drummer closely resembles none other than Landaluze himself is no mere coincidence:
Llaguno's Charanga de Villergas design is adapted from the cover
illustration of *La Charanga,* the first Cuban journal of social caricature, cofounded, in 1857, by Juan Martínez Villergas and Landaluze.[73] Under the pseudonym Bayacito, Landaluze also drew caricatures for the periodicals *Moro Muza* and *Don Circunstancias,*

Figure 10. "El que siembra coje" (He who sows reaps), n.d., cigarette litho-graph, La Charanga de Villergas (reprinted with the permission of CENDA)

both published by Villergas, and he himself edited *Don Junípero.* The best known of Landaluze's cartoons is the series entitled "Lectura en los talleres" (Factory reading, 1866–69).[74] The importance of Landaluze to nineteenth-century Cuba's material culture, as well as the extensive imbrication of his work with the iconography of that culture, is nowhere more explicit than in the La Charanga *marquillas.*

"Vida y muerte de la mulata" contains yet another allusion to Landaluze: The black *calesero,* one of his (and Mialhe's) favorite Cuban types, appears in two of these genrelike scenes. In each instance, the coachman's conspicuous idleness, accentuated by his drinking,[75] both anticipates and reinforces the mulata's demise. His in visual terms unambiguous blackness is thus metaphorically extended to the light-skinned female figure. We first encounter the *calesero* as an iconographic accessory to the mulata's illicit conception. He is a background figure (fig. 10) having a drink in a store

whose cigar-smoking(!) owner, seated in the foreground, is captured in the process of paying a poorly dressed, barefoot black
woman for services whose nature is discernable from the ironic
caption: "El que siembra coje" (He who sows reaps). (The fact
that many of the captions in these three series take the form of
popular proverbs is another authenticating mechanism that lends
the pictorial messages an air of "timeless truth" and thus inevita-
bility.[76]) When the coachman reappears later in this series, it is of
course to confront the mulata with her origins and thus to destroy
the visual illusion of her whiteness. As he accosts the mulata with
the words, " Caridad, quieres mecha? Siaa!!" (Caridad, do you
want me to light your fire? Yeaah!), we also notice that the bottle
has changed hands: it is now the mulata who appears to be drunk.
In a print that is part of La Honradez's chronicle "Vida de la mulata," the coachman berates a mulata, who probably has slighted
him, with the words, "Ya tú ni chicha ni limona [sic]" (You are
neither fish nor fowl)(29), a confrontation reminiscent of that between Dionisio and Cecilia. The *calesero*'s accessory function in
these scenes is similar to that of the older black woman in Landaluze's *La mulata,* in that his presence helps contemporaneous viewers identify the mulata's hidden blackness as a condition of sociosexual delinquency. The black pallbearers in "La conducen al
hospital" (They take her to the hospital) (see fig. 17) and the half-
clad black man who jeers at the mulata and her gentlemanly ad-
mirers from a nearby park bench in "Nueva sistema de anuncios
para buscar colocación" (New system of position wanted ads) (26)
are similar witnesses.

Prints 3 and 4 in the "Vida y muerte de la mulata" series return
to the iconographic setup of Landaluze's *La mulata.* The first scene
(fig. 11), set at a street corner, shows a black woman with the product of the "unwanted harvest" announced in print 2: her two fair-
skinned daughters, one a mere infant. The paternal figure of the
white shopkeeper is visible in the background. The older child,
who is the visual center in this print, wears a bright red dress, and
though restrained by her mother's hand, she invitingly gestures toward a white boy to her right. The caption, "Promete ópimos
frutos" (She/he promises the best results) seems deliberately vague
about the presumed speaker of these lines. Not only does the girl's

Figure 11. "Promete ópimos frutos" (He / she promises the best results), n.d., cigarette lithograph, La Charanga de Villergas (reprinted with the permission of CENDA)

outstretched hand recall her darker mother's gesture from the first print of this series, replete with its commercial overtones. The entire scene evokes Landaluze's *La mulata* in its contrasting representation of the alluring young mulata and the distant dark (grand)-mother—with the difference of course that the male viewer is now very much part of the picture. His solicitous (and controlling) presence is even more pronounced in the next *marquilla,* where the frame of the street corner has given way to that of the drawing room (fig. 12). The girl, having blossomed into a "high-yellow" beauty, is now confronted with the promises of a distinguished-looking white patron—"Si me amas, serás feliz" (If you love me, you will be happy)—whom her darker mother silently and critically contemplates. A similar configuration recurs in the "Vida de la mulata" series in "El nacimiento" (The birth) and "Dios te guarde, sabrosona" (The lord watch over you, honey) (27–28).[77]

Figure 12. "Si me amas, serás feliz" (If you love me, you will be happy), n.d., cigarette lithograph, La Charanga de Villergas (reprinted with the permission of CENDA)

Consistent with these iconographic patterns is that representations of the mulata's social success require the erasure of all images of blackness, which is the case in prints 5 through 11 of "Vida y muerte de la mulata." These lithographs depict the mulata in a sequence of suggestive situations, always from the single-point, masculine perspective embodied in the figure of a white patron. Even where it is erased from the actual prints, this masculine perspective remains implicit in the verbal commentary: For instance, the hurried departure of the fashionably attired mulata from the premises of what appears to be a sprawling estate is accompanied by the caption "Una retirada a tiempo" (A timely retreat), and when, back in the privacy of her boudoir, she scrutinizes her reflection in the mirror, the caption offers her thoughts as "Mi querido dice que tenga esperanza" (My sweetheart tells me not to lose hope). That mirror is immediately gendered in the next print, which elaborates the theme of narcissism: "Somos bonitas y por eso nos sigue" (We're pretty, and that's why he follows us)— "he" being represented as the caballero watching two mulatas pass by. In several of the prints that complete the series, such masculine voyeurism yields to more explicit (trans)actions. For instance, the dance in print 8 is readily transformed into a sexual market place when the foregrounded male figure, his back toward the viewer, appraises the mulata with a remark that picks up the initial harvest metaphor as well as reintroduces a familiar system of color classification: "Amarillo, suénamelo pintón" (High-yellow, just ripe). As the party continues in a more intimate setting in print 10, "Noche buena" (Christmas Eve), sexual allusions move from the verbal to the visual sphere: here, one of the male figures demonstratively fondles a mulata's buttocks, and almost always do we see a provocatively exposed female calf.[78]

By far the most consistent visual emphasis on sexual commerce appears in the second series, Eduardo Guilló's "Historia de la mulata." Unlike "Vida y muerte de la mulata" and "Vida de la mulata," the lithographs in this series do not constitute a narrative; they are all variations on the visual paradigm introduced in "Escuela de primeras letras" (Basic education).[79] Each *marquilla* depicts a different mulata in the company of either one or two white men, from whom she is usually receiving money. Dress and settings that alternate between street corners or market places and drawing rooms clearly indicate differences in the social status of the male figures. The mulatas in prints 2, 3, and 4, two of them fruit vendors, are all dressed poorly in both senses of the word. Their faces and bodies bear disfiguring traces of their presumed sexual and materialistic greed, and the symbolic association of exposed breasts with the fruit being sold can hardly be missed. The male figure in each case is either a shopkeeper or a sailor, in contrast to the fancy male company the more refined mulatas keep (see figs. 13 and 14). The respective captions further emphasize the theater of "vulgarities" in these three prints: "Poner los medios para conseguir los fines" (Ways to accomplish an end) (Fig. 13); "Percances del oficio" (The drawbacks of the job); and "Ataque directo al bolsillo" (Direct attack on the wallet)—not reproduced here. The unequivocal message of these pictorial anecdotes remains constant even as the settings change, so that no doubt is left in the viewer's

Figure 13. "Poner los medios para conseguir los fines" (Ways to accomplish an end), n.d., cigarette lithograph, Para Usted (reprinted with the permission of CENDA)

mind about the moral degeneracy of these women, even when such behavior results from poverty and necessity (see fig. 13). "El palomo y la gabilana" (Male dove and female hawk) (fig. 14) is most explicit in its representation of white men as victims of the mulata's ambitions, an argument that recalls Muñoz's "La mulata."

The additional presence in these *marquillas* of an icon that heralds "proper" femininity may be entirely coincidental, but it nevertheless has the effect of visually validating the implicit contrast between virtue and vice, innocence and corruption, that organizes these *marquillas*. That icon is the *tabaquería's* label, situated to the right of each lithograph. Its image of a flower-picking peasant girl in a bucolic setting conveniently clashes with the distinctly urban theater of the pictorial anecdotes. Within this country-city dichotomy, the mulata is resolutely constituted as an unnatural transgressor of the rules of social propriety. What significantly defines this offensive "unnaturalness" is her profitable position within a mas-

Figure 14. "El palomo y la gabilana" (Male dove and female hawk), n.d., cigarette lithograph, Para Usted (reprinted with the permission of CENDA)

culine economy of desire in which sex, stripped of all affective associations, is a commodity exchanged not for social status (as in
legal marriage) but for hard currency that, we are told in *Cecilia
Valdés,* is a great purifying agent: "Ya se sabe que el oro purifica
la sangre más turbia y cubre los mayores defectos, así físicos como
morales" (It is well known that gold purifies even the most turbid
blood and covers great defects, of the physical as well as the moral
kind).[80] The use of money obtained from illegal commerce of all
sorts—prostitution and concubinage, in fact, being by far the least
significant problems—as a substitute for pedigree and concurrent
social privilege is symptomatic of major socioeconomic changes in
nineteenth-century Cuba. In this sense, the *marquillas* of the Guilló
series in particular can be read as allegories of social crises and
transformations much more far-reaching than racial mixing. That
the figure of the mulata should nevertheless be central to these allegories is indicative of the attempt to produce an illusion of stability
by making race and gender the primary stage for social anxieties.

Figure 15. "Las consecuencias" (The consequences), n.d., cigarette lithograph, La Charanga de Villergas (reprinted with the permission of CENDA)

Representations of social control are crucial components in the "realistic" production and performance of this illusion. The final three prints of "Vida y muerte de la mulata" are as much a case in point here as the final chapters of *Cecilia Valdés* are. But unlike Cecilia's surreptitious abduction by the authorities, who act on behalf of her father, Don Cándido, the mulata's arrest in "El castigo" (The punishment) (17) is a public spectacle in which viewers are assigned a place that corresponds to a definite moral position. That place, represented by a group of well-to-do white spectators who are partially hidden behind a half-closed front door, is the security of home and family. "Las consecuencias" (The consequences) (fig. 15) shifts to the claustrophobic, institutional space of a prisonlike shelter or hospital, which is as reminiscent of both Rosario's and Cecilia's internment in Villaverde's novel as it is evocative of Foucault's remarks on the prison as a locus of thought control.[81] The final print, "Fin de todo placer" (The end of all pleasure) (fig. 16),

Figure 16. "Fin de todo placer" (The end of all pleasure), n.d., cigarette lithograph, La Charanga de Villergas (reprinted with the permission of CENDA)

foregrounds that angelic guardian of virtuous womanhood who is already present in the hospital scene and who now presides over the mulata's symbolic funeral. In the end, the figure of the white woman, who occupies a choruslike position in this print, has in fact visually replaced the mulata. An enclosed black carriage in the shape of an enlarged casket extends the earlier prison motif that attests to the mulata's successful removal from society as the music (in the frame) plays on. While the final print in La Honradez's series, entitled "La conducen al hospital" (They take her to the hospital) (fig. 17) does not completely erase the mulata's image, it accomplishes a similar narrative closure by openly displaying her social illness, inscribing it on her now-aged visage.[82] No white female guardian is included in this picture, only four black pallbearers, but the ever-present blindfolded figure of Justice in La Honradez's label may well serve as a substitute.

The ways in which each of the two pictorial narratives achieves

Figure 17. "La conducen al hospital" (They take her to the hospiral), n.d., cigarette lithograph, La Charanga de Villergas (reprinted with the permission of CENDA)

closure merits some additional commentary. The first series firmly reestablishes the authority of civil law, that agent of Reason: As at the end of *Cecilia Valdés,* social order and hygiene are restored by way of discipline and punishment. While the second series's visual translation of social "defects" into physical deformities is premised on natural law, it, too, ends with the triumph of Reason over what is set up as corrupt Nature. Both closures perform what Robert Brown calls a "reinvestiture in civil power through the medium of the non-civil," which is quite overt in the latter case and more veiled in the former. This process of reinvestiture, according to Brown, is itself "an essentially colonialist discourse."[83] Iconographically and ideologically, these social and political technologies are authenticated in much the same way that the sugar mill becomes the law of the land in nineteenth-century Cuba. The slave María de Regla in *Cecilia Valdés* cogently summarizes the mulata's

position before patriarchal Reason: "¡Yo sonsacadora! ¿Qué culpa
tenía de que los blancos se enamoraran de mí? Si les correspondía,
malo; si les rechazaba, peor" (A seductress, me! Is it my fault that
white men fall in love with me? If I humor them, bad; if I don't,
worse.)[84] Or, as the refrain of the *guaracha* in my epigraphs has it:
"My illness has no cure."

3

Plácido's Pastoral

Es más dulce que el azúcar
cuando quiere una mulata,
entre todas las mujeres
sin duda es la flor y nata.

Loving a mulata
is sweeter even than sugar,
among all the women,
she is definitely the cream of the crop.

Fictional characters and historical dignitaries, among them even
Domingo Del Monte, mingle freely and frequently in the pages of
Cecilia Valdés. In a memorable passage we find Cecilia rubbing
elbows with certain "Negroes born in Cuba who had received
some measure of education and knew how to treat women well."[1]
Among these more sophisticated mulatos paying their respects to
Cecilia are several supporters of the antislavery and proseparatist
conspiracy of La Escalera, many of whom, Villaverde informs us,
were executed in Matanzas in 1844.[2] There are, for instance, Juan
Francisco Manzano—the "sentimental poet who had just recently
received his freedom, thanks to the philanthropy of some members
of the Havana literati"—and of course Plácido, who is misidenti-
fied as José (rather than Gabriel) de la Concepción Valdés and
praised as "the most inspired poet Cuba has ever seen."[3]

Unlike Plácido, who was charged with being the head of La
Escalera and was executed in Matanzas on June 28, 1844, Man-

zano, whose manumission had been purchased in 1836, was spared and received only a jail sentence for his alleged participation in the conspiracy.[4] Villaverde's reference to Manzano as a "sentimental poet" is apt, even generous, given that the two volumes of poems he published, *Poesías líricas* (1821) and *Flores pasageras* [*sic*] (1830), are remarkable only for what Sylvia Molloy has called "mediocre Neoclassicism at its very worst."[5] "It is pointless," Molloy argues, "to search these poems for poetic originality, personal confessions or reflections on slavery; ludicrous to find them. . . . Manzano's poetry . . . is original precisely *because* it is so imitative, because it is such a deliberate and total act of appropriation."[6] What interests me about Manzano's "cold imitations," as he himself called his poetry, are their emphatically nonsexual representations of the poet's female muse, a "parda virgen" (dark virgin) whom he addresses respectively as Lesbia and Delia, presumably references to Manzano's first and second wives, Marcelina Campos and María del Rosario, a young free mulata. In "La música" (The music), for instance, "entusiasmo ardiente" (burning enthusiasm) and "volcánico ardor" (volcanic ardor) are immediately transformed into "fuego *celestial*" (*celestial* fire).[7] In the following lines from "Ilusiones" (Illusions), Manzano's procedure is not only more subtle but different enough to merit brief commentary.

> La tierna, juvenil, hermosa frente
> cual nítida amapola, los cabellos
> de ébano lustroso perfumado,
> las mejillas de rosas y violetas,
> los negros ojos y purpúreos labios,
> el aire fino de garboso talle
> *que ostentaba en su andar nada lascivo,*
> en un rincón de Cuba me ofrecían
> un ser divino bajo humana forma.

> The tender, young, beautiful forehead
> with its clear blush, the lustrous,
> redolent ebony hair,
> the cheeks of roses and violets,

the black eyes and purple lips,
the elegant air of her graceful waist,
without a trace of lewdness in her walk,
in some corner of Cuba I beheld
a divine being in human shape.[8]

If there is anything at all remarkable about this vapid adulation of feminine beauty, it is the poet's stress precisely on the absence of sexuality in her walk. Had he been describing a white woman, this would have been quite unnecessary, redundant even.[9] The extravagant and rather sensationalistic sexualization of female physiognomy in Muñoz del Monte's "La mulata" and in Landaluze's portraits of the same type makes Manzano's contrasting insistence on chastity conspicuous. However ephemeral, it is an inscription of racial difference. To be sure, that difference is introduced here only to be immediately erased. But the effect is not necessarily an uncritical endorsement of white womanhood, to which Manzano self-consciously, perhaps mockingly, refers as "dulce magia" (sweet magic) and "ingenioso artífice" (ingenious artifice).[10] Manzano, it would appear, was certainly aware of racial issues even before he wrote his *Autobiography* (1840), of his own "untidy" difference as a "mulato among blacks," and of the fact that his and other dark bodies, especially if they were female, were primary sites of exploitation, sexual and otherwise.[11] At rare moments like this one, his poetry reflects precisely that awareness, as well as the need to protect those bodies from further abuse by cloaking them in unobtrusive rhetorical clichés and thereby effectively rendering them invisible. It is not that Manzano's writings lack racial awareness, only that they do not celebrate racial difference in ways that some critics tend to expect of all black writers, quite regardless of their specific and varied historical circumstances.[12]

The critical reception of Plácido's poetry has suffered from a similar imposition of twentieth-century cultural politics and notions of political correctness. A free mulato with little formal education who earned a living carving tortoiseshell combs of the kind that Adela and Cecilia wear in Villaverde's novel,[13] Plácido was a legend in his own time, albeit a controversial one. His popularity as a poet was second only to that of José María Heredia (who was already living in exile in Mexico at that time), and Plácido's execution made him a patriotic martyr in the eyes of many.[14] However, since Plácido did not care to identify himself as a "Negro writer" and indeed devoted precious little of his poetry to overt commentaries on racial issues, his poems have, more often than not, been criticized, and in fact dismissed, for their alleged preoccupation with white themes and forms and their overall lack of a clear, coherent racial identification.[15] This, on the other hand, did not prevent North American slave narrator and novelist William Wells Brown from including Plácido in his *The Black Man, His Antecedents, His Genius, and His Achievement* (1863), even though Brown, like others, mistook Plácido's biography for Manzano's. James Weldon Johnson's *The Book of American Negro Poetry* (1922) devotes several pages to black poets in Hispanic America, singling out Plácido as "in some respects the greatest of all the Cuban poets" who, "in sheer genius and the fire of inspiration . . . surpasses his famous compatriot Heredia."[16] Johnson even includes a translation of Plácido's famous (and controversial) sonnet "Despedida a mi madre" (Farewell to My Mother) in the appendix. But most notable are Johnson's meditations on the situation of what he calls "the Aframerican poets of the Latin languages."

Up to this time the colored poets of greater universality have come out of the Latin-American countries rather than out of the United States, they will continue to do so for a good many years. . . . the colored poet of Latin America can voice the national spirit without any reservations. And he will be rewarded without any reservations, whether it be to place him among the great or declare him the greatest.

So I think it probable that the first world-acknowledged Aframerican poet will come out of Latin America.[17]

Though the international careers of Machado de Assis, whom Johnson mentions along with Manzano and Plácido, and especially of Nicolás Guillén, would seem to bear out Johnson's prophecy, his claim that these and other black Hispanic American poets could voice the national spirit of their respective countries "without reservation" is at best problematic. Even Johnson, it seems, would have had to admit that Plácido's execution was something of a dubious reward for poetic genius.

Although Plácido's fame among nineteenth-century readers—that is, when they did not confuse him with Manzano—rested largely on the sensational aspects of his life and on his late "prison poems," later critics have invariably emphasized the aesthetic superiority of his presumably apolitical explorations of indigenous themes (notably in the acclaimed "Jicotencal") and his "charming" descriptions of the Cuban landscape in the so-called blossom poems.[18] This apparent consensus has led many critics and historians to deny altogether the possibility of Plácido's involvement in La Escalera and to portray him as a tragic victim of the militaristic regime of captain-general Leopoldo O'Donnell.[19] If few critics have attempted to make a solid case for Plácido's social and political interests, even fewer have been concerned with discovering resonances of those interests in his *siboneísta* poetry.[20] It would seem that the subtleties of Plácido's work have eluded his readers as persistently as they did the colonial government's censors.

It is true that Plácido rarely wrote *about* Cuba's slaves and *gente de color,* one exception of sorts being the poem "El Diablito." But, as Castellanos points out, it was surely risky enough, perhaps worse, to call himself a Cuban—for instance, in "La sombra de Padilla" (Padilla's shadow), a birthday ode to Queen-Regent María Cristina—to support sedition (in "¡Habaneros, libertad!"), and to invoke in his poems the names of José Antonio Saco, Félix Varela, José de la Luz y Caballero, and other opponents of Spain. There can be little doubt that Plácido, jailed several times for his politics,[21] was as wise to the salient ideological contradictions that were part and parcel of the island's sugar and slave economy as he was enamored of Cuba's natural beauty. He was an unrelenting, at times quite explicit, critic of his society's hypocrisy. For instance, in "Que se lo cuente a su abuela" (Let him tell that to his grandmother), he satirizes the mulato class's social aspirations as he ridicules the very idea of racial purity.

> Siempre exclama Don Longino:
> —"Soy de sangre noble y pura,"

Con una pasión más dura
Que cáscara de tocino,
Y con su rostro cetrino
Que africana estirpe indica
Alucinado publica
Ser de excelsa parentela!
Que se lo cuente a su abuela.

Don Longino always exclaims:
—"I am of noble and pure blood,"
With a persistence tougher
Than the rind of bacon,
And with a sallow face
That shows his African extraction,
Deluded, he proclaims
To be of highborn parentage.
Let him tell that to his grandmother.[22]

The black (grand)mother who "stains" supposedly pure Hispanic lineages is a familiar figure in Caribbean literature.[23] Plácido's mockery of a widespread social practice in Cuba, namely, the concealment of the nonwhite mother's name in the registration of newborn children,[24] raises the specter of miscegenation and, in that respect, may be seen as a prelude to another one of Plácido's poems, "La flor de la caña" (The sugarcane blossom). The portrait in that poem of a woman of uncertain color and origin is an almost uncannily precise commentary on Cuban history and society, one that merits detailed attention. Here are the poem's first three stanzas.[25]

Yo ví una veguera,
Trigueña tostada,
Que el sol envidioso
De sus lindas gracias,
O quizá bajando
De su esfera sacra,
Prendado de ella,
Le quemó la cara.
Y es tierna y modesta
Como cuando saca

Sus primeros tilos
La flor de la caña.

La ocasión primera
Que la vide, estaba
De blanco vestida,
Con cintas rosadas.
Llevaba una gorra
De brillante paja,
Que tejió ella misma
Con sus manos castas,
Y una hermosa pluma
Tendida canaria,
Que el viento mecía
Como flor de caña.

Su acento divino,
Sus labios de grana,
Su cuerpo gracioso,
Ligera su planta:
Y las rubias hebras
Que a la merced vagan
Del céfiro, brillan
De perlas ornadas
Como con las gotas
Que destila el alba,
Candorosa ríe
La flor de la caña.

I once knew a tobacco picker,
a tawny, brown-skinned woman,
as if the sun,
of her pretty graces envious,
or perhaps coming down
from his sacred sphere,
enamored of her,
had burned her face,
and she is tender and modest,
like the first shoots
of the sugarcane blossom.

The first time
I saw her, she was

dressed in white
with rose-colored ribbons.
She wore a hat
of brilliant straw,
woven with her own chaste hands,
on it a beautiful canary feather,
that swayed in the breeze
like the sugarcane blossom.

Her accent is divine,
her lips scarlet,
her body graceful,
her step light,
and her blond tresses,
at the mercy of
the Zephyr, shine
like ornate pearls,
like the dewdrops
that dawn distills,
innocently laughs
the sugarcane blossom.

At first glance, this is just a simple love poem, reputedly one of
Plácido's best. Though still constituted by the male poet-lover's
gaze in predominantly neoclassical terms, the female object of desire here bears little resemblance to the ethereal, laurel-decorated
nymphs with lily-white fingers in poems like "El sueño" (The
dream), which, in this respect, harkens back to Silvestre de Balboa's *Espejo de paciencia* (Mirror of patience), that first Cuban
epic of 1608. This difference might be a first hint that this graceful,
brown-skinned beauty is not just tanned —it is only *as if* the sun
had burnt her face. Almost by default, this uncertainty introduces
the possibility that the woman is of mixed racial origin, perhaps
like Plácido's beloved mulata Fela, a slave who died in the 1833
cholera epidemic in Havana and to whom he dedicated a considerable number of poems, among them "Los ojos de mi morena" (The
eyes of my dark woman).[26] To be sure, the polite euphemism *trigueña,* both a colloquial variation on *mulata* (much like *morena*)
and a term of endearment without differential connotations (like
the Cuban phrase *mi negro*), does not definitively establish the

woman's identity as nonwhite but, in leaving it undetermined, implicitly calls into doubt the reliability of systems of racial classification influenced by Linnaean rationalism.[27] Like Plácido himself, and like his poetry, the *veguera* is *al parecer blanca,* white in appearance, and invested with all the uncertainties and ambiguities of that phrase (Morúa's novel *Sofía* raises similar questions about phenotype). I take the poem's equivocation on the issue of racial origins, plus the fact that legal practice in nineteenth-century Cuba tended to "darken" white women desirous of interracial alliances,[28] as license to refer to this female figure as a mulata, in the sense of *amarilla,* which would translate as high-yellow. Further support for this kind of reading comes from the fact that, while only the initial four stanzas explicitly compare the *veguera's* physical and spiritual attributes to "sugarcane blossoms," stanza eight extends the simile to include the poet himself.

> Ya no me es posible
> Dormir sin besarla,
> Y mientras que viva
> No pienso dejarla.
> Veguera preciosa
> De la tez tostada,
> Ten piedad del triste
> Que tanto te ama;
> Mira que no puedo
> Vivir de esperanzas,
> Sufriendo vaivenes
> *Cual flor de caña.*

> I cannot sleep
> without kissing her,
> and as long as I may live,
> I will not leave her.
> Precious tobacco picker
> of the tawny skin,
> Take pity on one so sad
> Who loves you so much:
> You see, I cannot
> Live on hope alone,
> tossed to and fro
> *Like a sugarcane blossom.*

Cecilia Valdés offers a notable variation on what Plácido conceives as an image of amorous torment. Approaching the sugar
mill La Tinaja, Diego Meneses compares "los güines," the tassels
of the blooming sugarcane, "con las garzotas de innumerables
guerreros en marcial arreo, mecidos blandamente por la gentil
brisa de la mañana" (to the helmets of countless warriors in mar-
tial formation, swaying gently in the morning breeze). This image
recurs several pages later in the narrator's casual remark that the
fiery afternoon sun made the sugarcane leaves shine "cual si fueran
bruñidas espadas" (as if they were polished swords).[29] The virile
bellicosity of Villaverde's image is indeed jolting in its denial of any
bucolic comfort one might have expected. Yet, in order for this
image to be perceived as impressive *and* beautiful in the eyes of
both Meneses's female companion and the reader, its violence has
to be tempered by the December wind's gentleness, a representation of benign nature whose authenticating function we have already had occasion to observe in some detail in the preceding chapter. The recurrence of this strategy, on whose deployment in *Cecilia
Valdés* I have remarked previously, is noteworthy, since Villaverde's image of "sugarcane blossoms" appears to be so radically
different from Plácido's. But appearances are precisely what is at
issue in this poem, as the next (and final) stanza confirms.

> Juro que en mi pecho
> Con toda eficacia,
> Guardaré el secreto
> De nuestras dos almas;
> No diré a ninguno
> Que es tu nombre Idalia,
> Y si me preguntan
> Los que saber ansian
> Quién es mi veguera,
> Diré que te llamas
> Por dulce y honesta
> *La flor de la caña.*

> I swear that in my heart
> I will forever
> guard the secret
> of our two souls.

> To no one shall I proclaim
> that Idalia is your name,
> and if the curious inquire
> whom exactly I desire,
> I will say that I call you,
> for being sweet and honest,
> *the sugarcane blossom.*

That the speaker, even within the presumed intimacy of his direct address, reveals "the secret/of our two souls," along with the woman's name, at the same time that he vows to protect it flags the poem's duplicitous strategies. But what is actually being revealed here is not the "secret" itself, but the fact that "the secret of our two souls" is not simply a trite metaphor for the clandestine love affair the poem narrates but a metonym for the unreliability of poetic representation. This becomes even clearer when one considers what the name Idalia actually tells about the *veguera's* identity. An allusion to Venus/Aphrodite, the name Idalia initially seems to confer a false identity that idealizes and idolizes the mulata in the best of neoclassical fashions. But this is not the only reading possible of Idalia. The both luminous and dark Aphrodite, aquatic mother-seductress and patroness of prostitution, shares those mythic attributes with the African-Cuban deity Ochún, both of which are aspects of the "supersyncretic" figure of the Virgen de la Caridad del Cobre, Cuba's dusky patron saint and another "ideal" that lurks behind Plácido's mysterious *veguera*.[30] The combination Venus-Aphrodite-(Ochún), abbreviated, condensed, and disguised in the name Idalia, makes accessible a messy, promiscuous syncretism that is clearly a form of cultural miscegenation.

There is still more. In order to restore the specific historical dimensions of miscegenation, that other clandestine affair that is the poem's *real* secret and the origin of its textual double play, the mulata has to be renamed. However, the Adamic thrust of this poetic gesture, quite different from the naming in Muñoz del Monte's poem, is deceptive to the extent that this new, "honest" and "sweet" name, is conceived as a protective metaphoric cloak, designed for an anxiously inquisitive audience. Significantly, the poet does not ally himself with these presumably male questioners, implying through his distance their unreliability. For a different kind of readership, the mulata's new name—"the sugarcane blossom"—proves most revealing.

Racially mixed characters, as we have seen in "Que se lo cuente a su abuela" and elsewhere, are primarily used to raise questions about racial ancestry as well as cultural origins. But whereas the former poem is content with ridiculing the social apprehensions that inevitably attended such questions in colonial Cuba, "La flor de la caña" complicates the issue of cultural origins by historicizing it in rather unexpected ways. At the beginning of the second stanza, for instance, the *veguera* is described as "dressed in white/ with rose-colored ribbons," attire immediately suggestive in this context of the tobacco flower with its white corolla and pink-edged petals. This nature image, predictably representative of feminine beauty, innocence, and purity, was later to become a symbol of Cuban nationalism: For Martí, the single star of the Cuban flag represented the five-pointed star of the tobacco flower.[31] Plácido's text, however, forecloses this mythic reading of the mulata's dress by insisting on sugarcane blossoms as the poem's dominant simile. Sugarcane displaces tobacco in a poetic gesture replete with historical resonances that contextualize what might have been a patriotic icon within the realm of colonial Cuba's economic development: the conflicts and complicity between the tobacco planters and the nascent Havana saccharocracy.

Plácido's strange hybrid, at once tobacco flower and sugarcane blossom, resonates with the multifaceted historical entanglement of tobacco and sugar within the realms of economics, politics, and culture. In this image, the delicate pinkish whiteness of the tobacco flower blends with the chemical whiteness of refined sugar—*flor* also refers to high quality sugar, as in *blanco florete* or *azúcar de flor.*[32] Plácido's is a "blossom" ironically (dis)colored by its historical and economic origins, slave labor and the sugar industry, whose insatiable appetite for land had, at the time, already defaced much of the indigenous landscape through deforestation and had set in motion almost irreversible changes in both the island's socioeconomic infrastructure and its intellectual life. Sugarcane, it seemed, could "blossom" only where tobacco did not, and the fact that Vuelta Abajo proved after all to be an excellent location for growing tobacco was purely a fortuitous coincidence.[33]

That "La flor de la caña" could just as easily have been the name of a sugar mill (such as La Flor de Cuba) tellingly distinguishes this poem from Plácido's other "blossom poems," as well as from *indigenista* poems featuring native caimitos, papayas, and *mameyes,* whose sexual investments, in part due to the fact that female slaves used some of these fruits and plants for contraceptive and related purposes, survive even in today's Cuban Spanish. Its metaphoric association with sugarcane blossoms makes Plácido's image of a mulata considerably different from the ways in which this figure is constructed in the poems by Muñoz del Monte and Crespo y Borbón, as well as in the popular visual arts. By linking the brown-skinned *veguera* to sugar production, slavery, and Cuba's imminent industrialization, Plácido's text on the one hand severs the mythic ties of women and blacks with nature, ties that nineteenth-century natural science cited as evidence of inferiority. On the other hand, the poem removes culture's conceptual dependency on nature by locating Cuba's cultural origins in history: in the brutal socioeconomic realities that attended "el arte de hacer azúcar" in nineteenth-century Cuba. That "art" of making sugar was of course as much a profit-oriented economic enterprise as it was an intellectual adventure.[34]

Though the antislavery narratives of that period were on the whole quite vociferous in criticizing the conditions on the sugar plantations,[35] they did not bring into focus the conflict between national interests and the steadily increasing political power of a small economic elite, the Havana sugar barons. Though Heredia, in his renowned "Himno del desterrado," had already constituted his native land—"¡Dulce Cuba!" (Sweet Cuba)—in the contrast of the beautiful external world and the horrifying moral world, "La flor de la caña" is the first poem to situate that contradiction in the specific context of sugar production.[36] It predates by almost a decade Agustín Acosta's *La zafra* (The sugar harvest) and Felipe Pichardo Moya's *El poema de los cañaverales* (The poem of the sugarcane fields), both published in 1926. While "La flor de la caña" cannot properly be labeled social-protest poetry, sugarcane's displacement of tobacco and the iconographic link the poem establishes between sugar and the mulata are at least indirect criticisms of the far-reaching consequences of the sugar economy's ruthless expansion. Within this historical framework Plácido's sugarcane blossom emerges as a representation not of Cuba's tropical splendor but of Cuban culture and its messy historical foundations. Cuba *is* "la flor de la caña," "dulce por fuera/y muy amarga por dentro" (sweet on the outside/and very bitter on the inside),[37] like the mulata herself. "Sugar was mulatto from the start," writes Fernando Ortiz, "for the energies of black men and white always went into its production."[38] Yet the equality Ortiz casually implies, the same idea of equality that underlies popular notions of Cuba's *mestizaje* and Caribbean muticulturalism, is no less deceptive than the sugar's sweetness.

Insofar as Plácido's mulata embodies the process of cultivating the land both in economic and imaginative terms, she ceases to be part of nature, of that unchanging realm of the Other. In "La flor del la caña," she unfastens the conventional anchorage of culture—by definition male and white—in nature and its concomitant elimination of history, the only realm in which differences, be they sexual, cultural, or racial, have to be actively confronted.[39] One result of this disruption is that the historic violence at the origin of the figure of the mulata can no longer be justified as a necessary (and thus "reasonable") violation of nature; that is, it cannot be contained within a readily available mythology. Here, sugarcane "blossoms" only by being transformed into sugar, and this refinement is historically the product of monstrous violations of social contract: *con sangre se hace azúcar* (Sugar is made with blood).[40] By describing the mulata as a sugarcane blossom, that is, by proffering a natural image that ultimately proves resistant to being read as one and, as it fails to represent nature, emerges as a figure for history, Plácido exposes the most volatile and seemingly inescapable paradox at the core of the discourse of sugar. That paradox would be more explicitly articulated by Acosta in 1926: "Grano de nuestro bien . . ./clave de nuestro mal!" (Grain of our well-being . . ./key to our evil!).[41]

Once again, it is instructive to turn to Villaverde, and specifically to his image of "las flores o güines *color violado* claro, de las cañas en sazón" (the light violet flowers or tassels of the sugarcane in season).[42] Of course, "violado," in this phrase, refers to the color violet or purple, and it would not make sense to translate it in any other way. At the same time, however, it is impossible to turn a deaf ear on the semantic resonances of "violado"—that is, violated, ravished, raped—particularly in the context of the present discussion; after all, other adjectives could have easily been used to render a similar color. It is entirely consistent with the ways in which Villaverde represents the sugar plantation elsewhere in the novel to discover within this natural image traces of the same "unnatural" violence inscribed in Plácido's "sugarcane blossom."

I have already commented at length on the pervasiveness of the discourse of sugar in nineteenth-century Cuba and on that discourse's desire to legitimate the economic and social violence of the sugar plantation in order to nourish the illusion of ideological stability that would facilitate national unification and ultimately bring about liberation from Spain. In particular, I have traced the iconographic strategies deployed in popular lithography and commercial art forms such as the cigarette *marquillas*. Bearing the latter discussion in mind, I now turn to the fifth stanza of "La flor de la caña" which includes a reference to those colorful advertisements.

> Halléla en el baile
> La noche de páscua,
> Púsose encendida,
> Descogió su manta,
> Y sacó del seno
> Confusa y turbada,
> Una petaquilla
> De colores varias.
> Diómela al descuido,
> Y al examinarla,
> He visto que es hecha
> *Con flores de caña.*

> I met her at the dance
> on Christmas Eve,
> she was blushing,
> picked up her coat,
> and took from it,
> confused and troubled,
> a little tobacco case

of many colors.
She gave it to me unexpectedly,
and upon examining it,
I saw it was decorated
with sugarcane blossoms.

The importance of this other, nonliterary text, the one on the outside of the container,[43] is that it frames the secretive, private exchanges between the two lovers—represented by the note or letter and the lock of hair—that constitute the poem's sentimental or romantic conceit. The sudden shift in stanza 5 from the singular to the plural "flores de caña," the only time the plural form occurs in the poem, underscores this contextualization of romance within a historically specific public discourse. That discourse, in its turn, instantly appropriates (and effaces) the figure of the mulata/*veguera* and reproduces her as a commercial commodity, as a fetishized cultural *text*. "Ella" in the next stanza refers now to the "petaquilla," while the beloved woman has been metonymically reduced to a lock of her hair.

En ella hay un rizo
Que no lo trocara
Por todos los tronos
Que en el mundo haya;
Un tabaco puro
de *Manicaragua,*
Con una sortija
Que ajusta la *capa,*
Y en lugar de *tripa,*
Le encontré una carta,
Para mí mas bella
Que la flor de la caña. (emphases in original)

Inside it was a lock of hair
that I will not trade
for all the kingdoms
of this world;
Pure tobacco
from *Manicaragua,*
with a band

that holds the *wrapper,*
and instead of *filler,*
I found a letter,
more beautiful to me
than the sugarcane blossom.

Instead of using poetry to transcend socioeconomic history, which is of course what is implicit in the charge that Plácido's poetry is generally unconcerned with themes black, Plácido takes great care here to prevent such a disengagement. The poetic voyeurism of the opening stanzas ("ví una veguera," "la vide") has given way to different kinds of activity: writing and reading, which enable a kind of reciprocity between the poet and the woman— even if this mutuality is initiated and still framed by a masculine consciousness. Note that the two lovers never speak to each other but, beginning in stanza 4, secretly *exchange* letters.

El domingo ántes
De Semana Santa,
Al salir de misa
Le entregué una carta,
Y en ella unos versos.

The sunday before
Holy Week,
upon leaving Mass,
I slipped her a letter,
that contained some verse.

This situation is substantially different from what we find in the poems by Manzano, Crespo y Borbón, and Muñoz del Monte, not to mention Landaluze's *La mulata*—all discursive environments in which such reciprocal exchanges are impossible, unthinkable even, because in each case they would imperil representational and thus social hierarchies. However, this difference in "La flor de la caña," produced by the (acknowledged) racial proximity of the poet to his female muse, does not readily dissolve all hierarchies. The lovers' gift exchanges remain framed by a hegemonic discourse that would (and does) censor and distort them. Within that discourse, for instance, the offering of tobacco Plácido's persona receives from his chaste beloved would become a sexualizing gesture that precedes the mulata's commodification in the image of the *marquilla*. But, intertwined as they are in the (partially) shared metaphoric space of the "sugarcane blossom" and of the pronoun "ella," these two discursive fields are nevertheless distinguishable in the poem, in part because of the shift between present and past tenses ("hay," there is; "encontré," I met), *and* because they are assigned different (aesthetic) value. The letter inside the tobacco case, obviously of greater value to the poet than both the lock of hair and the tobacco, is described as "more beautiful" than its decorative outside, perhaps because it, unlike the outside "text," contains no dehumanizing "fiction."

> No hay ficción en ella,
> Sino estas palabras:
> "Yo te quiero tanto
> Como tú me amas".
> En una reliquia
> De rasete blanca,
> Al cuello conmigo
> La traigo colgada;
> Y su tacto quema
> Como el sol que abrasa
> En julio y agosto
> *La flor de la caña.*

> There is no fiction in it,
> only these words:
> "I love you as much
> as you love me."
> On a band
> of white satin
> I hang it
> from my neck;
> and its touch burns
> like the sun that,
> in July and August, scorches
> *the sugarcane blossom.*

This is a gesture somewhat reminiscent of Muñoz del Monte's fetishization of the mulata as a male "charm," but with a major difference: the fetish here is a letter written by a mulata, *not* a physical attribute (hair or skin color) enlarged into a representative icon.[44] No matter how brief, no matter how unoriginal, the woman's letter is an articulation of female desire. Nor is its "burning" touch simply a sexual metaphor—no more, at any rate, than sugarcane "blooms" in Cuba during the summer months. What makes Plácido's "La flor de la caña" exceptional, then, is the extent to which it is able to resist the sentimental and sexual commodification of race and its attendant feminization in the literary and nonliterary discourses on Cuban society at a time of social crisis.

"La flor de la caña" is not an attempt at erasing racial differences; nor does it seek to mythify the origins of Cuba's colonial regime. That the poem, in the process of commenting on nineteenth-century Cuba's various "mixed" economies, should, among other things, direct us to the *marquillas* as representative of a hegemonic discourse is telling, given that the emergence of this popular art form was symptomatic of, and coextensive with, the island's socioeconomic and cultural transformation under the impact of modern technologies. Unlike the majority of Plácido's poems, "La flor de la caña" does not attempt to reverse the effects of industrialization and the rise of capitalism by seeking refuge in pastoral romance (in the form of the *vega,* the tobacco farm, or the *cafetal* in Vuelta Abajo, those classic Cuban pastorals[45]). Instead, it dramatizes, however subtly, the impossibility of a pastoral vision in the presence of the sugar plantation and slavery. Plácido's pastoral, as I have called it, is a space not of leisure but of labor. As "la flor de la caña" multiplies into decorative "flores de caña," we move from an already contaminated and dislocated pastoral to a space defined primarily by mechanical reproduction, commodification, and commercialization. Within that space, represented by the sugar plantation, all pastoral images are decentered, pushed to the outer fringes of the picture. As in La Honradez's reproductions of Laplante's sugar mills, pastoral images become decorative, authenticating frames for simultaneous visions of economic progress. In these lithographs, the Machine has not only invaded the Garden; it has completely taken it over.

There is nothing natural or reasonable about such an invasion, whose sexual overtones would become the subject of Morúa Del-

gado's *Sofía*. If anything, "La flor de la caña" reveals Nature to be
a socially constructed text that functions as a powerful ideological
alibi for "the culture that sugar created" and its history of atrocit-
ies. Only by erasing that history could later Cuban poets—no
longer subject to the same kinds of social anxieties and pressures
Plácido's white and nonwhite contemporaries experienced—so exuberantly celebrate the mulata as a figure for their own cross-
cultural imagination and make her the object of and vehicle for
nationalist fervor.

4

Filomena's Law

No sé lo que tengo aqui,
ni lo que me da;
¡ay, ay, ay!
No tiene cura mi enfermedad.

Don't know what's the matter,
nor what's happened to me;
ay, ay, ay!
My illness has no cure.

en esa blancura inocente
se esconde el secreto.

in this innocent whiteness
the secret lies hidden

—Francisco Dominguez Charro,
"Azúcar blanca"[1]

I

It has been argued that the waning of *Cecilia Valdés*'s brand of
romantic realism and the impact of "modernist" naturalism on
late-nineteenth-century Hispanic-American fiction contributed significantly to the humanization of black literary stereotypes.[1] Ra-

món Meza's *Carmela* (1886), Martín Morúa Delgado's *Sofía* (1891), and Félix Soloni's *Mersé* (1924), whose title characters are all mulatas of sorts, are the most frequently cited examples of this trend in the Cuban novel.[2] *Sofía,* however, is a special case, the only one among the three novels that is explicitly conceived as a corrective to what many still believe is the most Cuban of novels, *Cecilia Valdés.*[3] Although both novels share similar plot structures and the thematics of incest, Morúa's revisions are rather unusual modulations of the topic of *mestizaje* and its discursive channeling through the figure of the mulata.

What he called "the terrible case" of Cirilo Villaverde was something of an obsession for Morúa, a free mulato who wrote fiction, journalistic pieces, and literary criticism and who emerged as one of Cuba's most powerful and controversial nonwhite politicians by the turn of the century.[4] To say that Morúa was critical of Villaverde's novelistic efforts and of his textual politics would be putting it very mildly indeed. "Las novelas del Sr. Villaverde" (1891), a long essay Morúa wrote while he was working on *Sofía,* contains abundant evidence of outright hostility. After quickly dismissing Villaverde's previous novels, "Las novelas" turns to *Cecilia Valdés,* which Morúa finds "extremely defective" and not at all worthy of the unqualified praise it had received.[5] If indeed *Cecilia Valdés* is the best novel Cuba produced in the nineteenth century, this, Morúa fumes, is so only by default. Morúa's misgivings about the novel are indeed numerous. He derides Villaverde's alleged lack of imagination, accuses him of "sociohistorical inaccuracies" and "unforgivable barbarisms," and complains about his graceless representations of Afro-Cuban vernacular.[6] But above all, Morúa denounces Villaverde's "social ethics," pronouncing him guilty of nothing less than "premeditated intellectual violence and repression."

Veo que el autor no ha podido aún desposeerse del maligno espíritu de aquellos tiempos, y se manifiesta poderosamente inficionado de la endemia colonial. . . . En toda la obra se nota el censurable y deliberado empeño de justificar las líneas divisorias trazadas y conservadas por el exclusivismo colonial. Vese que el autor acepta el orden establecido, y sigue rutinariamente la desgraciada argumentación de los que aspiran a subir, reteniendo bajo su planta a los infortunados que allí colocará el regimen autoritario que combaten a juro de aniquilamiento.

The author [of *Cecilia Valdés*] has not yet been able to divest himself of the malignant spirit of those [earlier] times, and he appears powerfully infected with the colonial disease. . . . Throughout the entire work one notices the lamentable and deliberate zeal to justify the divisive lines drawn and maintained by colonial exclusivity. It is evident that the author accepts the established order, and he routinely follows the disgraceful argument of those who aspire to advance themselves, keeping down the unfortunate people placed there [at the bottom of the social hierarchy] by an authoritarian regime that they fight at the risk of death.[7]

These accusations are harsh but, as my own brief remarks on *Cecilia Valdés* suggest, not altogether undeserved. His separatist sympathies notwithstanding, Villaverde, son of a sugar-plantation physician, tended to be more of an apologist for than a rigorous critic of Cuban colonialism's classism and racism. Yet, there is no particular reason to single him out for blame. After all, the kinds of contradictions that *Cecilia Valdés* exhibits were salient characteristics of nineteenth-century Cuban reformist ideology, a complicated legacy from which Morúa himself only partially escaped. A former insurrectionist who became increasingly conservative during his distinguished political career—in 1902 he voted for the Platt Amendment as a delegate to the Cuban Constitutional Assembly—Morúa's own political views were not unproblematic. On the one hand, he ardently supported education for nonwhites as a vehicle for greater social acceptance and advancement. On the other, as president of the Cuban senate he drafted and sponsored the so-called *Ley Morúa*, which prevented the formation of political parties on the basis of race or color.[8] The passage of this controversial bill in 1910, after his death, did not exactly contribute to easing racial tensions in Cuba.

It is consistent with Morúa's concerns about social integration that the aspects of Villaverde's supposedly limited and compromised novelistic vision he found most offensive were the former's portrayals of Cuba's *gente de color*.[9] Yet, anyone who approaches

Sofía with the expectation of mimetically "accurate," psychologically complex portraits of the island's slave and free nonwhite populations will be surprised: all of the novel's main characters, including Sofía herself, are whites. Characters of African extraction, among them the mulata Teodora and the coachman Liberato, all play only minor roles with little psychological texture. Sofía's friend Teodora, a streetwise "mulata in her best years, with excellent, though a bit flabby, skin" and "one of the most recent fruits of Mongolian extraction,"[10] is clearly modeled on Cecilia's confidante, Nemesia. In his capacity as assassin, Liberato, in his turn, is cast in the role of the musician José Dolores Pimienta, Cecilia's jilted mulato lover and the murderer of Leonardo. Morúa finds Pimienta's name—it translates as Pepper—understandably offensive, but he himself does little better with a character like the old *negra* Maló.[11] The situation improves somewhat in the second novel in this projected series, *La familia Unzúazu,* where Liberato, for one, moves closer to the center of the novel's action and a new character, the mulato Fidelio, who can be read at least partly as an autobiographical figure, joins what remains of the previous novel's cast.[12] One might be tempted to speculate that had Morúa lived to complete the "Cosas de mi tierra" series, his later novels might have featured blacks and mulatos in increasingly prominent roles. But such conjectures are pointless, especially given the vision of a raceless future Morúa projects in *La familia Unzúazu.*

But the absence of "realistically" (which usually means sympathetically) depicted nonwhite characters from *Sofía*'s central plot is hardly an adequate measure for the political perspective Morúa brought to bear on his novelistic constructions of late-nineteenth-century Cuban society—Richard Jackson calls it, much too generally, a "black perspective."[13] Morúa's scrutiny of the aesthetic and moral "defects" Villaverde and other reformers habitually perceived as evidence of racial pathology is not, as we shall see, contingent on the represented "humanity" of his black and racially mixed characters. My point is that to provide psychologically complex narrative portraits of blacks and mulatos does not per se constitute a break with the representational politics of literary realism. It certainly does little to shake readers' faith in language's "objective" mimetic capacities, not to mention in the idealist notion of essential humanity so crucial to literary realism and related discourses.[14] *Sofía,* in many ways, can be read as a parody of the nineteenth-century Cuban antislavery novel and of its costumbrista realism to the extent that Morúa mocks and ultimately explodes his fellow countrymen's continued belief in the reliability of appearances. A remark from "Las novelas" clarifies this. Here, Morúa notes Villaverde's repeated insistence that Adela and Cecilia look very much alike. He comments that, regardless of their resemblance and regardless even of Pancho Solfa's warning that, in the case of Spaniards and Cubans, "purity of blood" is a very tricky concept, the reader is nevertheless expected to take Adela's whiteness at face value.[15] According to Morúa, this preposterous proposition indicates an unwillingness to interrogate normative whiteness.

Sofía, by contrast, is a novel in which that norm is dissolved rather than confirmed, as a white character is ironically coerced into "passing" for a mulata.[16] Barreda suggests that Morúa is experimenting with two ideas in *Sofía:* "first, that society and heredity—ethnic heredity is not implied here—condition the individual, and second, that racial differences do not exist, because a white placed in the same circumstances as a black reacts in the same way as a black."[17] But Morúa does more than simply turn the tables on his readers in order to prove racial prejudice a logical absurdity. Rather, Morúa's project is to show the disfiguring and, in the end, lethal effects racial prejudice had on slaves *and* masters alike.[18] The novels's point is not to have whiteness replace blackness as the primary signifier of social pathology but to demonstrate the effects of slave economics on an entire society. As most of the characters Morúa invents are little more than clinical symptoms of what he calls "the colonial disease," *Sofía* does fit the mold of literary naturalism.[19]

Writing at a time when slavery had legally been abolished in Cuba—its last vestige, the *patronato,* or patronage system, lingered until 1886—Morúa was interested in the *codes* according to which colonialist power represented itself in late-nineteenth-century Cuba, in the strategic (and perverse) deployment of race and sexuality through which it continued to legitimate and consolidate itself after the official end of slavery. According to Morúa, these practices would prove to be the very instruments of colonial Cuba's demise. On the one hand, then, *Sofía* is a diagnostic portrait of social "disease" and decadence, of a society enslaved and warped by its irresponsible pursuit of profit, power, and pleasure. In this respect, what we have of the "Cosas de mi tierra" series may well be dubbed Cuba's *Fall of the House of Usher*. On the other hand, *Sofía* chronicles, as well as anticipates, imminent shifts in the distribution of economic and political power in Cuba (more on this in the following chapter).

II

Set in 1878–80 during the turbulent aftermath of the Ten Years War (1868–78), when Cuba teetered on the brink of an economic depression that would last from 1883 until well into the 1890s, *Sofía* seems at first curiously devoid of any signs of strife, economic or otherwise. The novel's exuberant opening pages are a case in point: "¡Qué vista más encantadora! ¡Qué hermoso panorama! ¡Diríase que la naturaleza desarrolló esta concepción sublime y regaló con ella al hombre, para demostrarle incontestablemente su munificencia y su imponderable fuerza creadora!" (What a most enchanting view! What a beautiful panorama! One could say that nature developed this sublime conception and made of it a gift to man, in order to demonstrate incontestably her munifience and her imponderable creative force!) (1). Morúa's imaginary Cuban city of Belmiranda (possibly his native Matanzas),[20] whose picturesque setting is what is being admired in this citation, is indeed aptly named—much like Justo Cantero's sugar plantation Buena Vista in Laplante's lithograph. But what one sees, the reader is quickly reminded, does of course depend on one's location: "Estamos en el mar, a la entrada de un puerto de la costa norte" (We are at sea, at the entrance to a port on the northern coast), reads the following sentence, and the lengthy paragraph extolling the city's charms concludes by reiterating: "Todo esto lo admiramos desde el mar, desde la cubierta de uno de los infinitos barcos de diferentes naciones que visitan el puerto" (All this we admire from the sea, from the deck of one of the countless ships from different countries that visit the port) (2). From this (physical and conceptual) distance, even the rustic, disorderly fishing shacks that provide an "inevitable contrast" to the city's refined splendor become invisible as they blend in with the lush vegetation (2).

What is interesting about this opening is Morúa's attention to perspective. The anonymous narrator, who functions almost like a dramatist introducing the set before turning to the cast of actors, takes great care to distinguish his own location or positionality from that of a foreign observer who, like Columbus and other travelers before him, marvels at what would appear to him or her as an earthly paradise, a space in this case where nature's sublime grandeur combines gracefully with the lavish achievements of human civilization: a magnificent theater, elegant schools, capricious and splendid structures. Harmony reigns here, and prosperity, products of "good taste" and "artistic refinement" (1). As with Laplante's sugar mills and Villaverde's description of La Tinaja, this "enchanting" effect—and it is only an *effect*—requires the near or total absence of human beings, so that society, represented by its material accomplishments and its cultural institutions, may assume an incontestable and imponderably mythic status akin to that of a natural force. What is visible from this viewpoint is surely not a society in turmoil.

But the attractive facade begins to crumble ever so slightly when the narrator briefly steps out from behind the screen of consensus provided by the first-person plural to identify himself as a Cuban: "*mi* noble tierra" (*my* noble land) (2, my emphasis). As a Cuban, he is aware of certain "inimitable changes" that elude both foreign travelers and artistic representation ("los inimitables cambiantes que tanto desesperan a la impotencia del arte"). He is capable of perceiving things, as it were, in a different "light." One suspects that what is at issue here are more than changes in the sunlight. The exclamation "¡Oh sí!" punctuates the prior statement just enough to jolt the reader and introduce a slightly unsettling note into the tranquil procession of ships from all kinds of different nations. Suddenly one wonders about the identity of these foreign "observers" (are they Europeans? African slaves perhaps?) whom the narrator has once again rejoined at the end of this paragraph ("admiramos"; we admire). One also wonders about the narrator himself and his allegiances. Due to this subtle change in perspective and the questions it poses about the narrator's identity, the initial "enchantment" takes on an ambiguous quality, as if all the splendor and luxury were hiding a terrible, unspeakable secret. Our attention is turned away from Belmiranda's "beautiful panorama" and to the less attractive "imprint" of slavery and colonialism, which the novel begins to bring into focus as a different lexicon ruptures its aesthetic and ideological screen: Descriptions of nature's splendor now give way to a view of the "sistema social" (social system) and the "régimen gubernativo" (government regulations) (2).

The narrative trajectory in the no less enchanting description of Sofía is structurally analogous to this introduction of Belmiranda. We first encounter the young woman in the Plaza de Armas, the main recreational site for "all classes of Belmiranda's society," above all Spaniards and criollos "atraídos por el grato olor de la 'canela'" (drawn by the pleasant smell of "cinnamon"). The latter phrase, to which the narrator takes exception by framing it in quotation marks, is a by-now familiar derogatory reference to the mulatas who frequent that spot to mingle with prospective white suitors. But Sofía, the narrator insists, is different from those women.

Entre las manejadoras, jóvenes y bonitas con muy contadas excepciones, había una *trigueña* que se distinguía de sus demás compañeras por el carácter reposado y los dulces modales que realzaban su belleza natural; porque Sofía era una muchacha de mucho atractivo. Su estatura, más que mediana, una de esas estaturas de juventud eterna, lucía un talle largo, bien contorneado, y unos hombros con gracia tal colocados, que formaban un tronco perfecto, sobre el cual descansaba su hermosa cabeza ostentadora de una cabellera negra, reluciente, ondeada, magnífica; y cuyo rostro oval, de finísimas facciones, estaba iluminado por dos rasgados ojos de negras pupilas que derramaban torrentes de ternura, cautivando a cuantos las veían, admirando acaso más que todo aquel conjunto encantador, su habitual tristeza que le daba una expresión la más interesante.

Among the maidservants, who, with few notable exceptions, were young and pretty, there was a *brown-skinned girl* whose peaceful character and sweet manners enhanced her natural beauty and made her different from the rest of her companions; for Sofía was a very attractive girl. Of more than medium stature, one of those figures of eternal youth, she was tall, well shaped, with graceful shoulders that formed a perfect line on which rested her beautiful head that was adorned by a magnificent mane of black, shiny, curly hair. Her oval face, with its fine features, was lit up by two almond-shaped eyes with black pupils that overflowed with torrents of tenderness, captivating all who saw her and who admired, even more perhaps than this enchanting combination of physical features, a habitual sadness that gave her a most interesting expression. (3; my emphasis)

The unreliable appellation *triguéña*, familiar from Plácido's "La flor de la caña," does not so much identify Sofía as a mulata as it problematizes her race.[21] Morúa does not subject Sofía to the same painstaking scrutiny with which Villaverde probes Cecilia's physical appearance for imperfections attributable to racial descent. One could of course argue that since Sofía, unlike Cecilia, not only looks but *is* indeed white (she is one of the daughters of the slave trader Don Sebastián Unzúazu, a piece of information, however, to which the reader does not have access at this point in the novel), she would obviously not have any such "flaws," so that to look for them would be ridiculous. But such logic has limited validity once we consider that race—in this case, blackness—is an ideological construct capable of operating independently of physical appearance. Once pronounced a mulata and a slave, Sofía's white skin offers her no protection whatsoever. For none of the novel's characters, sympathetic though they may be to Sofía's predicament, question her slave status. That, in Sofía's case, white skin alone does not guarantee a privileged identity throws into hopeless confusion any system of racial stratification based on phenotype.

Interestingly, what most sets Sofía apart from other slaves in the novel is her complete submissiveness to her tragic fate,[22] an attitude the narrator seems to attribute to her innate moral superiority, not simply to an extraordinary naïveté. "Poor girl!" the narrator exclaims at various points in the novel. "She was born with the soul of an angel, and the whims of the egotistical world subjected her to the tortures of hell" (16). However, Sofía's saintliness cannot be read as a function of her racially "pure" genealogy. For

Sofía's legacy is hardly pure in any moral sense: she turns out to be the daughter of a slave trader and a prostitute. Is it possible, then, to detect a note of irony in the narrator's sentimental outbursts on her behalf? Why, after all, would a white Cuban reader—and there is no question that this novel was written for a predominantly white audience[23]—feel sympathy for Sofía? For the same reason that some of the novel's characters do, because it is an injustice that "aquella mulatica tan blanca fuese esclava" (so white a little mulata would be a slave) (71)? Because the returns promised by the reader's presumed investment in a specific ideological position (that is, the belief in social advancement through whitening and thus in white superiority) have been withheld? Because Sofía has been deprived of what is due her?

Sofía's origins may be biologically "pure," but historically they most certainly are not. To the extent that it delegitimates white superiority and ruptures the ideology of whitening, her fate has an aspect of poetic justice, extreme though it may be. If this sounds too much like blaming the victim, let me suggest that Sofía occupies a precarious position in the novel: She represents both the victimized, because of her gender, *and* the victimizer, because of her color *and* her family history. Moreover, it is her gender that serves as the main source of the reader's (and the narrator's) sympathy *and* attraction—this novel's protagonist could clearly not have been male. Along similar lines, what Sofía is deprived of (her money, her social position) is hers only *by law,* the same law of "blood" that also underwrites Don Acebaldo's patriarchal power. This is also precisely why it becomes impossible for Sofía to be reinstated after her true origins are revealed. What is at issue in this novel is not freedom through the acquisition of social privilege but the persistence and function of racism within Cuba's society at a time when slavery has been officially liquidated. To allow Sofía to survive as a white woman, that is, to free her from slavery and restore her honor through marriage to Federico, would have severely compromised Morúa's project. It would have provided an emotional and ideological escape hatch for the contemporary reader by restoring confidence in the deplorable values of Cuba's upper classes. As a mulato, Morúa might have been too acutely aware of racism's subtle deployment to let his readers get away with a simple moral lesson about social injustice. The question is not whether Sofía *deserves* to be either slave or mistress; she deserves to be neither. The novel's point is that, like Sofía, all Cubans are caught up in a web of power relations and conflicting impulses from which there is no easy escape. "She struggled, caught between her modesty that rebelled against any moral degradation and her desire for improving her humiliating condition that was destroying her" (7).

It is perfectly in keeping with naturalism's philosophical underpinnings that Sofía's struggle is quite in vain, that her belief in individual agency is but a delusion. This lack of control over social practices and discursive conventions is abundantly clear from the following passage, which anticipates Sofía's own trajectory.

¿Quién podía asegurarle que entre la juventud enriquecida que concurría a las tales reuniones no podía encontrar su Ricardo [*sic*] Bonanza[24] que la libertase y se casara con ella *secretamente? Esto le atraía con fuerza incontrastable.* Pero su incertidumbre duró sólo algunos instantes. Luego recordó otros casos en que lo único que habían logrado las confiadas esclavas era aumentar el número de los criollitos de la dotación de sus dueños. Y ¡qué dolor para Sofía, verse como la pobre Filomena, la costurera de su propia casa, que tuvo un hijo con no se sabía quién, y fue a criarlo a un ingenio donde por castigo las habían mandado sus amos; porque ensoberbecida se atrevió a decirles que "el padre de su hijo tenía dinero sobrado para libertarla a ella y a él!" ¿Quién quitaba que cualquier mocito sin conciencia se burlase de ella, dejándola en peor situación de la que ella se encontraba? *Más valía no exponerse. . . .* Asi pensaba Sofía, sin imaginar un momento que aquello del *casamiento secreto podía ser todo una grosera artimaña. . . .* ¿Lo creía de la misma suerte la bachillera Teodora? Podría sospecharse que no.

Who could assure her that among the wealthy young men who attended such gatherings she would not meet her Ricardo [*sic*] Bonanza, who would liberate her and marry her *secretly? This [possibility] attracted her with undeniable force.* But her uncertainty lasted only for a few brief moments. Then she remembered other cases in which the only thing the gullible slaves achieved had been to increase the number of children their masters owned. And, how painful had it been for Sofía to watch how the poor Filomena, the seamstress of her own house, left with a child by God knows who, was forced to raise it on a sugar plantation, where her owners had sent her as punishment; because she had proudly dared to tell them that "the father of her son had enough money to buy her freedom and that of her child"! Who prevented some brat without a conscience from making fun of her, leaving her in a worse situation than she had already been in? *Not worth taking the risk.* . . . This is what Sofía thought, without imagining for a moment that a *secret wedding could be one big joke.* . . . Did the unmarried Teodora believe this as well? One would think not. (7–8; my emphases)

"Secret marriage" is of course a euphemism for concubinage, an arrangement without binding legal consequences and in that sense "one big joke." *Secret* is the operative modifier here; the passage clearly associates it with white, male power that is invisible, hidden, absent—like the unknown father of Filomena's child, represented solely by his purported financial prowess and his unfulfilled promises, and like the God in which Sofía places so much "good faith." Only the discursive effects of this power are visible in the text, as a conflict between "risky" (that is, sexual) desire and the dangers of moral (and physical) "exposure" (*exponerse* is indeed a highly charged verb here): pregnancy, banishment to the sugar mill, and death.

The reference in the above passage to the mulata Filomena (Filomela?) and her "tropiezo moral" (moral mishap) (31) is significant as a prophecy of Sofía's own fate, which unfolds according to a particular set of laws operative in the Unzúazu-Nudoso family: "El ejemplo dado con Filomena sería *ley eterna* en aquella casa *en que debía imperar constantemente la moralidad más estricta*" (The example made of Filomena would be *eternal law* in this household *in which the very strictest morality always had to reign*) (89; my emphasis). What is "law," however, is not only the example *made of* Filomena, that is, her punishment, but, more importantly, the *example* of sexual exploitation and abuse her case sets for Sofía's. Though only a memory for the novel's characters, Filomena/Filomela—the resonances of her name are too tempting to pass over— is perhaps the most significant, mythic trace of a discourse and a social practice in whose mutually reinforcing play of pleasure and power Sofía becomes helplessly and hopelessly entangled. That discourse deploys sexuality and race in ways that ultimately crush Sofía like a stalk of cane in the grinders of a sugar mill. The "eternal law[s]" of this discourse originate of course in a very specific and familiar place: the sugar plantation. This setting is central to the next stage in Sofía's metamorphosis.

Though the events narrated in the novel's chapter 2 predate those in chapter 1, they are part of a process that unfolds independent of chronology: chapter 2 marks Sofía's progress from *trigueña* to "mulata." The term appears in Sofía's second textual portrait, as painted by Don Acebaldo Nudoso del Tronco, that epitome of social petrification and "one of the most solicitous and expeditious promoters of the false integrity of those days" (36), who takes the place of Villaverde's Don Cándido. Nudoso challenges Sofía's status as the presumed daughter of Doña Brígida, her guardian: "'¿Y tú por qué le dices mamá a doña Brígida? *¿Tú no ves* que eres una mulata y que ella es una señora blanca? Tú no tienes madre, ni padre'" (And you, why do you call Doña Brígida mother? *Can't you see* that you are a mulata and that she is a white lady? You have neither a mother nor a father) (15–16, my emphasis). Similar to Muñoz del Monte's "You are not white, mulata" both in intent and effect, Don Acebaldo's's "can't you see" is less a question than a declaration designed to put Sofía in her place. This operation requires a series of *dis*placements, for one, the girl's own and her mother's. Sofía is excluded from the Unzúazu family because of her alleged race, a fiction that is installed literally in loco parentis, a place Nudoso can usurp because it is unoccupied (Don Sebastián is deceased). Sofía's uncertain (and illegitimate) origins make it possible for Nudoso to assume paternal(istic) prerogatives. By forcing Doña Brígida to vacate the maternal position she had "illegally" occupied—he discredits her authority and expels her from his home—he then fills that position with a fictive mother who, according to the logic of the times, had to have been black. In fact, Sofía's mother is believed to have been a mulata; had she been white, so the argument goes, social convention would have forced Sofía's father to marry her. The same logic resurfaces later in the novel in Magdalena's argument that since Sofía is really white, her lover can be compelled to restore her and her unborn child's social "honor" (see 145). In other words, the female absence in Sofía's lineage, which Doña Brígida presumably attempts to conceal, is read not as blank but as black. (Tellingly enough, there is not even a hint at the suggestive possibility that, as a mulata, she might equally as well have been the offspring of a white mother and a black father.) Quite in keeping with the norms of his social environment, Nudoso invents for Sofía a history of sexual transgression complete with a fictitious female ancestor. Filomena, in whose image Sofía is remade, is in some sense a representation of that female ancestor. Nudoso's patriarchal power, then, is doubly constituted: What authorizes his actions, establishes his despotic claims on life and death, is sexual and racial difference rooted in "natural" law enacted through human effort. Sofía's delegitimation is a measure of the extent of his own "rights" (*derecho*) (17).[25]

The fact that Nudoso's words to Sofía are quoted in her brief autobiographical narrative confirms his seeming omnipotence. Even when he is physically absent, Nudoso still silences her. The extent to which Sofía's language is a reflection of his is already evident from the first sentences of that narrative that she tells to a fellow slave: "Yo no tengo padre ni madre. No los he conocido nunca. Yo no tengo familia" (I have neither a father nor a mother. I never knew them. I have no family) (15). In the same way that Nudoso's gaze reinvents Sofía by making her *see* herself as something she is not—a situation that recurs when Sofía looks in her bedroom mirror and sees not herself but Federico (40)—his language invades and replaces hers; he also renames her.[26] The text articulates this process in the form of the narrator's seemingly casual remark that Nudoso "se desataba . . . en denuestos contra la muchacha, *pintándola con los más detestables colores* (exploded . . . with insults against the girl, *painting her in the most detestable colors*) (28, my emphasis). Nudoso almost literally paints her black (to him the most detestable of colors) by racializing her: that is, he investing her with precisely the kinds of moral deficiencies emphatically absent from the text's initial portrait of her.[27]

The girl, however, is blackened not by her imputed race but by Don Acebaldo's avarice:[28] "Nephew of an old mate of a slave ship that, under the command of the veteran captain Unzúazu, had plundered the West African coastal areas," Don Acebaldo "had a cruel and unjust disposition, and was always avaricious when it came to his insatiable appetite for wealth" (51–52, 95). Greed motivates Nudoso's (re)construction of Sofía as racial Other and his "aversión instintiva . . . a 'la maldita muchacha'" (his instinctive aversion . . . to "the accursed young woman") (48). The deployment of race is the only way in which Don Acebaldo can legally claim for himself Sofía's 10,000–peso inheritance, with which he had been entrusted after having already obtained a portion of the Unzúazu fortune through no-less-conventional means: his marriage to Ana María Unzúazu, oldest daughter of the dead patriarch and slave trader Don Sebastián Unzúazu, and a lesser version of *Cecilia Valdés*'s Doña Rosa (note that both Nudoso and his literary precursor Don Cándido marry money). In order to possess Sofía's fortune, Nudoso literally has to turn her into his property; since he cannot make her his wife, he makes her his slave. Here, slavery works much like marriage to transfer financial resources and thus social control from female into male hands. That Sofía and Ana María are half sisters helps establish the ironic interchangeability of their seemingly very different positions.

But Nudoso's materialistic appetites are not the only thing Sofía mirrors; she is also inscribed with his sexual desires. A woman and a slave, Sofía is doubly objectified. She is constituted at the intersection of desire for wealth with sexual pleasure, a "vital adjunct to power" that furthers its workings.[29] As far as the novel's plot is concerned, Don Acebaldo's interest in Sofía may be entirely based on economic motives. But these motives have a distinct sexual subtext independent of the represented actions of this particular male character, whose exercise of power produces pleasure in excess of material benefits. For instance, the fact that her husband never even attempts to seduce the "mulatica" does not prevent Ana María from suspecting Nudoso of being the father of Sofía's unborn child: "Suddenly, like an electric shock, a terrible thought crossed her mind: the child's father. Yes, the father. Who was the father? Was perhaps Don Acebaldo's tremendous dislike of the little mulata nothing but an odious farce?" (88). That Don Acebaldo already has two children with "una arrogante mestiza" (131), in front of whose house he is murdered, confirms the specifically sexual (and adulterous) dimensions of his "dishonest desires" (114). But the significance of Ana María's question about the father of Sofía's child extends well beyond its immediate context. Reaching back to the mysteries surrounding Sofía's own parents, that question conjures up the image of Don Acebaldo not as the father of the child but certainly as implicated in her pregnancy: he after all creates the very conditions that lead to Sofía's rape, even serves as the final catalyst for the girl's seduction.

That "abominable crime" (90), the third stage in Sofía's development, is prefigured in the novel's singular, most explicit representation of sexual violence: Sofía's nightmare, in which Nudoso's desires assume their most revealing shape.[30] In this dream, which plagues Sofía during her punitive exile on the sugar plantation Candelaria, her self-appointed master

tomaba la forma de una bestia feroz, aterradora, que se le echaba endura con sus venonosos dientes afilados, puntiagudos, y *su lengua mortífera, garfilanceada, que se estiraba, se estiraba hasta alcanzarla en el rincón en que casi muerta de miedo se había acurrucado, y al tocarle con la punta en su enervado cuerpo, vomitaba una volcánica escoria* que la martirizaba atrozmente; y lanzando blanquecinas llamas por las narices y los ojos, poco a poco transformábase en hombre nuevamente, e íbase luego por grados ennegreciendo, y convirtiéndose en algo como un demonio de peludo cuerpo, de cuernos retorcidos, de horrorizante risa, *de ojos como ascuas cuya mirada quemaba cual la luz de la lente a la trasmisión del sol; y al sentir en el rostro aquellas persistente mirada, no pudiendo sufrirla porque le abrasaba las carnes,* dio la niña un grito y un salto para huir de sus trituradoras garfas que ya se extendían para cogerla . . . y despertó bañada en un sudor frío, abundoso, y dominada por una terrible congoja que no la dejaba moverse.

assumed the shape of a terrifying wild beast that moved toward her with its venomous, pointed, sharp teeth and *a deadly tongue that, like a spear, penetrated into the corner where she was hiding, almost dying from fright. And when he touched her frail body with the tip of his tongue, he spewed forth a volcanic scoria* that made her suffer atrociously. White-hot flames shooting from his nostrils and his eyes, he slowly returned to being a man. Then his skin darkened gradually, and he changed into something like a demon with a hairy body, twisted horns, a horrifying laugh, *and eyes like live coals whose look burned like rays of sunlight intensified by a magnifying glass; and feeling in her face that persistent look, unable to bear it because it scorched her flesh,* the girl screamed and jumped in order to escape the crushing claws reaching out for her . . . and she woke up bathed in a flood of cold sweat and in the grip of such terrible fear that she could not stop shaking. (20–21; my emphases)

By far the most significant instrument of violence in this scene is the beast's elongated and rather phallic tongue that tortures Sofía in the same way that Nudoso's words did. If this tongue is symbolic of language—*lengua(je)*—then the implication is that pronouncing Sofía a mulata is already an act of violence whose sexual undertones emerge more fully in the silence and secrecy of her nightmare. The flames shooting from the monster's eyes elaborate upon the initial image of aggressive male sexuality. As they parch Sofía's skin, these flames become representations of the unbearable male gaze that constructs Sofía as a mulata. What we see here is what remains invisible in the previous passage, whose emphasis on the visual is now identified as phallic. It is part of a gendered discourse that generates female sexuality as a discursive effect.

Similar imagery is associated with Federico Unzúazu, Morúa's version of the vain and irresponsible Leonardo Gamboa—whom he calls "un modorro que no sabe nada ni estudia nada" (a bore who knows nothing and studies nothing).[31] The text repeatedly draws attention to Federico's persistent gaze: "Teníale ... un miedo instintivo, al extremo de sentir muchas veces en sus espaldas *el fuego de las intensas miradas del mancebo, a pesar de cuyo ardor le causaba frío* (She [Sofía] had ... an instinctive fear of him, especially when, on many occasions, she felt on her back *the fire of the young man's intense stare, which, in spite of its heat, gave her chills*) (33, my emphasis). Federico's "venom"—he is described as a "sátiro ponzoñoso" (venomous satyr) (44)—recalls the dream's scoria-spewing beast. Even Don Acebaldo's "horrifying laugh" reappears in the "mefistofélica sonrisa" (devilish smile) (34) that lights up Federico's face as he devises his "cálculo maligno," his malicious scheme for seducing Sofía.

Interestingly enough, the only color reference in the entire passage, the verb *ennegrecer* (to blacken), pertains to the male monster into which Don Acebaldo is so appropriately transformed. While it is tempting to conclude that the dream reveals his true colors, the implications of this are hardly unproblematic. Another aspect of a racialized discourse inserts itself into the citation at the very point where the beast returns to a somewhat more human shape: the mythic phobia of black male sexuality on which Landaluze plays in his painting of a black slave kissing a white female bust (see chapter 2). The image of a white man sexually assaulting a (presumably) nonwhite woman receives an unexpected twist as the body of the assailant darkens to produce a scene of a black man raping a white woman! In addition to prefiguring Liberato's rape of Ana María in *La familia Unzúazu,* this visual overlay is, however, by no means as paradoxical or even as counterproductive as it may seem at first. If one of the discursive effects of white masculine power is the "blackening" of the female body in the process of sexualizing it, if sexuality, in other words, is a function of race, then it is appropriate for Don Acebaldo to become himself blackened as that discourse, the wellspring of his power and privilege, is turned against him. He is now the one who is disfigured by the same racial biases and phobias that inform his own actions and legitimate the horrors he indiscriminately inflicts on Sofía and Filomena alike. The transformation he undergoes in Sofía's dream ironically shows him not to be in control of the very power he abuses.

Yet another aspect of Sofía's dream merits attention. As a representation of psychological and physical torture, it is implicitly connected with Morúa's chronicles of the brutalities systematically visited upon the slaves of Cuban sugar plantations. These accounts frame Sofía's nightmare.

Desde su tarima oía Sofía el monótono cantar de la negrada que todavía trabajaba alimentando el conductor a los cilindros moledores, cargando las *fornallas,* trasegando las *templas,* removiendo los carros cargados de dorada granza que diez minutos más tarde quedaría convertida en el más rico azúcar granulado, por medio del procedimiento centrífugo que tanto maravillaba a los sencillos guajiros. La triste y acompasada canción selvática de los maltratados esclavos resonaba en los oídos de Sofía como un lejano canto a muertos, algo como la fúnebre oración ceremoniosa que había presenciado indiferente algún tiempo antes en la iglesia catedral de la ciudad. . . . *La música del órgano religioso la suplían tormentosamente para ella el torbellino que le envolvía el cérebro, y el continuado* chi-qui-chic-chac *de la máquina de vapor.* . . . Aquella finca [Candelaria], como casi todas por aquellos tiempos en Cuba, era un infierno terrenal, un lugar de tormento, donde los gritos de las víctimas se confundían con las imprecaciones de los victimarios, donde los juramentos de los condenados eran amortiguados por el ruido de los hierros que les aprisionaban y los estallidos del foete sobre sus laceradas espaldas.

From her bench Sofía heard the monotonous singing of the masses of blacks who were still working, feeding the rollers of the grinder, loading the *furnaces,* decanting the *boiling liquids,* moving along the carts loaded with the golden substance that, ten minutes later, would become converted into the richest granulated sugar by means of the centrifugal method that so amazed the simple peasants. The sad and rhythmic jungle song of the abused slaves resonated in Sofía's ears like a distant song to the dead, something like the ceremonious funeral oration in the city's cathedral to which she had been an indifferent witness some time ago. . . . *For her, the religious music of the organ tormentingly replaced the turbine that whirred in her head, and the continuous* chi-qui-chic-chac *of the steam engine.* . . . This plantation [Candelaria], like almost all sugar plantations in Cuba in those days, was hell on earth, a place of torment where the cries of the victims mingled with the curses of their torturers, where the oaths of the condemned were muffled by the noise of the irons that shackled them and the cracking of the whip on their lacerated backs. (21–22; my emphases)

In this passage, the still-human monster from Sofía's nightmare assumes the shape of the complex "infernal" machinery of the steam-powered sugar mill, a giant mechanical creature ceremoniously tended by an indistinct, anonymous black mass of slaves (*la negrada*). The entire scene is compared to a solemn mass held for a dead patriarch, whose passing marks the advent of the machine, of a new religion represented by the unceasing rhythm of the steam engine that accompanies the funereal chants of the abused slaves. As they merge in Sofía's mind, the precise technical vocabulary Morúa employs in his description of the marvelous art of making sugar (I have italicized the Cubanisms in the first sentences of the above passage) and the religious imagery he attaches to the slave songs become part of a familiar process of authentication in which the sugar mill takes onto itself the omnipotent prerogatives of divinity.

The technical precision that characterizes the discourse of Cuban sugar production conspicuously recurs a few pages later in a slightly different, though crucially related, context. What is described here is a different kind of technology, a by-product, if you will, of sugar production: the "science" of discipline, or what Morúa calls, advisedly, "la peculiar legislación del negrero" (the peculiar legislation of the slave driver) (25).[32]

En muchas ocasiones la rompía, o lo que es igual, descuartizaba al esclavo con el boca-abajo de veinticinco a cincuenta azotes a piel desnuda; en otras usaba el cepo, máquina de tormento, compuesta de dos tablones en cuyas junturas formaban agujeros en que cogídos de los pies por los tobillos, o de la cabeza por el pescuezo, sufrían los esclavos una tortura verdaderamente horrible; . . . o si no, usábase "el collar," otro instrumento más degradante aún, cuanto que consistía en un aro de hierro que se colocaba en el cuello al penado, cerrándose con llave o a remache; de este aro partían dos a modo de cuernos, también de hierro, que sobresaliendo por los lados a la cabeza, tenían en los extremos superiores una campanilla cada uno, como las que se acostumbra poner a las vacas de cría, y así adonde quiera que se dirigía el esclavo llevaba consigo el sonsonete ominoso que le denunciaba. . . . en fin, la escalera (azotes, amarrado el delicuente de pies y manos en ella), el pregón (esto es, el castigado a más de ir cargado de hierros, debía ir pregonando, por ejemplo; "Aquí va Fulano—su nombre—que robó una lata de miel" . . .); esta variedad . . . limitábase donde se limitaba el refinamiento cruel de los aplicadores del tormento, el cual quedaba al libre albedrío y natural condición del poderoso feudatario, puesto que no había código ni ordenanza superior que seriamente señalara el correctivo de cada falta o delito.

On many occasions the slave was broken, or what amounts to the same thing, torn into little pieces with the *boca-abajo* of twenty-five to fifty lashes on the bare skin. At other times, a *cepo* was used, a torture instrument that consisted of two planks, at whose joint two holes had been left in which, the feet held by the ankles or the head by the neck, the slaves suffered a truly horrible torture. . . . Or if not that, "the collar" was used, another even more degrading instrument, because it consisted of an iron ring that was fastened around the delinquent's neck and closed with a key or rivet; attached to this hoop were two others, also made of iron, which stuck out to the sides of the head like horns. At the end of each hung a little bell, like those that one usually puts on pregnant cows, so that wherever the slave went he was accompanied by the ominous ringing that betrayed him. . . . finally, the ladder (a flogging administered to a delinquent tied to it by his hands and feet)[33] and the shout (the punished slave, in addition to carrying irons, had to go around shouting, for example: "here comes so-and-so—his name—who stole a can of honey" . . .). This variety . . . was a result of the cruel refinement of those who applied the tortures, the nature of which was left up to their whims and to the natural resources of the feudal power, since there were neither slave codes nor government ordinances that specified the kind of punishment appropriate for each offense or crime.[34] (25–26)

Where Villaverde provides a meticulously detailed account of the sugar mill's technical apparatus and data, Morúa focuses on the very aspects of the picture that would most definitely spoil the view. *Refinement* here is a term that applies not only to sugar but also to methods and degrees of sadistic torture. The almost clinical tone and precision of Morúa's catalog of "Cubanisms" is indeed striking in its departure from the pious formulae of antislavery rhetoric, of which the novel itself includes a few choice samples: Phrases such as "How those unfortunate souls suffered! How cruel those soulless slaveholders were!" (22), ring hollow when compared with the above chronicle of horrors, which are all the more effective and all the more troubling for their seeming lack of compassion. No less disturbing is Morúa's emphasis on the *systematic* nature of the practices of physical torture that, in the absence of specific legislation regulating the treatment of slaves—there were in fact no slave codes of any significance in nineteenth-century Cuba: none, at any rate, that were obeyed[35]—had become a law unto themselves, complete with a discourse all its own: *el boca-abajo* (or *bocabajo*), *el cepo, el collar, la escalera, el pregón.*[36] There is no individual case study here to soften the shocking impact of this social technology and its discursive representations by allowing the reader to take refuge in his or her compassion for a particular character, such as María Regla in *Cecilia Valdés.* Nor does the above passage indicate what specific offenses or crimes merit such cruel sentences. In addition to stressing the arbitrariness in the meting out of the punishment that actually contradicts any claims to systematicity, this omission also accentuates questions of fairness and justification, not to mention justice. What Morúa's language represents here is naked power in no need of legal or moral justification. What authorizes that power are the perversely "scientific" procedures it applies to the management of the sugar mill's human labor force, and this is what his rhetorical strategies make available for criticism. Harder work, then, is not the only reason why so many slaves tried to escape from the modernized sugar plantations.

Sofía, "'la engreída esclava'" (the spoilt slave) (17) whom Don Acebaldo had secretly hauled off to La Candelaria, is made to conform to the rules of the sugar plantation almost immediately: "She had not spent more than two days in this country residence and already her head had been smashed in, she had been hit in the face, her hair had been cut off, she had been threatened with having to work in the cane fields and the *boca-abajo* and the *cepo* had been hinted at" (20). All this because one of the house slaves had compared her to the overseer's daughter, suggesting that "parecían hermanitas" (they looked like sisters) (17). This resemblance, based of course on the fact that Sofía looks white, has violent consequences, as the overseer's wife, jealous of the supposed mulata's beauty, puts Sofía in her "place" by way of a brutal beating. In order for Sofía to become distinctive—that is, in order for others to perceive her as someone of inferior status—she has to be visibly marked. Cutting off her luxurious black tresses, "that hair which they had so admired in the city" (19–20), serves that very purpose. Morúa's characters construct racial difference much like Villaverde's narrator does in his portrait of Cecilia Valdés: as a deficiency, an imperfection.

When Sofía is finally allowed to return to Belmiranda after six years that "were for her six centuries of unspeakable pain and suffering" (26), the sugar plantation has left its distinctive marks on her: "acá . . . en la ciudad a la moda, *necesitaba algunos afeites que le quitasen aquel sello montuno que la disfrazaba,* presentándola tan desfavorablemente" (here in the fashionable city, *some cosmetics were needed that would remove the rustic marks that disguised her* and gave her such an unbecoming appearance), (29; my emphasis). Even "su lengua debía ensayar, ejercitándose hasta readquirir sus primeros movimientos y modular *sonidos más en armonía* con el círculo en que habían de escucharse" (her language needed readjusting, and she had to practice until she regained her initial skills and produced *sounds more in harmony* with the circle in which they were heard) (29; my emphasis). The blemishes of slavery have to be removed to make Sofía's appearance and her language more compatible with the urban environment. She has to be refashioned, and this particular reconstruction involves yet another erasure of history, whose visible manifestation would disrupt (social) harmony by providing evidence of Don Acebaldo's crime. The recurrence of a crucial phrase, "parecían hermanitas" (31), this time applied to Sofía and Magdalena, a character who combines the beauty of Adela Gamboa with the piousness of Isabel Ilincheta,[37] signals that the marks of the sugar mill have been successfully removed. But it also signals something else: it is the first subtle trace of the "crime" that seals Sofía's fate.

III

Federico is first mentioned in the novel when Sofía, after her conversation with Teodora, notes his absence from the Plaza de Armas that afternoon (8). Indeed, his conspicuous absence from places where he is expected to be (such as the *tertulia*) is a central feature of this character, who is invariably described as ungallant and ill-mannered. I mentioned before that Federico shares with Don Acebaldo a taste for deception and secrecy—with all the sexual resonances this word has by now acquired. But they also share an interest in legal matters. They are brothers-*in-law* in more respects than one. If Don Acebaldo's dishonest desires for Sofía can only be represented in the self-censored secrecy of her dream, then it is clearly appropriate that Federico's sexual conquest, that "demented impulse," be situated in the seclusion of the young woman's room. Nowhere is Federico more out of place than in "aquel limpio santuario de una virgen pura" (that clean sanctuary of a pure virgin) (34). His desecration of this "sacred" abode is a prelude to his violation of Sofía's body. He examines the room in the same way that he scrutinizes Sofía herself: "he resembled an artist who studied the details of his ambitious model" (33). His single-minded glance is replete with all the voyeurism familiar from the work of Muñoz del Monte, Landaluze, and Villaverde. The difference is that Morúa is considerably more explicit about the gaze's violence, which Federico insinuates in his initial threats to Sofía.

Tal vez asi tendrías tú más cordura y me atenderías como debes, contri-
buyendo a tu felicidad y a la mía . . . Escucha lo que tengo que decirte
y no seas tonta; y si no lo haces, bien, allá tú. No tendrás a quien que-
jarte de cuanto te suceda. De todos modos yo no he de salir de aquí
hasta por la mañana; me verán todos los criados, lo sabrá Ana María,
lo sabrán todos, y . . . *¿te acuerdas de Filomena?* . . . Reflexiónalo
bien . . .

Perhaps you might have more good sense and treat me as you
should, contributing to your own happiness and mine . . . Listen to
what I have to say to you and don't be crazy; and if you don't, fine,
have it your way. You won't have anyone to complain to about what
happens to you. In any case, I'm not going to leave here until the morning; all the servants will see me, Ana María will know, everybody will
know, and . . . *remember Filomena?* . . . Think about it carefully . . .
(40–41; my emphasis; ellipses in original)

Consistent with the systematic and conspicuous elision of
white male sexuality in this brief passage, the opening sentence
echoes Don Acebaldo's earlier words to Sofía: "eres ya muy zanga-
letona para que no sepas que tu obligación es servir en lo que se te
mande, y nada más" (you are indeed a very stupid girl for not
knowing that your duty is to obey orders, and nothing more) (16).
The ellipses are the loci of those unspoken and unspeakable desires
with which the rules that govern social relations are saturated and
which are throughout encoded in the name Filomena. For Federico
to evoke that name is to comply with the "eternal law" of the
Nudoso household (and, it seems, of Cuban society): that is, always to hide any and all evidence of immoral and shameful acts
("inmoralidades, desvergüenzas, eso no lo admitiría nunca Ana
María") (89). Sofía's imaginative reconstruction of Filomena's demise as "a procession of wax figures" (42) significantly connects
this particular social practice with the sugar plantation and its
"laws."

Cuando aquel brutal salteador de muchachas indefensas pronunció el
nombre de Filomena, *sintióse Sofía presa de un temblor convulsivo, ano-
nadante.* ¡Filomena! Este nombre, y en tales circunstancias, era para ella
toda una revelación fatídica, aterradora, una predicción horrible.
Apenas había oído la joven más que *el ritmo amedrentador del estudi-
ado discurso* de aquel abusador infame, que le hablaba de su deshonra,

amenazándola embozadamente con el martirio más cruento. Porque la recordación de aquel nombre evocaba en su desconcertado espíritu los primeros tiempos de su azarosa existencia, los sufrimientos que experimentara en la finca-infierno a que la confinaran en su niñez durante seis agonizantes años. Recordó los dolorosos sufrimientos de los demás esclavos; vió materialmente a Filomena en un lugar desconocido . . . ; y oyó el chasquido del latigazo que sobre las espaldas le daba el negro contramayoral . . . ; y vio al hijito de la infortunada Filomena, . . . se frotó los ojos con las manos como para quitarse la visión que tanto daño le hacía.

When that brutal attacker of defenseless young women pronounced Filomena's name, *Sofía felt herself shaking convulsively, uncontrollably.* Filomena! This name, and spoken in such circumstances, was for her an ominous, terrifying revelation, a horrible prediction. The young woman barely heard more than *the terrifying rhythm of the studied speech* of that infamous victimizer, with which he spoke to her of her dishonor, *secretly threatening her with the bloodiest martyrdom.* Because the mention of that name evoked in her disconcerted mind the first times of her hazardous existence, the suffering she experienced on the infernal sugar plantation to which she had been confined during her childhood for six agonizing years. She remembered the painful suffering of the rest of the slaves; she literally saw Filomena in an unknown place . . . ; and she heard the cracking of the whip with which the black overseer was lacerating her back . . . ; and she saw the little son of the unfortunate Filomena, . . . she covered her eyes with her hands as if to stop this vision that was hurting her so. (41; my emphases)

In its prophetic quality, this nightmarish vision is closely related to Sofía's dream, which induces the same uncontrollable trembling. But what conjures up the image of the sugar plantation is not so much the content of Federico's speech as its "rhythm," terrifying because it evokes the steam engine's rhythmic accompaniment to the slave's songs, a rhythm whose power over their lives is as total as the power Federico now exercises over Sofía's in the form of veiled threats. This rhythm identifies Federico's speech as part of the discourse of sugar, the inevitable locus of Cuban society's deep, dark secrets, the place where those secrets originate and to which they return to be hidden from public view. In a sense, Filomena is a name that designates not an individual, not even a person, but a practice comparable in its effects to the *boca-abajo*, the "ladder," and other Cubanisms that refer to similar disciplinary measures. Filomena's Law is part of Cuba's "peculiar legislation."

As Federico's words do not produce the desired results, he switches to a different kind of suasion with "rhythms" no less conventional than those of his threats, except that they draw their authority from a different social institution: that of marriage.

No era posible que pensase en tí como en cualquiera de esas muchachas de por ahí; no, no era posible, cuando veo que tú no has nacido para ser esclava. Tu natural delicadeza, tu condición moral, tu color, todo se opone a tu triste posición social. Tú estás destinada a ser la esposa de un hombre capaz de labrar tu felicidad. ¿Podría yo hacer esto aquí? No. Pero, deseándolo como lo deseo, mi pasión por tí, mi cariño inquebrantable me había sugerido la idea de pagar por trasmano tu libertad, llevarte a los Estados Unidos y casarme allí contigo. ¿Quién había entonces de ponernos trabas? Tú eres tan blanca como cualquiera señorita. Allí no serías la esclava, serías la señora.

It is not possible that I could think of you as one of those girls out there; no, impossible, when I see that you were not born to be a slave. Your natural delicacy, your moral condition, your color, all that is contrary to your sad social position. You are destined to be the wife of a man capable of bringing you happiness. Could I do that here? No. But, wishing it as much as I do, my passion for you, my unyielding affection has given me the idea of having someone pay for your freedom, taking you to the United States and marrying you there. Who could put obstacles in our way then? You are as white as any respectable lady. There, you would not have to be a slave, you would be a mistress. (42–43)

While even in the nineteenth century North America was a haven for many an exiled Cuban, among them Morúa himself,[38] Federico's ideas about the post-Reconstruction United States as a land of liberty for anyone of African descent are as false as his formulaic marriage proposal. In the previous chapter, Morúa makes explicit reference to racial prejudice in the United States by noting, among other things, that "*the friends* [Quakers] of the neo-Anglican brotherhood had an extreme aversion to the mixing of the human races" (30). The narrator also takes this as an occasion to stress that such sentiments are of course alien to a character like Magdalena, even though "she had received a brilliant semi-Quaker education" (27) during her five-year stay in the United States. Magdalena, after all, "era cubana de corazón, y no alimentaba el odio de raza" (was Cuban in her heart and did not harbor any racial hatred) (30). This, however, does not prevent her from taking Sofía's "ungratefulness," that is, her failure to confide in her mistress about the father of her child, as proof of "'la bajeza de su condición. ¡No podía negar que era negra, aunque su piel fuese casi blanca!'" (the lowliness of her condition. One could not deny that she was black, even if her skin was almost white!) (91).[39]

Federico, much like his sister, pretends to be offended at Sofía's "desconfianzas" (mistrust) (91). Yet, his rhetoric is no more an attempt at soliciting Sofía's consent to sexual intercourse than it is a proposal of marriage. On the one hand, it is precisely her consent that would make her unfit for marriage, as it would provide incontrovertible evidence of sexual promiscuity and thus of black origins. On the other hand, as Federico's previous threats imply, since Sofía is believed to be a mulata, her consent is already a fait accompli, so that her withholding it makes no real difference. That Sofía literally has no voice in the matter is clear from the fact that her only response to Federico's proposition is a desperate appeal to the Holy Virgin. There is no doubt that Federico's words are as much of a sham as is a "secret marriage." His rhetorical appeal to the institution of marriage serves no other purpose than to provide him with a discursive framework in which his sexual desires would appear legitimate. Little does he know that the relationship between him and Sofía is governed by legal conventions quite different from the ones that make possible his self-serving sentimental fiction of the "marido amantísimo" (most loving husband). Exactly what those conventions are is hinted at in the following account of Federico's "triumph" over Sofía.

El camisón de grano de oro que de su desecho le regalara Magdalena, detallaba las esculturales formas de su cuerpo virgen, permitiendo adivinar la tersura de aquellas contorneadas carnes de inmaculada vestal. Atrájola hacia sí Federico, y en lúbrico acceso estrechóla entre sus brazos con nerviosa presión; y la joven no pudo ni supo hacer otra cosa que abandonar el cuerpo y reclinar la cabeza en aquel pecho fementido,

y llorar *silenciosamente,* llorar un mar de lágrimas que no había de ser
bastante para lavar la impura mancha de su inevitable deshonra.

*The gold-grained nightgown, a castoff that Magdalena had given her
as a present,* outlined in detail the sculpted contours of her immaculate
body, allowing one to surmise the smoothness of her vestal virgin's sup-
ple flesh. Federico pulled her toward him, and in a lubricous fit of excite-
ment he grabbed her; and the girl could neither do nor think of anything else to do than abandon her body and rest her head against that
perfidious chest, and sob *silently,* but even the ocean of tears she shed
would not have been enough to wash away the impure legacy of her inevitable dishonor. (44; my emphases)

It is perhaps needless to point out that what Hortense Spillers
has called the "unrelieved crisis" of "the customary lexis of sexuality, including 'reproduction,' 'motherhood,' 'pleasure,' and 'desire,'" extends well beyond the sphere of "familial arangements
under a system of enslavement," though not always safely beyond
the borders of the master's house.[40] In *Sofía* sexuality is not
"clean" even within that "sphere of domesticity," especially if we
consider, with Morúa, that the offspring of female servants like
Sofía herself "could easily be a brother or nephew of their masters"
(90).[41] Sex is always compromised by power, and particularly so
under conditions of slavery, where it is ruthlessly and arbitrarily
invaded by property relations. In *Sofía,* this is already quite clear
from the analogy between the theft of Sofía's money and the concurrent theft of her body, a "defenseless target for rape and veneration."[42] Such entwinement of rape and veneration, terms that are
more complementary than contradictory and ultimately insepara-
ble, is at the center of Federico's pursuit of Sofía. It is clearly spelled
out in the above passage, where Sofía is represented as both an
accessible sexual object and a forbidden sacred object, a "vestal
virgin" with smooth flesh. There is indeed nothing else to do for
her than to "abandon" a body thus inscribed to the violent and
perverse desires of its male "owner." These images actually antici-
pate a rape that has already taken place in a variety of ways, so
that the actual ravishing of the female body comes almost like an
afterthought. It has a different symbolic function, the key to which
is the nightgown Sofía wears. That nightgown does indeed reveal

more than it is able to conceal, and not only of the female body it covers.

For one thing, dressing Sofía's body in gold consolidates her status as a commodity as well as links sexuality to economics.[43] But much more important is the fact that this golden garment is a hand-me-down from "Malenita," Sofía's not-so-pious half sister, whose adulterous passion for Gonzaga is an important secondary plot in this novel. We read earlier that "estaba siempre Sofía vestida convenientemente con las ropas de su señorita, que le venían pintiparadas" (Sofía was always conveniently dressed in her young mistress's clothes, which fit her like a glove) (30). Morúa insists on a likeness between them no less than Villaverde does in the case of Cecilia and Adela, but for different reasons. At issue here is not only family resemblance produced by the adulterous commingling of different bloodlines—one black, the other white—but the illicit mingling of the *same* bloodlines. For the cameo in this climactic passage of Magdalena, who has inscribed and appropriated Sofía's body in her own way, serves subtly but unmistakably to identify the illicit sexual commerce between Sofía and Federico as incest. This is another instance in which mistress and female slave become "twin actants in a common psychic landscape."[44] To Federico, Sofía is a "darker" version of the suggestively named Magdalena, one sexually available to him because her lineage presumably places her outside the realm of legitimacy. As a mulata, Sofía would be incompatible with the family as a social institution pledged to maintain white supremacy. The situation is similar to that in *Cecilia Valdés,* except that this incest has different connotations and implications. Federico not only rapes his half sister; he rapes his biologically white half sister. And Sofía's resulting pregnancy makes this act irrevocable and unredeemable for *her.*

Sofía's genealogical whiteness of course breaks apart the unholy alliance of incest and miscegenation. Not only does racial purity offer no protection whatsoever against the dreaded possibility of incest in *Sofía;* ironically, it creates that very possibility. In more ways than one, this is not an incest that "everybody could have prevented."[45] The desire for racial purity is revealed to be incestuous in that it is a (sexual) desire for someone of the same blood and social position. The main crime commmitted in this novel, that from which all other instances of violence emanate, is not miscegenation but *consanguinity*. Its social practice, encoded in the institution of the family, ensures the transmission and circulation of wealth (and thus power) only among those of the same blood or race and thus maintains white supremacy. Consanguinity-as-(social-)incest is that which is most desired, because it serves as a strategy for managing the distribution of socioeconomic resources and political power. It is also that which is most feared because this desire is invested not only economically but sexually as well. It carries within it the seeds of its own undoing, that is, the possibility for the family to be turned into a site of unrestrained illict sexuality. Morúa's imagination systematically destabilizes the family as the seat of social and economic power in nineteenth-century Cuba and thus challenges claims to property and social status based on inheritance. Sofía's lack of parents is only the beginning of that challenge.

Sofía's pregnancy, then, is complicated in both medical and social terms. The product of compromised sexuality, her fetus, having lost "su posición normal" (its normal position) (144), endangers not only its mother's life but, even more significantly, the existence of "normal" kinship and property relations. For the status quo to be maintained, it is no more possible for Sofía, given "'the bad example of *her* immorality'" (92; my emphasis), to remain within the Unzúazu household than it is for her child to survive as evidence of the family's sexual and social crimes. The initial descriptions of her condition as an illness (see 87–88) already imply the abnormality of her pregnancy; it is as if the child were a malignant swelling of her body.[46] In addition, the precise medical language of Doctor Alvarez's diagnosis (see 144) belongs to the same order of scientific discourse the narrator employs earlier on in the novel to catalogue specific practices of physical abuse designed, among other things, to prevent "normal" sexual relations among slaves (see 19).[47] Both passages are instances of the same discursive formation, one that conceives especially of the black, female body as a mere site of cultural and political maneuvering. They indicate that this discourse simultaneously operates in different social environments, in this case, country and city.

Sofía is dispossessed of her motherhood in the same way, and for the same reasons, that she is stripped of her freedom and ultimately of her own life. In keeping with her dehumanized status and with the elusive anonymity of the system that produced her, she does not just die; she simply ceases to exist ("Sofía había dejado de existir"). The narrator's brief obituary resonates with the kinds of discursive alignments I am proposing: "Innocence had paid its tribute to evil. Vice and depravation, engendered by an infernal system, had added another victim to the immense catalog of its infamous relapses" (163).

Part of that system, whose property relations compromise both kinship and sexuality, is of course Sofía's prostitute mother. In the penultimate chapter of the novel, the plot takes a somewhat unexpected turn. Not only is it revealed that Doña Manuela de Corrales, who calls herself "the Mendoza Widow," is in fact not a mulata. We also find out that she poisoned Doña Brígida, Sofía's protectress, which makes her an accomplice, albeit an unwitting one, in Don Acebaldo's schemes (see 174–75). He and Doña Manuela share a single-minded interest in Sofía's monetary inheritance. In this sense, Sofía is no different from the "mulaticas" whose bodies her mother sells in a different kind of slave market.[48] Clearly, Sofía is a commodity that circulates among both genders. Morúa's version of a mother-daughter reunion is harshly different from Villaverde's quasi-sentimental confirmation of the joys of motherhood in the tearful encounter of Rosario and Cecilia. That Rosario, in the end, regains her mental health is but little consolation in view of the fact that Don Cándido's patriarchal control over his daughter remains intact, even if the price he pays for this is the life of his only son.[49]

Unlike his counterpart, Leonardo, in *Cecilia Valdés*, Federico is, at least temporarily, allowed to survive, even if not in blissful ignorance of his deeds. He even takes a new mistress, "una mulatica de buen corte, cuyos padres decían que 'estaban por el adelanto de la raza'" (a little mulata from a good crop, whose parents claimed "to be in favor of advancing the race") (151). In *La familia Unzúazu*, Federico appropriately dies in the arms of his mulata mistress. The other characters, however, including Federico's sisters, are left in the dark about the incest, so that Magdalena, in a passage of supreme irony, can comfortably believe that she discovers in her brother's shock at the news of Sofía's death "the sign of an exquisite sensibility which she had never before suspected in him. The good young woman believed that Federico's reaction had been caused by his grief about the death of his unknown sister" (186). There is no evidence of repentance here, only a momentary flash of guilt on Federico's part that evaporates as rapidly as Sofía's memory.

The circle of exploitation and violence in *Sofía* is partly broken with the murder of Don Acebaldo at the hands of an anonymous assassin believed to be a ñáñigo (129). Due to the craftiness of the ironically named lawyer Justiz and the "secret plan" he hatches at the behest of Ana María (185), Liberato's guilt, the subject of yet another secondary plot, is "disproved." The novel ends with Ana María's paying the lawyer's fees for the defense of a slave who killed her husband and who will later rape her. Her triumphant words, the novel's final lines, are not exactly those of an aggrieved widow. But more than anything, they attest to the fact that, despite Nudoso's death, things have changed very little; for one thing, money and sex remain most intimately associated: "Sí, es subida; pero lo doy todo por bien empleado. ¿Había de quedarse la mulata esa riéndose de mi? . . . ¡Ca-a-chor-r-rra!" (Yes, it [the bill] is high; but I consider it money well spent. Should I have let that mulata laugh at me? . . . The sly bitch!) (194). The reference is of course to Don Acebaldo's mistress, in front of whose house he dies. What motivates Ana María's words and actions is hardly a desire for justice and truth but the need to reassert her social position at a time of crisis by making sure that racial divisions are kept intact, especially as the social institution of the family disintegrates.

Ana María's schemes shrewdly manipulate the separation of public reason and private desires and emotion. This manipulation makes all the more perplexing Morúa's later faith in the impartiality of the state's legislative bureaucracy, an impartiality that presumably transcended individual and group interests in the name of the political good of the new nation. In authoring his bill, Morúa once again separated public and private spheres of existence in Cuba. To the extent that the *Ley Morúa* was based on ignoring the specific political needs and interests of Cuba's black population, it forced them into privacy by denying them public articulation.

The character who represents that public realm's supposed color blindness in *Sofía* is of course Eladislao Gonzaga, Morúa's romantic hero, who has no counterpart in *Cecilia Valdés*. In *Sofía,* Gonzaga is Morúa's model insurrectionist—he is no longer quite that in *La familia Unzúazu.*[50] "They say he was an insurrectionist .. leader .. head .. " of the first Cuban War of Independence (39; ellipses in original). One reason for adding this male character is clearly to counterbalance the loathsome presence of both Don Acebaldo and his brother-in-law and to provide something of a mouthpiece for the author and his political beliefs.[51] Another is to lend social respectability to the Cuban Separatists: "the Cuban insurrectionist was a refined and even elegant man, not the brainless monster that we have usually imagined him to be" (35). That it is the liberal white intellectual Gonzaga who comes to replace Don Acebaldo as head of the Unzúazu family and subsequently unravels the mystery of Sofía's origins (see 135, 140) is not very surprising, especially since the character may well have been inspired by José Martí.[52] This may also explain why Morúa's otherwise astute and harsh criticisms of colonial Cuban society so consistently and quite unself-consciously exempt this figure, the only one who forms social alliances across class and racial boundaries without encountering any resistance. Morúa offers a vision of a new patriarchy, one in which certain nonwhite men, such as Fidelio from *La familia Unzúazu,* may participate. But this new Cuban nation still has no room for the Sofías and the Filomenas, not even for their memory.

5

Antidotes to Wall Street

I

Vedlos: son los colosos, los gigantes, los dueños . . .
No son obra gloriosa de ideales empeños,
sino la cristalización del latifundio . . .
Tienen la actualidad máxima de un gerundio
y la determinante pesadez de un adverbio.

Look at them: they are colossi, giants, proprietors . . .
They are not the glorious work of pawned ideals,
but the crystallization of the latifundium . . .
They have the maximum actuality of a gerund
and the determining weight of an adverb.

—Agustín Acosta, *La zafra*

Early-twentieth-century Cuba witnessed massive shifts in socio-economic and political power relations. By far the most important of those changes was that, by the turn of the century, sugar was fast becoming a hegemonic discourse of a very different kind. That sugar production affected everything in Cuba, including the country's intellectual climate, was hardly a novel situation. The difference was that, when the Cuban republic was inaugurated in 1901, the controls were no longer in Cuban hands. Since the growing dependency of the island on the United States is more than a historical backdrop to the rise of Afro-Cubanism in the twenties and

134

thirties, which I discuss in the second part of this chapter, I begin with a sketch of the economic and political changes in Cuba since the eve of the second War of Independence.

In 1894/95, the island's sugar crop for the first time exceeded one million tons, only to plunge down to record lows for the next few years as a result of Máximo Gómez's wartime moratorium on all economic activity.[1] The general vowed to destroy the sugar mills, burn the crops in the fields, and execute all workers who refused to comply with his decree.[2] It was not until almost ten years later that Cuban sugar production recovered from the effects of a three-year separatist revolution that ended up as the so-called Spanish-American War.[3] But at that point everything had changed, and not necessarily for the better. It quickly became apparent that Cuba's liberation from Spanish colonial rule meant forfeiting independence for decades to come.

The changes to which I am referring began with the Ten Years War (1868–78), a costly and protracted struggle that brought the Cuban economy to the brink of collapse. The Pact of Zanjón, Pérez notes, "marked more than the end of the war—it announced the passing of an age. For the million and a half inhabitants of the island, life soon returned to normal, but it would never be the same."[4] The fact that sugar production, both during and after the war, did not seem to fluctuate quite as much as it would during the early decades of the twentieth century is somewhat deceptive. Much more telling is the sharp decline in the overall number of *ingenios* (sugar mills), from 2,000 in 1860 to 1,190 in 1877. By the turn of the century, barely 200 sugar plantations were left in Cuba, which means, in effect, that a mere 10 percent of the plantations were producing more than twice the amount of sugar that had been harvested in 1860, but at prices considerably lowered by increasing competition in the world sugar market.[5] Nothing illustrates better the rise of the Cuban latifundio or *central*, as the sugar plantation was now known, during the post-Zanjón economic depression. This development would have been impossible without the massive influx of U.S. capital to bail out already bankrupt Cuban planters who were unable to meet the immense financial requirements for rebuilding and modernizing sugar production. "Planters survived the crisis of the 1880s, but only at the cost of their traditional supremacy over production. The price of solvency was displacement and ultimately dependency. Cuba's efforts to recover its former primacy [in the world sugar market] announced the reorganization of the production system and the restructuring of property relations. A new stage of capitalist organization was about to transform sugar production, and with it all of Cuba. It would be a recovery from which the planters in increasing numbers would be excluded."[6] Many, in fact, were reduced to the status of *colonos* (farmers) growing cane for the ever-expanding North American *centrales.*

The statistical data for 1927, the year when Ramiro Guerra published his now-famous twenty-one essays collected under the title *Azúcar y población en las Antillas* (Sugar and population in the Antilles) and Alejo Carpentier completed the first version of his Afro-Cuban novel *¡Ecue Yamba-O!* (God be praised!) in a Havana prison, are unambiguous: A mere 185 *centrales* produced 4.5 million tons of sugar for the U.S. market. The majority of these plantations were owned by North American companies such as Hershey, Henry O. Havemeyer's American Sugar Refining Company, and of course the notorious United Fruit Company and its myriad subsidiaries. Benjamin points out that "the value of U.S.-owned land on the modest-sized island surpassed North American holdings in any other foreign nation," and "by 1927, U.S.-owned mills accounted for about eighty-two percent of Cuban sugar production."[7] There was indeed little left for Cubans in their own country.

The ever-expanding sugar plantations dominated Cuba to such an extent that Guerra called the island "un inmenso cañaveral" (one immense cane field), and he concludes, wistfully and somewhat apocalyptically, that "dentro del latifundio no hay esperanza" (the sugar plantation leaves no room for hope).[8] In retrospect, Guerra's words have an almost uncannily prophetic quality, prophetic most immediately of the 1929 stock-market crash and the *vacas flacas* (lean cows) of the depression, which was already well under way in Cuba by the time *Azúcar y población* saw print. (The depression hit Cuba five years earlier than it did the United States.) World War I had given a tremendous, but only very temporary, boost to the Cuban sugar economy. In 1919, sugar production for the first time exceeded the four-million-ton mark, with world sugar prices soaring to unknown heights of almost twelve cents a pound. In 1929–30 the crop was a veritable bonanza of over five million tons, but prices began to drop precipitously (to less than two cents in the following year and to well below one cent in 1932–33). The total value of the harvest in those two years barely reached that of 1885. If one of the most notable results of the post-World War I economic crisis had been Antonio Machado's rise to power in 1925, which more or less coincided with the founding of the Cuban Communist Party and the National Workers Union (CNOC), then the aftermath of the Wall Street catastrophe set the stage for his political undoing in 1933.

The same years in which Machado's presidency, along with the Cuban economy, took a sharp turn for the worse were also the years of the Afro-Cuban or Afro-Antillean movement, with which Guerra's book shared a significant element: its opposition to U.S. economic and political intervention in Cuban affairs (both really amounted to the same thing). Guerra urged that measures be taken against latifundism, but without destroying the sugar industry in the process.[9] He was careful to emphasize that the economic reform program he advocated—including government controls directed against overproduction, importation of foreign workers (mostly from Jamaica and Haiti), and reliance on foreign capital— was "no . . . antiazucarero, ni anticapitalista, ni antiextranjero, sino un ideal cubano de defensa colectiva . . . ; de noble y elevada justicia humana, sin la cual ni el orden, ni la paz, ni el progreso, ni la concordia pueden imperar en el mundo; ideal constructivo, realizable y patriótico, que brota de esa consciencia nacional" (not antisugar, neither anticapitalist nor antiforeign, but a Cuban ideal of collective defense . . . ; of noble and sublime human justice, without which neither order, nor peace, nor progress, nor harmony can rule in the world; a constructive, pragmatic, and patriotic ideal born from this national conscience).[10] For Guerra, to rescue the Cuban sugar industry and the Cuban worker from North American domination was more than an economic necessity. It was a noble patriotic cause, and one that inevitably clashed with the United State's rapid economic expansion and dollar diplomacy in the Caribbean.

By the beginning of the twentieth century, however, the threat the United States posed to Cuba was no longer one of either military intervention or annexation. Since 1909, when the United States once again restored sovereignty to the island after a second period of military occupation (1906–9), North American policy toward Cuba had undergone significant reformulations. The reinterpretation of the Platt Amendment made prevention rather than "pacification" the new function of intervention, and prevention meant "the creation of an infrastructure of hegemony in which the United States appropriated authority over the national system." But "ironically, the exercise of hegemony in the pursuit of [economic and political] stability became itself the principal source of instability."[11] Benjamin explains:

Washington never fully understood Cuban nationalism. It was treated as an atavistic phenomenon that would abate as accumulating U.S. influence led to a mature society. The State Department did realize that opposition to U.S. policy often served as an outlet for an emotional Cuban patriotism. It did not, however, consider the possibility that the U.S. presence in Cuba was the principal source of such nationalism. By inextricably mixing its rewards and punishments and by continually requiring Cuban society to recast itself, the United States assured that the question of Cuban independence—both in its practical and ideal forms— would never stray far from its original focus on North American power over the island's affairs.[12]

Racism had begun to emerge as a significant factor in U.S.-Cuban relations as early as the 1870s. If, for most of the nineteenth century, the United States had considered annexation a "natural fate" for Cuba, that "confident expansionism" was significantly qualified by the fear of absorbing the island's nonwhite population. This first became an issue due to the failure of Reconstruction, which "exposed a northern racial prejudice that had been obscured by the crusade against slavery."[13] Similar fears resurfaced in a heightened fashion during the massive wave of immigration around the turn of the century, whose effects were to boost the membership of the Ku Klux Klan and to plant the seeds for American Nativism. If earlier fears of Cuba's potential for becoming a second Haiti had served to justify the expansionist desires of those in favor of the island's annexation to the United States, now increasing opposition arose to the possibility of acquiring an island filled "with black, mixed, degraded, and ignorant, or inferior races."[14] It is telling that popular support for Cuban independence during the 1890s was helped along by the fact that the Cuban rebels as pictured in North American journals were not "a black rabble in the fashion of the Haitian revolutionaries of the early nineteenth century" but "white warriors, neatly ranked behind the banner of liberty."[15] The American soldiers who landed in Cuba in 1898 were rather surprised when they did not find many such republican gentlemen among the members of the separatist army. After all, about 40 percent of the senior officers of the rebel army were black:[16] "After the war, as U.S. soldiers returned home with stories of lazy, cowardly, thieving Cubans, the once-discredited Spanish view of their incompetence gained currency and was reinforced by the social Darwinism and racism with which most North Americans already viewed 'tropical' peoples."[17] Given their racial biases, North American officials were "instinctively" drawn toward the whiter, wealthier Cuban planters, which led them to ignore the growing black classes as well as the racial tensions that would soon challenge the rule of the island's native elite.

So despite the fact that the Partido Revolucionario Cubano (PRC), founded in 1892 in Key West, Florida, attracted substantial numbers of nonwhite Cubans, and despite the hopeful call for racial integration José Martí issued in 1893 in "Mi raza" (My race), racial discrimination in Cuba was once again on the rise—barely two decades after slavery had been legally abolished. There is no question that racial prejudice was in part fostered by the initial U.S. occupation of the island (1898–1902), a period during which military units were segregated for the first time in Cuban history and severe restrictions were placed on the immigration of black workers from Haiti and Jamaica.[18] But job discrimination in the sugar and especially the tobacco industries, often in the form of *sobrinismo* (nepotism) facilitated by the continued arrival of large numbers of Spaniards during the early years of the republic, contributed its share to heightening racial tensions.[19] In the same year that the Platt Amendment was ratified, making Cuba a virtual U.S. protectorate, a general strike was organized to protest such discriminatory hiring practices, while a group of university-educated black profes sionals successfully petitioned the government of Tomás Estrada Palma to ban comparsas and other, to them embarrassing, Afro-Cuban cultural institutions. The Partido Independiente de Color (PIC) was founded in response to the 1908 elections, when, despite campaign promises from both the Moderate and the Liberal parties to end racial inequality, not a single black politician was elected to office.[20]

The desirability of an independent party—an idea inspired by Evaristo Estenoz, Lucas Marrero, and other members of the so-called Negro Protest Movement that was active particularly in eastern provinces such as Camagüey—had been debated in the papers since 1906, the year when Fernando Ortiz published his seminal study of Havana's black proletariat, *Los negros brujos: Hampa afrocubana* (The black sorcerers: The Afro-Cuban underworld). There was a good deal of opposition from those who felt that the formation of such an organization would be inappropriately divisive at a time of this second U.S. occupation.[21] But that opposition did not die down even after the departure of the American troops in 1909. On the contrary, during the first year of the Liberal government of José Miguel Gómez, installed with U.S. help, a bill to outlaw the PIC was introduced in the Cuban senate by the former *independista* Morúa Delgado, whose early efforts to organize workers in Matanzas had led to his arrest and deportation in 1880–81. Morúa—at the time a staunch enemy of Juan Gualberto Gómez, another prominent mulato politician who, together with Generoso Campos Marquetti, had presided over the founding of the Comité de Veteranos de la Raza de Color in 1902—was the only nonwhite member of the first Cuban senate and the only "person of color" to become its president. After the *Ley Morúa* was passed in 1910, the PIC was promptly dispersed, and its leaders arrested.

But the issue was far from resolved, and the worst confrontation occurred two years later, when the 1912 elections provoked an armed rebellion demanding the legalization of the PIC. Race riots broke out in Havana and Oriente Province, posing a threat to North American-owned sugar mills and mining companies, particularly in southern Oriente. The Gómez government, ironically with the loyal support of the same veterans who had been at the forefront of the 1902 labor unrests, brutally crushed the insurrection when faced with the growing possibility of another U.S. military intervention.[22] One year later, it also banned the secret society of the ñáñigos—recall, for instance, that Morúa's Liberato, for one, was supposedly a ñáñigo. The society was not revived until the mid-twenties when, due mainly to the anthropological work of Fernando Ortiz, *ñañiguísmo* and other Afro-Cuban religious practices were beginning to acquire some intellectual currency and literary value.

A prominent example is Carpentier's *¡Ecue Yamba-O!* often cited as the only novel Afro-Cubanism produced.[23] *Ecue* features ñáñigo dances and religious ceremonies as "therapeutic" alternatives to the culture sugar created during the tumultuous first decades of the twentieth century, when sugar production was so closely tied to United States economic, political, and cultural imperialism. According to Carpentier, "Sólo los negros . . . conservaban celosamente un carácter y una tradición antillana. ¡El *bongó,* antídoto de Wall Street! ¡El Espíritu Santo, venerado por los Cué, no admitía salchichas yanquis dentro de sus panecillos votivos . . . ! ¡Nada de *hot-dogs* con los santos de Mayeya! (Only the blacks . . . fervently preserved an Antillean character and tradition. The *bongó* drum, antidote to Wall Street! The Holy Spirit venerated by the Cué family did not allow Yankee sausages between pieces of his votive bread . . . ! No *hot-dogs* for the saints of Mayeya!)[24]

The contrast is even more pronounced in an earlier passage. *Ecue* opens with an poetic image worthy of Laplante's nineteenth-century estate portraits: "Anguloso, sencillo de líneas como figura de teorema, el bloque del Central San Lucio se alzaba en el centro de un ancho valle orlado por una cresta de colinas azules" (Angular, with the simplicity of a theorem, rose the block of the Sugar Mill San Lucio at the center of a sprawling valley framed by a crest of blue hills). Carpentier succeeds in condensing the entire authenticating machinery of the discourse of sugar into an image compelling in its starkness and almost mathematical precision. But then the focus abruptly shifts to a figure systematically erased from Laplante's picturesque scenes: "El viejo Usebio Cué había visto crecer el hongo de acero, palastro y concreto sobre las ruinas de trapiches antiguos, asistiendo año tras año, con una suerte de espanto admirativo, a las conquistas de espacio realizadas por la fábrica. Para él la caña no encerraba el menor misterio" (The old Usebio Cué had seen how the steel, sheet iron, and concrete sprouted like mushrooms on the ruins of the old sugar mills; filled with a sort of admiring terror, he witnessed, year after year, the conquest of space achieved by the factory. For him, the sugarcane did not hold the slightest mystery).[25] This old black farmer, about to lose his land to the foreign-owned sugar company, is only the first black character Carpentier would cast in a double role as both witness to the workings of (neo)colonial power and redemptive signifier of an authentic Cuban or Antillean culture.[26]

Carpentier was neither the first nor the only Cuban writer at the time who perceived Afro-Cuban secular and religious culture as a cultural alternative to North-Americanization and as a political vehicle for national integrity and survival. For many of the mostly white members of the Cuban intelligentsia, Afro-Cuban culture, much like the image of the Santa Teresa candle burning in front of a picture of the deity San Lázaro-Babayú-Ayé that closes *Ecue*,[27] was a talismanic presence that would somehow avert or transcend the dangers posed by Wall Street and the *central*.

Afro-Cubanism or Afro-Antilleanism as a politico-literary practice began to take shape during the Machado regime in the mid-twenties and ended, according to its early commentators, around 1940. Rather than constituting a literary movement unified by an aesthetic program, Afro-Cubanism can more profitably be seen as a historically specific instance of *cubanía*.[28] Fernando Ortiz's term for what he understood as a spiritual condition, *cubanía*, unlike the more passive national identification expressed by the concept of *cubanidad*, signifies an active desire to be Cuban, and its various articulations in literature, the arts, and the social sciences were to provide indigenous ideological antidotes to the economic, social, and political crises induced by United States interventionism.[29] There is no doubt that Cuban nationalist politics of the kind that undergirded the launching of journals such as *Revista de Avance* (1927) and *Atuei* by the "grupo minorista" and that became audible in the notes of social criticism that began to sound in the poetry of Acosta, Felipe Pichardo Moya, Lino Novás Calvo,

Regino Pedrozo, Félix Pita Rodríguez, and others between 1926 and 1928, served as a major catalyst for Afro-Cubanism. This was particularly so since the specter of U.S. military intervention had been successfully invoked by a number of Cuban presidents to manipulate the island's domestic politics, especially but not exclusively when it came to racial conflicts. At the same time, racial prejudice was by no means just a North American import, even if it had been aggravated by the presence of increasing numbers of "Yankees," military and otherwise, since the Spanish-Cuban-American War. Though it had somewhat different manifestations in the Hispanic Caribbean, racism had not exactly been extinct from that region prior to the North American occupation(s), as is evident, among other things, from the growing disdain with which the socially more "advanced" class of mulato professionals in Cuba treated the "uncultured" masses of black laborers, augmented by immigrants from Jamaica and Haiti, whom they perceived as an insult to Cuban civilization.

Afro-Cubanism was an exemplary instance of Cuba's ambivalence toward racial matters. Not unlike many of the nineteenth-century costumbrista representations of Cuba's free or enslaved people of African descent on which I focused in my earlier chapters, this "movement" and its literary products, mainly poetry, contained and defused potential ethnic threats to national unification by turning them into original (and originary) contributions to Cuban culture. In a poignant passage from the introduction to his 1938 anthology *Orbita de la poesía afrocubana*, Ramón Guirao, himself the author of several well- known *poemas negros/mulatos*, attempts to distinguish Cuba's sensibility from postwar Europe's faddish embrace of "things black."

Hoy, al amparo de una comprensión más cabal de los tratos y contratos desfavorables que gravitan en nuestra economía y dificultan la afirmación de nuestra naciente nacionalidad, se intenta propagar, movido de la necesidad de que la población negra y mestiza participe responsablemente de este momento crítico, que la poesía afronegrista, esto es, de tema negro, es la más genuina manifestación de nuestra sensibilidad insular. . . . Esta vigilante pasión de lo negro nos hizo pensar . . . en la posibilidad de que el negro adquiriera su igualdad de oportunidades, el derecho a convivir en un plano armonioso de comprensión y entendimiento mutuos. *Hemos visto que estas incursiones a las ricas vetas de la cantera negra no han alterado el destino social del hombre negro. La realidad es otra.* Situados a una distancia prudencial de aquella racha de negrofilia se hace necesario confesar que el objetivo era más cruel. Se trataba de añadir una cuerda más al arco del artista occidental para solear un poco su arte. . . . *Si se invitó a los negros a que compartieran el pan, si se les sentó por unos instantes a la mesa, fué con el propósito de que dejaran algo original sobre su mantel de albura almidonada.*

Today, with the benefit of a more accurate understanding of the unfavorable bargains and contracts that burden our economy and make difficult the affirmation of our nascent national identity, one wants to propose, motivated by the necessity that the black and mixed population participate responsibly in this critical moment, that *afronegrista* poetry, that is, poetry about black themes, is the most genuine manifestation of our insular sensibility. . . . This vigilant passion for blackness made us believe . . . in the possibility that the Negro could achieve equality of opportunities, the right to coexist [with the whites] on a harmonious plane of mutual comprehension and understanding. *We have seen that these incursions into the rich veins of the black quarry have not changed the social destiny of black people. The reality is different.* A careful distance from that [European] spell of negrophilia makes it necessary to confess that its objective was very cruel. It was a matter of adding another string to the bow of the Western artist to give his art a little luster. . . . *If one invited the blacks to share the bread, if one seated them at the table for just a few moments, it was with the expectation that they would leave something original on the starched white tablecloth.*[30]

Echoes of Langston Hughes's poem "I Too" (sing America, that is) are not the only ones that resonate in the final sentence of this passage.[31] Perhaps more importantly, Guirao's polemic against Europe's *vogue nègre* recall the much earlier remarks in which José Jacinto Milanés identifies Cuban blacks as "the mine of our best poetry."[32] Given his interest in nineteenth-century Cuban poetry written by blacks, Guirao would no doubt have been familiar with this and other, similar pronouncements. Despite his disclaimers, and despite the fact that Cuba's political circumstances and ideological motives were very different from Europe's, it is nevertheless true that, in both the nineteenth and early twentieth centuries, *los negros* added luster ("originality"?) to the island's otherwise rather dull literary scene.

The early ethnographic writings of Fernando Ortiz were instrumental in this process. Most notable here is his *Hampa afrocubana* (Afro-Cuban underworld) (1906), subtitled "Apuntes para un estudio de etnología criminal" (Notes for a study of criminal ethnology) which, together with *Los esclavos negros* (The black slaves) (1916), the *Glosario de afrocubanismos* (Glossary of Afro-Cubanisms) (1924), and the dozens of articles he published in the *Revista Bimestre Cubana* and elsewhere,[33] became an important launching pad for *poesía negra/mulata*. Ortiz also founded the journal *Archivos del Folklore Cubano*, whose inaugural issue appeared in 1924, and became president of the Sociedad de Estudios Afrocubanos in 1937.[34] Anthropology and literature collaborated in amalgamating nationalism and culture into a depoliticized ethnographic discourse whose effect was both to recuperate and to absorb *la gente de color* through their folklore. While this affiliation does not invalidate Ortiz's work, it does situate it within what Depestre calls "the reciprocal relations . . . anthropology maintained with the scandals of the colonial era."[35] Not unlike nineteenth-century costumbrismo in the service of reformist abolitionism, Afro-Cubanism had all the makings of a folkloric spectacle whose political effect was to displace and obfuscate actual social problems and conflicts, especially racial ones. The mythic Afro-Cuban underworld Ortiz and others constructed was more than a cultural origin; it was the only Cuban space seemingly beyond the reach of the United States.

II

Dale a la popa, mulata,
proyecta en la eternidad
ese tumbo de caderas
que es ráfaga de huracán, y menéalo,
de aquí payá, de ayá pacá,

menéalo, menéalo,
¡para que rabie el Tío Sam!

Shake your butt, mulata,
project into eternity
this beat of your hips
that's the hurricane's gale, and shake it,
back and forth, forth and back,
shake it, shake it,
to make Uncle Sam rage!

—Luis Palés Matos, "Plena de menéalo"
(Shaking it)

In 1928, the conservative *Diario de la Marina,* the daily with the largest circulation in the island until 1936, printed a public announcement of the founding of the Ku Klux Klan (La Orden de los Kaballeros) in Camagüey, the birthplace of later poet laureate Nicolás Guillén and many other renowned Cuban writers.[36] Although this Havana newspaper had a reputation for championing antinationalist causes and foreign interests in Cuba, it had also published the series of Guerra's articles on the sugar industry on its front page during the previous year; this may in part account for Guerra's conspicuous attempts at tempering his nationalist sentiments with pro–United States disclaimers. And only a few months later, on November 25, 1928, Gustavo E. Urrutia's section, "Ideales de una Raza" (Ideals of a race), made its first appearance in the Sunday Literary Supplement that *El Diario* had carried since early 1926. Under the editorial direction of José Antonio Fernández de Castro, the Supplement had become an important cultural forum, one of whose functions was to keep Cuban readers abreast of the latest developments in the arts, at home and abroad. Contributors included Miguel de Unamuno, Jorge Luis Borges, Miguel Angel Asturias, Agustín Acosta, Ramón Guirao, and of course Alejo Carpentier. Carpentier in those days wrote mainly on painting and music, taking every opportunity to report on the international successes of Cuban composers Amadeo Roldán and Alejandro García Caturla.[37] On the one hand, there were articles on more staid topics like the work of Cervantes, Góngora, Calderón, Byron, and Hardy (not to mention on the purple poetry of Mrs. Calvin Coolidge[38]). On the other, feature articles appeared on surrealism, futurism, and feminism; on recent poetry in Cuba, Mexico, and the United States; on José Martí, Antonio Maceo, Domingo Del Monte, Waldo Frank, H. L. Mencken, Booker T. Washington, Fernando Ortiz, Carpentier, José Enrique Rodó, and José Carlos Mariátegui; and there were one-page spreads on the theater of Eugene O'Neill, the poetry of José Manuel Poveda—including a reprint of his "El grito abuelo" (The grandfather's cry)—José Zacarías Tallet, Regino Pedrozo, and José Ortega y Gasset's *La deshumanización del arte* (*The Dehumanization of Art*). The books that were reviewed in the "Libro de hoy" (Today's book) section ranged from José Vasconcelos's *La raza cósmica* (The cosmic race), Jorge Mañach's *Indagación del choteo* (Investigation of *choteo*), Guerra's *Azúcar y población,* and Juan Luis Martín's *Ecue, Changó, y Yemayá,* to Waldo Frank's *The Dark Mother,* Mary White Ovington's *Color Portraits,* and Josephine Baker's *Memoirs.*

As early as 1926, the Supplement had also begun to spotlight the work of nonwhite Cuban painters and sculptors such as Pastor Argudín y Pidrozo, Andrés Alvarez Naranjo, Jaime Valls, Hernández Cardenas, and Teodoro Ramos, many of whom lived in Paris at the time.[39] It had also printed *negrista* short stories and poetry, such as Gerardo del Valle's "El bongó" (The bongo drum) (1927) and "Seboruco" (1928), as well as Palés Matos's "Danza negra" (Black dance) (1927) and Guirao's "Bailadora de rumba" (The rumba dancer), which was dedicated to Valls and accompanied by Valls's *La Rumba* (1928).[40] But with "Ideales de una Raza," which editor Urrutia described as a "modesto exponente de la cultura de nuestra raza negra" (modest forum for the culture of our black race),[41] accounts of black artistic achievement for the first time became a regular feature in the *Diario de la Marina.*

"Ideales" was by no means exclusively devoted to literature and the arts. Notwithstanding his inaugural disclaimer that this page was "nonpolitical," Urrutia published articles on a wide array of social, economic, historical, and political topics pertaining to blacks in Cuba and elsewhere in the Americas. One of Urrutia's favorite targets in his weekly editorial column—tellingly, and perhaps somewhat ironically, titled "Armonías" (Harmonies)—was racial discrimination and segregation in the United States, which gave him the opportunity to emphasize, time and again, how much better race relations were in Cuba.[42] In fact, it would seem that the primary purpose of "Armonías" was to assure white Cubans that their nonwhite fellow countrymen were not engaged in hostile competitions for socioeconomic privileges but were thoroughly dedicated to patriotic causes.

Among many others things, "Ideales" printed translations from W. E. B. Du Bois and Atenor Firmin,[43] as well as providing weekly bibliographies of the work of nonwhite authors in Cuba. It reported extensively on the visits to Havana by Langston Hughes and Federico García Lorca, as well as printing *negrista* short fiction. But, most importantly, it regularly featured *poesía negra/mulata* from Cuba and Latin America: Ildefonso Pereda Valdés's "Canción de cuna para dormir un negrito" (Lullaby for a black child) and his "La guitarra de los negros" (The guitar of the blacks);[44] Palés Matos's "Danza negra," which was reprinted in October 1930 from the supplement;[45] and an assortment of poems by José Manuel Poveda (July 1929), Regino Boti, Regino Pedrozo (June 1930), the Panamanian Rogelio Sinán, and, above all, Guillén. It is admittedly difficult to define an exact starting point for what is frequently called the Afro-Antillean movement. Even though Luis Llorens Torres had included a handful of poems about blacks in his *Sonetos sinfónicos* (San Juan, 1914), the first to popularize *poesía negra* in Puerto Rico was Palés, a founding member of the magazine *Los Seis* (1924). "Los seis" (the six) was a group of Puerto Rican *modernista* writers whose proindependence sentiments were similar to those of Cuba's *minoristas* (minorists) and who began to turn to social and racial issues as part of their war on romantic/lyric poetry. Palés's earliest *negrista* poems, "Africa" (later retitled "Pueblo negro" [Black people]) and "Danza negra"—possibly inspired by Vachel Lindsay's "The Congo" (1914) and by the famous Cuban reciter Eusebia Cosme, who had visited Puerto Rico in 1925—appeared in 1926, the same year in which Langston Hughes published his influential manifesto "The Negro Artist and the Racial Mountain" in the *Nation*.[46] Alfonso Camín's

"Elogio de la negra" (The black woman's eulogy) had already appeared in 1925.

To be sure, "Ideales" was by no means the only place where *negrista* poetry was being popularized. In Cuba, the *Revista de Avance* printed Alfonso Camín's "Damasajova" and "La negra Panchita" in March 1927 and January 1928, respectively; Guirao's "Bailadora de rumba" (Rumba dancer) in September 1928; Ballagas's "Elegía de María Belén Chacón" (María Belén Chacón's elegy), and Carpentier's "Liturgia" in 1930. *Atuei* published Tallet's "La Rumba" in 1928. *Social* reprinted Guillén's "Hay que tiene boluntá" (One Must Have Willpower) in July 1930 and published Hernández Catá's "La negra de siempre" (The same old black woman) in July of the following year. In addition, the *Revista Bimestre Cubana,* which had reviewed Pereda Valdés's *La guitarra de los negros* in 1929, published a considerable number of articles on *negrista* poetry and Afro-Cuban music between 1932 and 1940. In Puerto Rico, *La Democracia* published Pedro J. Brull's "Canto a la negra" (Song to the black woman) in 1927 and Palés's "Canción festiva para ser llorada" (Festive song to be cried) in 1928. The two journals that devoted most attention to racial matters were the newly founded *Hostos,* followed by *Indice* which printed "Falsa canción de Baquiné" in 1929, "Bombo" in 1930, "Elegía del duque de la mermelada" (Elegy of the Duke of Marmalade) in 1930, and "Ñam-ñam" in 1931.[47] Still, it is safe to say that "Ideales," that modest one-page, presumably unpolitical forum for black culture—which would be discontinued at the beginning of 1931 precisely because it was too political—was the principal showcase for Afro-Cubanism/Afro-Antilleanism and its various manifestations in literature, music, and the visual arts.

If the impressionistic *poesía negra/mulata* written by Ballagas, Guirao, Tallet, Carpentier, Palés, and others cannot be separated from their ideological resistance to U.S. imperialism any more than can some of the politically more astute poems by Guillén, Arozarena, Boti, and Pedrozo, the impact on these writers of the *vogue nègre* that swept from postwar Europe to the Americas is equally undeniable. France and Germany's "rediscovery" of non-Western, especially African cultures, had begun during the final quarter of the nineteenth century with the wholesale "transferral" of African art objects, primarily sculp tures, to museums in London, Paris, Berlin, Leipzig, Dresden, and Brussels. That rediscovery continued as modernism made European painters such as Picasso, Matisse, Juan Gris (and, to a lesser extent, Kandinski, Modigliani, and Marc) more receptive to African aesthetics. Escalated by World War I, the modernist crisis, fueled by the work of ethnographers Leo Frobenius and Maurice Delafosse and conceptualized by Oswald Spengler's *The Decline of the West* (1918 and 1919–22), spread from the visual arts to other areas of artistic representation, especially to music (Dvořák, Bartók, Stravinsky) and to poetry (Blaise Cendrars, Guillaume Apollinaire, Philippe Soupault, Paul Morand, André Gide).[48] In Hispanic America Spenglerian ideas were disseminated mainly through Ortega y Gasset's *Revista de Occidente,* which also published a translation of Leo Frobenius's *The Black Decameron* (1910) in 1925. Spengler's work was reviewed in the *Revista Bimestre Cubana* the following year.[49] As an avant-garde "movement" that, on the one hand, belonged squarely in the context of cubism, fauvism, futurism, dadaism, surrealism, and especially Hispanic American *posmodernismo* while, on the other, being firmly entrenched in concurrent national struggles for decolonization, Afro-Antilleanism was an amalgam of different cultural and political trends that derived much of its momentum and its coherence from the urgent need to formulate alternatives to what was quickly becoming an intolerable situation. What was at stake, especially for Cuba, was economic, cultural, and political survival in the face of mounting pressures from what Martí had dubbed the "colossus of the North."[50]

Much like Afro-Cubanism, the various movements of "black consciousness" that have emerged in different parts of the Caribbean since the beginning of the twentieth century have almost invariably been inspired by foreign intrusion. Haitian *indigenisme,* another ideology of national consciousness that developed almost simultaneously with Afro-Cubanism and centered around journals such as *Les Griots* and *La Revue Indigène,* can be attributed to the invasion of the U.S. marines in 1915. Francophone Caribbean negritude, with Aimé Césaire's journal *Tropiques* as its focal point, was partly a response to the racism of the French army that occupied Martinique and Guadeloupe from 1940 to 1943. The presence of the Shell petroleum refinery in Aruba prompted such Dutch-Caribbean statements as the poet Frank Martinus Arion's *Stemmen uit Afrika* (Voices from Africa) (1957). The presence of U.S. military personnel in Trinidad during World War II had similar effects. The popularity of Garveyism especially among the large Caribbean populations in Panama and Costa Rica was likewise a response to the Jim Crowism practiced during the construction of the Panama Canal and later in the factories of the United Fruit Company.[51]

Parallels of the literary kind have been drawn primarily between Afro-Cubanism/Afro-Antilleanism and the Harlem Renaissance, while comparisons with *indigenisme* and negritude are less frequent.[52] Since much has been made in particular of the friendship between Guillén and Langston Hughes, a brief digression to Hughes's visit to Cuba seems in order. Hughes came to Havana in late February of 1930, hoping to find a librettist for his "singing play"—he had just finished his first novel, *Not without Laughter.* Hughes had with him a letter of introduction from Miguel Covarrubias to Fernández de Castro, through whom Hughes met Urrutia, Marinello, Conrado Massaguer, Tallet, the painter Eduardo Abela, Ramos Blanco, and, of course, Guillén. The great Negro poet from the United States was received warmly. Guillén in particular was both fascinated with and perplexed by this North American "mulatico" (little mulatto). Guillén recounts at the end of an interview he did with Hughes for "Ideales," that during a visit to a local dance hall the latter exclaimed, "Yo quiero ser negro. Bien negro. Negro de verdad!" (I want to be black. Really, truly black).[53] Hughes, who had by then published two volumes of poetry, *The Weary Blues* and *Fines Clothes to the Jew,* urged Guillén to use Afro-Cuban music as a basis for his poetry. Although Guillén dedicated *Motivos de son* (*Son* motifs) to Fernández de Castro, not to Hughes, this dedication seems like an indirect homage to the latter: it was, after all, Fernández de Castro who had introduced Guillén to Hughes and who had first translated some of Hughes's poems into Spanish.

Yet, just how much of a specific impact Hughes and his blues poetry ultimately had on the writing of *Motivos* is difficult to ascertain. Guillén's English was precarious; it is unlikely that he was able to read Hughes's poems in the original. Hughes, on the other hand, with the collaboration of Ben Frederic Carruthers, would later translate a significant number of Guillén's poems into English.[54] By the same token, despite Urrutia's exuberant claim that Guillén's verse was "the exact equivalent of [Hughes's] 'blues,'" a comment that seems to have inspired several critics,[55] it is as problematic to liken the Cuban *son,* and Guillén's *poemas-son* (*son*-poems), to the North-American blues, and to the blues poetry of Hughes and even Sterling Brown, whose more consistent use of Afro-American vernacular speech in *Southern Road* (1930) would seem to place his work in closer proximity to *Motivos* than Hughes's. While it is useful to compare aspects of North American blues poetry to Guillén's *poemas-son,* greater care has to be exercised in contextualizing such formal and thematic similarities so as not to elide social, historical, and ideological differences.[56] One major difference is that Afro-Cubanism, unlike the Harlem Renaissance, was not supported, financially or otherwise, by a nascent African-American middle class surrounded by a host of wealthy white patrons.

A case in point is that the "black" bourgeoisie of Havana's Club Atenas, which made up most of the readership of "Ideales," were less than enthusiastic about the publication of Guillén's *Motivos de son.* Not even José Zacarías Tallet's "La rumba," published in *Atuei* in 1928 and an immediate object of controversy because of its overtly sexual language, had elicited this kind of a reaction. If many showered Guillén with praise—Juan Marinello, Fernando Ortiz, and others admired the poems' compelling rhythms, and Urrutia exultantly called *Motivos* "the best kind of Negro poetry we ever had," in fact, the only "authentic" Negro poems ever written in Cuba[57]—the members of the Club Atenas were exceedingly skeptical about the *Motivos,* even offended. They voiced strong reservations about the propriety of Guillén's poetic use of the vernacular of Havana's poor blacks in conjunction with the dance form of the *son.*[58] Although the *son,* descended from the famous "Son de la Ma Teodora" (presumably dating back to 1580) and popularized in the 1920s and 1930s by Eliseo Grenet and especially Miguel Matamoros,[59] had by then achieved respectability in the salons of Havana, its transformation into a literary form was quite a different matter, with unsettling political implications.

Guillén's *Motivos* did lend formal emphasis to the African presence in Cuba.[60] Despite their problematic representations of women, on which I shall comment later, these poems, unlike so many other *poemas negros/mulatos,* did not uncritically celebrate the picturesque contributions of black folklore to Cuba's national cultural landscape. Instead, *Motivos* raises questions about social inequality in what to many middle-class blacks were loathsome vernacular voices from the notorious "Afro-Cuban underworld." Guillén's poems were indeed different from García Lorca's exuberantly musical "Son de los negros en Cuba," published in *Musicalia* that same April, and indeed from most of the *poesía negra/mulata* his fellow countrymen produced. Topics such as racial shame and color hierarchies, poverty, prostitution, and economic exploitation did not sit well with Cuba's mulato professionals, the same class that had previously effected a ban on Afro-Cuban comparsas. What Guillén's representations of working-class Cuban blacks lacked, to be sure, was social (and linguistic) decorum. To the members of the Club Atenas, these poems were what Paul Laurence Dunbar would have called "jingles in a broken tongue" that washed Cuba's dirty laundry in public, a charge to which Guillén himself cheekily alludes in *El diario que a diario (The Daily Daily)* (1972).[61]

Little is gained by debating whether Afro-Antilleanism was a truly indigenous movement or an imported intellectual fad. Dismissing white *negrista* poets while praising writers of African descent for their presumably more authentic portrayals of blacks may help consolidate present ideological positions, but only at the expense of dehistoricizing and depoliticizing both the issues and the literature. It is equally fruitless, as I noted in my Introduction, retrospectively to blame Guillén and other nonwhite Cuban writers for their supposed failure to invest in a black aesthetic in the U.S. sense of that term. Among other things, such a view disregards the fact that the poetry of Afro-Antilleanism, no matter how inauthentic most of it may seem today, did set a precedent for nonwhite writers from other Hispanic-American countries. In that regard, it is quite significant that, with the exception of Guillén's first two books of poems, *Motivos* and *Sóngoro cosongo* (1931), all the major volumes of *poesía negra / mulata*, as well as Carpentier's *¡Ecue Yamba-O!* were published when Afro-Antilleanism was already on the decline (and in Cuba after Machado had been toppled): Pedrozo's *Nosotros* (We) appeared in 1933, Ballagas's *Cuaderno de poesía negra* (Book of *poesía negra*), Guirao's *Bongó*, Gómez Kemp's *Acento negro* (Black accent), and Guillén's *West Indies, Ltd.*, in many ways a transitional text that includes few *poemas negros*, in 1934. Palés's *Tuntún de pasa y grifería*, though completed by September 1933, was not published until 1937, the same year that saw the first issue of *Estudios Afrocubanos*, the official organ of the Sociedad de Estudios Afrocubanos contra los Racismos (Society for Afrocuban Studies against Racism), founded by Ortiz and others in 1936. And the two major anthologies, Ballagas's *Antología de poesía negra hispanoamericana* (Madrid) and Guirao's *Orbita de la poesía afrocubana* (Havana), did not come out until 1935 and 1938, respectively. José Sanz y Diaz's *Lira negra* (Madrid) and Ballagas's *Mapa de la poesía negra americana* (Buenos Aires) appeared even later, in 1945 and 1946. What these dates show is not so much a continuation of *negrismo* in the Hispanic Caribbean as the broader dissemination of texts written during the late twenties and early thirties, whose initial impact had been felt mostly in the Caribbean (and in Europe, for that matter), not so much in Hispanic America at large. This may well explain why *poesía negra/mulata* written outside of the Hispanic Caribbean did not really begin to flourish until the late thirties.[62]

Critics have tended to assume that the purpose of *poesía negra/mulata* in Cuba was to humanize racial stereotypes by replacing them with more positive, purportedly realistic, portraits of the local black population.[63] However, rather than being an image renovation, and a largely failed one at that, Afro-Cubanism was an attempt at making poetry a stage for nationalist discourse, not by turning it into a platform for political slogans but by tapping specific cultural institutions with a long history of resilience: the syncretic forms of Afro-Cuban popular music and dance became the new signifiers of a desire for cultural and political independence. In the tradition of José Martí, *poesía negra/mulata* sought to define an ideological space that all Cubans, regardless of color and caste, could presumably inhabit on equal terms.

It hardly comes as a surprise, then, that early collections of and commentaries on *poesía negra/mulata,* notably Guirao's *Orbita* and Ballagas's more wide-ranging volumes *Antología* (1935) and *Mapa,* would, in varying degrees, distance themselves from the "deterministic tyranny" of racial ancestry. In fact, the majority of the poets represented in these collections are not of African descent, a practice later anthologizers have largely maintained. Among the numerous collections of so-called Afro-Hispanic American poetry that have been published since, only one—Pereda Valdés's *Lo negro y lo mulato en la poesía cubana* (Montevideo, 1970)—focuses exclusively on the work of writers of African descent. In the case of Guirao's *Orbita,* this editorial policy is perfectly in keeping with the fact that Afro-Cubanism was the product of a predominantly white local intelligentsia. The logic behind Ballagas's *Mapa,* on the other hand, is more confusing, in part because, along with racial divisions, its broader scope does away with national and linguistic boundaries across the Americas. In the process, Ballagas dispenses with all kinds of historical, political, and cultural differences, most glaringly between the Hispanic Caribbean and the United States. *Mapa*'s section on North America places poetry by James Weldon Johnson, Cullen, and Hughes alongside verse by Whitman and Longfellow.[64] Even though, by 1931, "American Negro poetry," at least for Johnson, was no longer synonymous with any and all poetry written by American Negroes but carried a distinct thematic emphasis,[65] the kinds of historical continuities and literary lines of descent Ballagas's grouping suggests are aesthetically and politically misleading. Neither *poesía negra* nor *poesía mulata,* and terminological variations on those labels such as *poesía negrista,* are synonymous with "Negro poetry" in the sense that the anthologizers of the Harlem Renaissance understood that appellation: as poetry written by blacks and only by blacks.

In his introduction to *Mapa*—a shorter version of the essay "Situación de la poesía afroamericana," which was also published in 1946—Ballagas insists that "la poesía afroamericana no es obra

exclusiva de los negros, sino de colaboración blanca" (Afro-
American poetry is not the exclusive work of blacks but a collaboration of blacks and whites) with diverse thematic manifestations.[66] Terms such as *white poetry* and *black poetry,* he laments,
are not only too imprecise: "son terminos sospechosamente limi-
tadores que cortan a veces, hiriéndolo, el cuerpo viviente de la
poesía que, en definitiva, es una. . . . Presentamos aquí una suma
de poesía afroamericana y el rasgo definitivo de esta es el ser un
arte de relación, poesía negra con referencia blanca, o poesía de
blancos referida al negro y a su pecularidad americana" (are suspi-
ciously limiting terms that at times cut, and injure, the living body
of poetry that is definitely one. . . . We offer here a collection of
Afro-American poetry, and the definite feature of this poetry is that
it is an art of relations, "black poetry" with white references, or
poetry by whites about the Negro and his American peculiarity)
(*Mapa,* 9).

It is conspicuous that Ballagas mentions "black poetry" but
makes no reference to black writers. To acknowledge racial divisions, and with it the possible existence of a different group consciousness, within the realm of poetry and poetics is not just limiting; it is suspect, because it is harmful to a national unity so
"definite" in its existence that its dynamics are allowed to go entirely unquestioned. Another passage brings the dehistoricizing
thrust of Ballagas's argument into even bolder relief: "Esta expresión de la sensibilidad del hombre de color, pueden darla ca-
balmente el negro y el mulato desde *su propio centro intuitivo
lírico;* e igualmente el blanco, pero por un fenomeno reflejo, tan
diáfano a veces, que supone, no sólo una afortunada identifica-
ción, sino hasta que punto *el despojarse del lastre historicista y
sociológico* lleva de nuevo a la identidad de la especie humana y a
la idea cristiana de su origen común" (Blacks and mulatos, from
their own *intuitive lyric center,* can accurately offer this expression
of the sensibility of the person of color; and whites can do the same
thing, but as a reflected phenomenon, at times very diaphanous,
which supposes not only a fortunate identification but beyond that
a throwing off of the historicist and sociological burden that leads
again to the identity of humanity and the Christian idea of its
shared origin) (*Mapa,* 46, my emphases).

Whites, in other words, can identify or empathize with blacks only in a quasi-mythic space untroubled by history and social realities. The racially charged contrast between lyric intuition on the one hand and burdensome historicism and sociology on the other recurs throughout Ballagas's essay. It undergirds his belief in the existence of "pure poetry," unaffected and thus uncontaminated by sociopolitical issues: "Nuestra actitud hacia la poesía negra no es la del etnógrafo ni la del sociólogo, mucho menos la del político velado quizás a través de la riqueza elocutiva y dialéctica" (My attitude toward the "black poetry" is not that of the ethnographer or the sociologist, much less that of the politician veiled perhaps by elocutionary and dialectical richness) (*Mapa,* 8). What is most important to Ballagas, then, is the kind of ideological impartiality based on a careful avoidance of concrete political issues, especially racial questions. As always in Cuba, this strategic avoidance is encoded in the idea of cultural synthesis: "Pensamos que una Antología Negra de Poesía Americana ha de recoger, para no ser parcial, el acento negrista del poeta negro y del poeta blanco en sintesis unitiva" (I believe that a Black Anthology of American Poetry, in order not to be biased, must represent the "negrist" accent of the black and the white poet in a unified synthesis) (*Mapa,* 31).

But what Ballagas offers is hardly a "saldo despasionado" (dispassionate balance) (*Mapa,* 7). This is perhaps most obvious from his reduction of African poetry—what he calls "poesía negra en toda su pureza, mitología y existencialidad africana, como la recogida por Frobenius, primero, y más tarde por Cendrars" ("black poetry" in all its African purity, mythology, and existentiality, like the one collected first by Frobenius and later by Cendrars)—to an "asombro ante la naturaleza y . . . idílica amistad a los animales" (awe of nature and the idyllic friendship with animals) (*Mapa,* 24–25). At the same time that he proclaims the existence of "una tradición cultural negra no interrumpida aunque sí transformada por el medio ambiente donde fueron trasladadas las diversas culturas africanas" (a black cultural tradition not interrupted though clearly transformed by the different environments into which the diverse African cultures were transplanted) (*Mapa,* 51), he relegates Africa to the realm of prehistory. The transformation he posits, then, amounts to little else than Western culture's "civilizing" influence, a positive factor despite the tragedies of the Middle Passage and of slavery.

Ballagas's effort to distinguish different currents within the "moda de lo negro" (the fashion of blackness) is no less revealing: superficiality, "el arte africano turístico" (the art of Africanist tourism), is pitted against profundity, "mirar al negro desde lo dentro" (to look at the black from the inside) (*Mapa*, 31).[67] At first glance, this might appear to be a perfectly reasonable distinction, laudable even for its (seemingly successful) avoidance of essentializing categories. However, Ballagas also avoids, or evades, something else. In his formulation, blacks and blackness become mere intellectual commodities to be *looked at* either from the outside or, more paradoxically, from the inside. Since those commodities are constituted in familiar fashion by a white, Western gaze, self-consciousness on the part of the nonwhite subject does not even arise as a possibility. Even the textual presence of nonwhite poets cannot outweigh this conceptual dominance of a white perspective, which finally, and inevitably, returns the argument to Europe: "la poesía negra que se cultiva en las Antillas hispánicas, en Colombia, en Venezuela o en el Ecuador, *no es en su origen otra cosa que poesía española.* No es sólo en el idioma que se vierte la emoción africanista, sino que el arranque creador también nos ha venido de España" ("the black poetry" cultivated in the Hispanic Antilles, in Colombia, in Venezuela, or in Ecuador *is not, in its origins, anything other than Spanish poetry.* It is not only that [Spanish] is the language in which the Africanist emotion flows, but that the creative impulse itself has also come to us from Spain) (*Mapa*, 52; my emphasis). Still and all, Góngora and Lope did not write in Afro-Cuban vernacular, no matter how much their "gracefully disfigured" (graciosamente disfigurado) linguistic forms may resemble it (*Mapa*, 30).

It is impossible to say if Ballagas held those same beliefs almost twenty years earlier, when he wrote his famed "Elegía a María Belén Chacón," a poem that Guillén praised as "a little masterpiece."[68] They are not as much in evidence in his introduction to *Antología* in 1935, the year after Ballagas published his own *Cuaderno de poesía negra. Antología,* however, compensates for this by way of contributor's notes that meticulously identify the race or racial mixture of each poet. In the case of nonwhite poets, this procedure assumes a painstaking (and embarrassing) precision: Regino Pedrozo, of African and Chinese descent, is curiously classified as "de raza amarilla (sin otra mezcla)" (of the yellow race [without any other mixture]), while Ignacio Villa's label reads "de color negro macizo" (of solid black color).[69] There are certain attributes, it seems, that rise to the top even in a Cuban melting pot. If the combination of poetry and politics was never a comfortable one for Ballagas, by the mid-forties they had become two completely separate and unrelated spheres. Significantly, Ballagas was now no longer writing *poesía negra*. Few, if any, traces of it remain in his later poems.

Like Ballagas, Guirao abandoned writing *poesía negra* in the late thirties, though, one suspects, not for the same reasons. Guirao's introduction to his anthology *Orbita* is explicitly and vehemently critical of the kind of apolitical impartiality with which Ballagas and others regarded *poesía negra:* "es imposible, al hablar de lo negro, limitarse a consideraciones de orden estético. Lo extraestético ha de servirnos, necesariamente, de clave y punto de partida" (it is impossible, when speaking of blackness, to limit oneself to aesthetic considerations. The extra-aesthetic must serve us, necessarily, as key and point of departure).[70] Unlike Ballagas, Guirao attempts to draw a clear line between fashionable European "negrism" and Afro-Cubanism. Rather than glorifying Frobenius, he calls attention to the existence of "antiblack traditions" both in France and in Germany (see *Orbita,* xvi-xviii). Even if "nuestra poesía afrocriolla es un eco de la moda negra europea; consecuencia más que iniciativa propia" (our Afro-criollo poetry is an echo of Europe's fashion of blackness; a consequence rather than an initiative), and even if, initially, "hemos adquirido la mercancía oscura en otros mercados estéticos y la hemos hecho aforar en las aduanas sin percatarnos de nuestra realidad negra" (we acquired the dark merchandise in other aesthetic markets and had it appraised at customs without taking into account our own black reality) (*Orbita,* xxii, xviii), Afro-Cubanism is a very different matter for Guirao. While Ballagas actually dismissed Afro-Cubanism as "un movimiento de importancia menor" (a movement of minor importance) (*Mapa,* 7), Guirao privileges Cuba's *poesía negra/mulata* as a literary phenomenon that "contiene una esencia más auténticamente nacional" (contains a most authentically national essence) (*Orbita,* xxiii–xxiv). He elaborates:

La modalidad afroantillana ha dado sus más cuajados frutos en Cuba porque *contamos con el documento humano vivo, presente, racial y económicamente en nuestros destinos históricos.* Con la aparición del negrismo se establece entre nosotros una corriente de simpatías, un ligamento, que nos lleva a una introspección más cabal, amplia y profunda del alma negra. La poesía afrocubana, anecdótica, jitanjafórica, onomatopéyica, a veces asistida de actitudes demasiado elementales o infantiles, por no decir caricaturescas y deprimentes, . . . entraña ya un acercamiento sincero, un deseo de acortar distancias, de salvar obstáculos que, *por razón económica más que de color o matices,* impedían la simpatía y la fraternidad. Este es a nuestro juicio el valor funcional de la poética negra. . . . El modo negro, pues, no nace en Cuba como en Europa, sin tradición y alejado del documento humano. Tiene perspectiva histórica y un futuro indefinible la lírica bilingüe de español y dialectos africanos, y puede, hermanada a la sensibilidad criolla, intregrar la gran poesía vernácula de que hablamos.

The Afro-Antillean modality has borne its ripest fruits in Cuba, because *we take into account the living human document, a racial and economic presence within our historical destinies.* The appearance of *negrismo* led to the establishment among ourselves of a stream of sympathies, a bond, which resulted in a more accurate, ample, and profoundly introspective view of the black soul. Afro-Cuban poetry, be it anecdotal, *jitanjafórica,*[71] onomatopoeic, at times accompanied by attitudes far too elemental or infantile, not to say caricaturesque and depressing, . . . nevertheless involves a sincere coming together, a desire to overcome distances, obstacles that, *for economic reasons more than for reasons of race or different shades of skin color,* have impeded sympathy and fraternity. This, in my opinion, is the functional value of black poetry. . . . The black mode, then, is not born in Cuba in the same way that it is in Europe, without tradition and alienated from the human document. The bilingual poetry made up of Spanish and African dialects has a historical perspective and an indefinite future and can, together with the criollo sensibility, integrate, make whole, the great vernacular poetry I am talking about. (*Orbita,* xviii–xx, my emphases)

Guirao's sense of the importance of *local* variations on what appears to be a global theme or preoccupation is substantially different from Ballagas's attempt to reduce all manifestations of *poesía negra/mulata* to a common denominator that can be traced back to Europe, particularly to Spain. For Guirao, what crucially distinguishes Afro-Antillean and particularly Afro-Cuban poetry from other manifestations of *negrismo* is its rootedness in Cuba's historically specific circumstances. Though Guirao's Marxist emphasis on historicism and economics, modified by the requirements of local specificity, is diametrically opposed to Ballagas's investment in the universality of pure formalism, it also leads him to underestimate the effects of racial conflict and discrimination in early-twentieth-century Cuba.

All his emphasis on the imbrication of economics and racism notwithstanding, Guirao himself shows a remarkable penchant for rather unhistorical analysis when it comes to things Afro-Cuban. At times, he even sounds like Ballagas. Guirao's avowedly historicist perspective falters quite miserably when it comes to acknowledging the cultural differences of Cuba's "people of color," who are not (yet?) included in the national collective voice he uses in the above citation and to whom he quite readily attributes "primitive ingenuity" and "telluric impulses" (see *Orbita*, xxiv). It seems that Guirao is much more comfortable with race as a conceptual abstraction—such as "the black soul"—or as a thing securely located in the past, that is, in the nineteenth century. It is important to note this uneasy evasiveness at the same time as recalling the fact that *Orbita* significantly includes Manzano, "poeta negro de acento blanco" (black poet with a white accent), whose autobiography and poetry Guirao had discovered a few years earlier. In fact, almost a third of his introduction is devoted to "black and mestizo/mulato poets of the epoch of slavery in Cuba."[72] Compared to Ballagas's preoccupation with the image of blacks since antiquity, which takes precedence over Manzano or any of the other slave poets Guirao lists (only Plácido gets a brief mention in "Situación"),[73] Guirao's recognition that Afro-Cubanism has extensive historical links to nineteenth-century developments in economics, politics, and literature is astute and certainly refreshing.

Yet, despite substantial divergences in their respective critical approaches to *poesía negra/mulata*, both Ballagas and Guirao are equally reluctant even to acknowledge, let alone to address directly, the existence of racial hierarchies and conflicts in their own contemporary historical setting. The difference between their essays, finally, is only one of degree. To dispel any notion that such reluctance was peculiar to Cuba's white elite, I quote Gustavo Urrutia: "la teoría de la afinidad racial falla con los poetas negros que han pretendido asir el nuevo género por los cabellos; y fracasa con Luis Palés Matos, hombre blanco y admirable poeta negro. El quid no está en la genealogía sino en el genio" (the theory of racial affinity does not work with the black poets who have sought to take hold of the new genre [of *poesía negra/mulata*]; and it falls apart with Luis Palés Matos, a white man and an admirable black poet. The quid is not in genealogy but in genius).[74] Urrutia's antiessentialist stance is certainly valuable, but why did he not pick a Cuban poet to make the same point? And what about his exuberant praise for Guillén's poetry as the only "authentic" Negro poetry written in Cuba?[75] Inconsistencies such as these go a long way toward demonstrating just how deeply contradictory a national ideology *mestizaje* really was in Cuba.

6

Sublime Masculinity

I

> [Latin America] is a vast zone for which *mestizaje* is not an
> accident but rather the essence, the central line: ourselves,
> "our *mestizo* America." Martí . . . employed this specific ad-
> jective as the distinctive sign of our culture—a culture of de-
> scendants, both ethnically and culturally speaking, of aborigi-
> nes, Africans, and Europeans.
>
> —Robert Fernández Retamar, "Caliban"

The poetic inscriptions of the mulata in the Hispanic Caribbean
both before and especially after the late 1920s are so numerous
that it is tempting to translate *poesía mulata* as "mulata [not mu-
latto] poetry." In Cuba, there is Felipe Pichardo Moya's "Filosofía
del bronce" (Philosophy of bronze) (1925) and of course Guillén's
"Mulata" from *Motivos de son* (1930), followed almost immediately by several other poems from *Sóngoro cosongo* (1931) and
West Indies, Ltd. (1934): "Madrigal 1"; "Rumba"; "Secuestro de
la mujer de Antonio" (The Abduction of Antonio's Woman), an
homage to Miguel Matamoros's *son* "La mujer de Antonio"; "Pa-
labras en el trópico" (Words in the tropics); another "Madrigal";
and "El abuelo" (The Grandfather). Among the better-known *poemas mulatos* are also Ballagas's "Elegía de María Belén Chacón"
(María Belén Chacón's elegy) (1930) and his "Nombres negros en
el son" (Black names in the *son*) (1931), as well as Marcelino Aro-

zarena's "Mulata rumbera" (Rumba-dancing mulata), "Caridá" (1933), "Liturgia etiópica" (Ethiopian liturgy) (1936), and his later "Amalia" (1957).[1] A Colombian version is Jorge Artel's "¡Danza, mulata!" (Dance, mulata!) from 1940. The most notable contributions from Puerto Rico include Luis Llorens Torres's "Copla mulata" (1929), Luis Palés Matos's "Mulata-Antilla" (1937) and "Plena de menéalo" (Shaking it) (1953), Fortunato Vizcarrondo's "La mulata" (1942), Alfonso Camín's "La Mulata Candelaria" (1952), Evaristo Ribera Chevremont's "Morena" (Brown girl) (1957), and José I. de Diego Prado's "Venus nubia" (1959). These are but a few examples of poems that explicitly focus on the mulata. Others could easily be added, especially if one were to extend the chronological range to the present and include the many poems in which this figure makes only a cameo appearance.[2]

Regardless of formal and thematic variations, regardless even of the different racial affiliation of their individual authors, these poems share one thing: they speak emphatically to what Teresa De Lauretis has called "the nonbeing of *woman*": "The paradox of a being that is at once captive and absent in discourse, constantly spoken of but of itself inaudible or inexpressible, displayed as spectacle and still unrepresented or unrepresentable, invisible yet constituted as the object and the guarantee of vision; a being whose existence and specificity are simultaneously asserted and denied, negated and controlled."[3] Far from redeeming or redressing entrenched racial and gender stereotypes, Afro-Cubanism's heavy ideological stakes in *mestizaje* create textual scenarios in which particular kinds of female bodies, in Lemuel Johnson's words, are "called into service as the vessel in which the body politic is (man)-made and (woman)-unmade."[4] I have argued throughout that the mulata and the ideology that represents itself through her in Cuba are products of a masculinist imagination, of what I would call, to borrow a leaf from Lemuel Johnson, a poetics of male bonding and bondage[5] that underwrites idealized views of race (and class) reconciliation and thus of national unity.

These narratives are bound up in a "compulsive [literary and/or cultural] thematics"—the perpetual search for a consciousness or identity, that is, for a legitimate origin, which fails almost as frequently as it is undertaken.[6] At the center of this frustrated, deeply romantic search or self-invention, the mulata is the inscription of a desire for cultural synthesis upon a field of sociopolitical contingencies that is accordingly distorted. To the extent that this process of self-invention is analogous to what Julie Ellison has called "the invention of the romantic subject as the hero of desire," it, too, "is wholly bound up in the feminine." At the same time, Ellison continues, "romantic writers suspect that desire may be a form of power . . . and woman a form of sabotage. Objects of desire are lost or violated in ambivalent allegories of the domestic and the maternal. Ultimately, the feminine becomes, first, wholly figurative or non-referential and then invisible," or, as De Lauretis has it, "*unrepresentable.*"[7] The mulata may be *the* signifier of Cuba's unity-in-racial-diversity, but she has no part in. For the mestizo nation is a male homosocial construct premised precisely upon the disappearance of the feminine.[8] To clarify this point, I return briefly to Carpentier's *The Lost Steps.*

Much indeed has been said about the failings and failures of Carpentier's would-be romantic hero. What has not been remarked upon, however, is that the very conception of the novel itself is predicated on the failure of the text's heterosexual and interracial romance.[9] Rosario's disappearance from the plot of *The Lost Steps* enables a different kind of communion at the fringes of El Dorado: that between the narrator and the Greek(!) miner Yannes, who offers him passage in his boat. Relevant to that final scene are the narrator's earlier, somewhat curious, musings on racial mixing, for which Rosario's first physical description serves as a catalyst: "I began to ask myself if certain amalgamations of minor races, without a transplanting of the stock, might not be preferable to the formidable encounters that occurred in the great places of such unions in the Americas."[10] Relative similarity, this passage suggests, may be more desirable in (re)productive cross-cultural encounters than difference; it may yield superior results. While the purported context here is *racial* mixing, racial difference is not the sole issue here. Rosario, after all, is not the product of the mixing of "minor races," so that these observations do not pertain to her. If anything, they would, and ultimately do, make her a less desirable presence in the novel. The character to whom they do pertain, at least indirectly, is Yannes, whose origins are Mediterranean and whose affinities with the narrator are encoded in the *Odyssey*, which Yannes carries everywhere. But literary symbolism is not the only thing that links the narrator and the Greek. In relation to the narrator, Yannes is both a racial and an ethnic other who is also of the same gender.[11]

The fact that the objects of the narrator's desire are not unequivocally female gives gender and male sexuality significance beyond the at-times deceptively heterosexual situations presented in *The Lost Steps*. Consider, for instance, the protagonist's uncontrolled anger at Mouche's sexual advances to the Greek, a response for which jealousy is hardly a sufficient explanation at that stage in the novel—unless it is jealousy of Mouche. And, most importantly, the affective ties between the two male characters outlast the narrator's sexual bond even with Rosario. In the end, heterosexuality is no more of a possiblity for Carpentier's artist than is a return to Paradise.

From the male homoeroticism that resides within the interstices of *The Lost Steps*'s heterosexual romance emerges a founding fiction similar to the one Roberto Fernández Retamar offers in his programmatic and controversial essay "Caliban: Notes toward a Discussion of Culture in Our America" (1971).[12] Written as a belated response to José Enrique Rodó's *Ariel* (1900), "Caliban" is one of the postcolonial Caribbean's many versions of Shakespeare's *The Tempest*, which range from Aimé Césaire's play *Une tempête* (1969) to George Lamming's novel *Water with Berries* (1971).[13] Though it may share little else with Carpentier's novel, Fernández Retamar's essay invents for Cuban and, by extension, Hispanic American culture a similar cross-racial male lineage: *Mestizaje,* the cultural "essence" of "our America," issues from the intellectual Ariel's embrace of a Caliban whose working-class status subsumes his racial difference, at times too conveniently so.[14]

The foundational myth operative in both *The Lost Steps* and "Caliban" can be traced to a text written significantly earlier: Guillén's "Balada de los dos abuelos" (Ballad of the two Grandfathers) from *West Indies, Ltd.* (1934). The primal cultural scene (if you will) in this poem is also a fraternal embrace of two men: one a

Spaniard, the other African. Note that their class differences, signaled initially by the respective appellations *Don* and *Taita,* are leveled in the final stanza, where Don Federico and Taita Facundo become simply Federico and Facundo.

> Don Federico me grita
> y Taita Facundo calla;
> los dos en la noche sueñan
> y andan, andan.
> *Yo los junto.*
>
>   —¡Federico!
> ¡Facundo! Los dos se abrazan.
> Los dos suspiran. Los dos
> las fuertes cabezas alzan;
> los dos del mismo tamaño,
> bajo las estrellas altas;
> los dos del mismo tamaño,
> ansia negra y ansia blanca,
> los dos del mismo tamaño.[15]
>
> Don Federico cries out to me,
> and Taita Facundo is silent;
> both of them dream in the night,
> and wander, wander.
> *In me they meet.*
>
>   —Federico!
> Facundo! The two embrace.
> The two sigh. They
> lift their strong heads;
> both of the same stature,
> under the high-up stars;
> both of the same stature,
> a black and a white longing,
> both of equal size.

To invoke the title of Robert Márquez's 1972 translation of his poems, Guillén's are indeed *"man*-making words" (my emphasis). Nowhere in this masculinist paradigm are women, especially non-white women, acknowledged as participants in and possible producers of the very culture that inscribes its identity through them.

Women's work, as an economic and a cultural reality, is systematically elided.[16] Once the evidence of messy (that is, sexual) female participation in historical processes of racial mixing is eliminated by being made unrepresentable, *mestizaje* becomes legitimated as an exclusively male project or achievement in which interracial, heterosexual rape can be refigured as a fraternal embrace across color (and, in this case, class) lines and, significantly, across a female body absented by rape.[17] The homoerotic connotations of this embrace and the concomitant appropriation of the female reproductive function in the form of masculine creativity cannot possibly be missed. Guillén's conception of a racial (or raceless) utopia in "Balada" is predicated on the erasure—the "mis(sing) representation," in Lemuel Johnson's coinage—of a black woman, the one in whose violated body the two races actually met. A masculine consciousness has now clearly usurped that site.

That traces of such violence would spoil the mulata's legendary beauty along with her order-maintaining male lineage is the logic behind another one of Guillén's poems, also from *West Indies, Ltd.* The sonnet is tellingly titled "El abuelo" (The Grandfather), telling because it constructs an interracial male lineage for its near-white female figure.

> Esta mujer angélica de ojos septentrionales,
> que vive atenta al ritmo de su sangre europea,
> ignora que en lo hondo de ese ritmo golpea
> *un negro* el parche duro de roncos atabales.
>
> Bajo la línea escueta de su nariz aguda,
> la boca, en fino trazo, traza una raya breve,
> y no hay cuervo que manche la solitaria nieve
> de su carne, que fulge temblorosa y desnuda.
>
> ¡Ah, mi señora! Mírate las venas misteriosas;
> boga en el agua viva que allá dentro te fluye,
> y ve pasando lírios, nelumbios, lotos, rosas;
>
> que ya verás, inquieta, junto a la fresca orilla,
> *la dulce sombra oscura del abuelo* que huye,
> el que rizó por siempre tu cabeza amarilla.
>
> This angelic lady with eyes from the North,
> who follows the beat of her European blood,

knows not that in this rhythm's thorough flood
a black man beats dark drums that are hoarse.

Beneath the straight course of her small, Nordic nose
her mouth traverses as thin, delicate line;
no crow flies to stain the solitary snow,
of her skin with its tremulous, naked shine.

Oh, my lady! Behold the mysteries below,
ride the live waters that deep inside you flow,
and watch lilies, lotuses, and roses as you go;

and on the fresh shore, restless, you will then see
the sweet dark shadow of the grandfather flee,
he who curled your yellow head indelibly.[18]

In his provocative reading of this poem, Gustavo Pérez Firmat ironically, though perhaps predictably, returns to the immaculately masculine conception of *mestizaje* encoded in Guillén's "Balada." According to Pérez Firmat, this "'ethnic' sonnet," like the figure of the mulata herself, is the aesthetic product not only of one elusive grandfather but indeed of a "marriage" between two grandfathers: the anonymous African maroon on the one hand and the Spanish poet Gutierre de Cetina on the other.[19] Guillén's "La canción del bongó" (The Song of the Bongo Drum) from *Sóngoro cosongo* renders the case of the missing grandfather even more plain.

> En esta tierra, mulata
> de africano y español
> (Santa Bárbara de un lado,
> del otro lado, Changó)
> siempre falta algún abuelo.

> In this land, a mulata
> of African and Spanish mixture
> (Santa Barbara on the one hand,
> on the other, Changó),
> there is always some grandfather missing.[20]

Yet another of Guillén's texts, "Mulata," part of his controversial first set of Afro-Cuban poems, presents evidence of a different kind of erasure of the black mother figure.

Ya yo me enteré, mulata,
mulata, ya sé que dise
que yo tengo la narise
como nudo de cobbata.

Y fíjate bien que tú
no ere tan adelantá,
poqque tu boca e bien grande,
y tu pasa, colorá.

Tanto tren con tu cueppo,
tanto tren;
tanto tren con tu boca,
tanto tren;
tanto tren con tu sojo,
tanto tren.

Si tú supiera, mulata,
la veddá;
¡que yo con mi negra tengo,
y no te quiro pa ná!

I've got news for you, Mulata!
Mulata, I know you go around talking
about my nose being big and wide
like the flattened knot on a tie.

Well, look at yourself for a minute:
you're a real sight to see,
with that big-lipped mouth
and hair that's nappy and red.

And how you twist that body of yours,
it's just too much!
How you lick those lips,
it's just too much!
How you roll those eyes,
it's just too much!

If the truth be told,
Miss High Brown:
I'm crazy for my coal black gal
and have no use for the likes of you.[21]

At first glance, this poem seems inconsistent with Guillén's advocacy of *mestizaje* and *poesía mulata* in his prologue to *Sóngoro cosongo,* from which I quote in the epigraph to my Introduction. The highbrow Miss High Brown, taken as representative of the desire for *blanqueamiento* in her denigration of the broad-nosed black man, is now rejected in favor of the not-so-hot, but much more *reliable,* "coal black gal." The male speaker of the poem gets even, as it were, by using familiar racial slurs: he points knowingly to the mulata's "nappy" hair and her too-big mouth. The latter may of course also be read as an allusion to sexual licentiousness and material greed (trading sex for material benefits[22]), features he readily seeks to equate with lack of social status—according to him, the mulata is not so "adelantá" after all. Then the speaker proceeds to dismember her body until, in the third stanza, she has become all hips, lips, and eyes. *Mi negra,* by contrast, emerges as symbol of a more authentic (that is, African) cultural heritage. Though as yet invisible in "Mulata," she becomes the prototype of Guillén's "Mujer nueva" (New Woman).

> Con el círculo ecuatorial
> ceñido a la cintura como a un pequeño mundo,
> la negra, mujer nueva,
> avanza en su ligera bata de serpiente.
>
> Coronada de palmas
> como una diosa recién llegada,
> ella trae la palabra inédita,
> el anca fuerte,
> la voz, el diente, la mañana y el salto.

> The circle of the equator
> wrapped around her waist like a little world,
> the black woman, the new woman,
> advances in her serpent robe.
>
> Crowned with palm trees
> like a newly arrived goddess,
> she brings the unknown word,
> the strong rump,
> the voice, the teeth, the morning and the leap.[23]

This displacement of the haughty mulata by the earthy "negra" with "sangre joven/bajo un pedazo de piel fresca" (young blood/ beneath fresh skin), a mythic Mother Africa whose robust physique signifies endurance along with purity and freshness, is by no means unproblematic, even if, or especially because, it supplies the ground for "an alternate mythology of poetic creation," that is, for Cuban vernacular verse.[24] For Guillén's "new woman" is a purified reinscription of black femininity that displaces, and in the process effaces, not just the mulata but also that *other* dark female body from which she literally and symbolically originates. Guillén's, then, is not necessarily a more positive and certainly not a more realistic portrayal of black womanhood, and is an eminently sexist one to boot. Pérez Firmat comments that "to take offense at Guillén's portrayal of black women is to err on the side of literalism, for in these poems Guillén is talking about his poetry as much as about anything else." I take this to mean that poetics and/or aesthetics are not gendered, which, especially in light of Pérez Firmat's own unbounded male enthusiasm for "uterine utterance," "thinking with your thighs," and "the tropical fruits of [the black woman's] womb,"[25] is preposterous. Besides, a feminist perspective on these poems is not a matter of "taking offense" at Guillén's representations. It is a matter of acknowledging the difference gender makes to them.

What is abundantly clear from these poems, and from the commentaries they have received in this instance, is that the kind of racial mixing the mulata represents is precisely *not* the *mestizaje*, or *mulatez* (mulattoness), that grounds Guillén's vernacular Cuban poetry. That *mestizaje*, like Guillén's "Cuban color," is a trope for racial mixing without female participation. For what the mulata, unlike the ideology of *mestizaje*, represents is not a stable synthesis but a precarious and tenuous multiplicity, "a concentration of differences," of "insoluble differential equations."[26] The mulata indexes areas of structural instability and ideological volatility in Cuban society, areas that have to be hidden from view to maintain the political fiction of cultural cohesion and synthesis. The key signifier of such instability and volatility is the nonwhite woman's body conceived as the site of troubling sexual and racial differences. As much as this site has all the attractions of a mythic place of intellectual and psychological refuge and "epistemological con-solation" in a society like Cuba, it is simultaneously feared as the locus of potential change, disruption, and complication.[27]

Not surprisingly, then, Guillén's poems do nothing to explode or vindicate the stereotype of the mulata. They carefully expel both the mulata and that other dark body hidden behind her from the realm of the poetically representable as embarrassing evidence of racial and sexual violence that, if acknowledged, would chip away at the pillars of poetic authority on which Cuban nationalism rests so comfortably. And that authority, quite regardless of a given po-et's color and gender, is conceived as strictly masculine, even in those instances where it appears in feminine garb. The remainder of this chapter concerns itself with some of those instances.

II

Soy la mulata rumbera
que baila al son del bongó;
nadie baila como yo
desde Güira a Caimanera.
Cuando muevo la cadera,
huele el aire a azúcar cruda;

I'm the rumba-dancing mulata
who moves to the bongo drum's sound;
from Guira to Caimanera,
there's nobody who dances like I do.
When I grind my hips,
the smells of raw sugar fill the air.

—Alfonso Camín, "La mulata Candelaria"

Even if few other *poemas mulatos* are as explicit in identifying themselves as self-engendered products of a distinctly masculine cross-racial synthesis, they still continue to predicate visions of ra-cial amalgamation on the exclusion, or what Sylvia Wynter has called the "ontological absence," of "Caliban's woman."[28] Along with nonwhite women, Cuban women believed to be of "pure [white] blood" because of their elevated social status were excluded from the domain of interracial alliances on the basis of their presumed (and enforced) sexual and political loyalty in matters of race. Despite the increasing politicization of those white women due to their involvement in patriotic causes such as Cuba's Ten Years War, they remained, as indeed they had declared themselves throughout the nineteenth century, the "exemplary companions" and allies of white Cuban men.[29] *Poesía mulata* has no place for them. So, for instance, the white woman who "comes looking" for Bito Manué in Guillén's "Tú no sabe inglé" (Don't Know No English) has to be "mericana," North American, a foreigner, a mere tourist.

The mulata as displayed in the poems I listed at the beginning of this chapter, then, is little more than a body inscribed with and subjected to male desire, sexual and political. That body may be feminine in appearance, but much more significant than its gender attributes is that it is the site of an erotic "performance" *represented* as feminine. The following autobiographical anecdote from Antonio Benítez Rojo's *The Repeating Island* (1989) renders this distinction that, to my mind, is a crucial ingredient of theories of Cubanness. The not-so-arbitrary setting for this scene is the imminent threat of nuclear catastrophe during the Cuban Missile Crisis.

I can isolate with frightening exactitude—like the hero of Sartre's novel—the moment at which I reached the age of reason. It was a stunning October afternoon, years ago, when the atomization of the meta-archipelago under the dread umbrella of nuclear catastrophe seemed imminent. . . . While the state bureaucracy searched for news off the short wave or hid behind official speeches and communiqués, two old black women passed "in a certain kind of way" [de cierta manera] beneath my balcony. I cannot describe this "certain kind of way"; I will say only that there was a kind of ancient and golden powder between their gnarled legs, a scent of basil and mint in their dress, a symbolic, ritual wisdom [una sabiduría simbólica, ritual] in their gesture and their gay chatter. I knew then at once that there would be no apocalypse. . . . In this "certain kind of way" there is expressed the mystic or magical (if you will) loam of the civilizations [el légamo mítico, mágico] that contributed to the formation of Caribbean culture.[30]

Some textual variations ought to be noted before we proceed toward a reading of this passage. James Maraniss's previous translation, possibly based on an earlier version of Benítez Rojo's Introduction, invokes the legacy of Fernando Ortiz's Cuban stew, *el ajiaco*, by turning "una sabiduría simbólica, ritual" into "a domestic wisdom, almost culinary." [31] This is hardly an inappropriate extrapolation given the importance of Ortiz to *The Repeating Island* as a whole, and given also the herbal fragrances in which Benítez Rojo's prose envelops the two black women. What this earlier translation brings out more clearly is the highly ambivalent disposition of Benítez Rojo's narrative toward the kind of feminine knowledge it extols. This ambivalence is already inscribed in its very conventional juxtaposition of masculine "reason" and racially inflected feminine "wisdom," a scenario in which both the racial attributes of the two women and their lower-class status jointly contribute to the mysterious, "magical," inarticulateness and unself-consciousness represented by their "chatter." The text's erotic investment in visual and olfactory metaphor circumvents this issue. What is valued about these women is how they look and smell, not what they might say. It is as if listening to them might interfere with such visual and "culinary" pleasures.

In the same earlier translation, the final sentence of the passage quoted above reads: "It is surely that 'something more,' that 'certain kind of way' in which those two old black women walked when they conjured away the apocalypse, that brings us back in contact with the primal gnostic or mythic ooze of the non-'scientific' civilizations that contributed to the formation of Caribbean culture." [32] This sentence makes explicit, much more explicit than its expurgated version in *The Repeating Island*, the Cuban metanarrative into which this anecdote inserts itself, despite the momentarily distracting reference to Sartre. The coming into consciousness, or into "reason," is a quasi-Carpentierian journey back to the source, an attempted immersion in the primal ooze or slime of mythic cultural origins that the two black women represent for Benítez Rojo. This episode, in other words, recasts a founding scene in Cuban literary and critical discourse, one that both desires "contact" and safeguards against it. For this is a familiar voyeuristic scenario, one in which a male and usually white writer observes, in this case from the lofty heights of his balcony, the quotidian activities of racial Others who, more often than not, are figured as female because of the regenerative potential presumably inherent in their cultural "performance" or "style." Though Benítez Rojo's "anti-apocalyptic old women" are neither young nor alluring, the ancient gold powder or dust between their legs, something barely within the observer's actual range of vision, is a mythic or "magical" commodity that more than compensates for the lack of an eroticized exterior. Their bodies, it appears, are the real El Dorado, that proverbial gold mine of Cuban writing. Here, as in Pérez Firmat's readings of Guillén's poems, it seems as if these female bodies know what it means to be Cuban, even if their minds do not: The black women's words are reduced to indistinct "gay" chatter, and it is apparently up to the male writer to distill ancient knowledge from those inarticulate sounds and gestures. Benítez Rojo's anecdote aligns itself neatly with the opening of Guillén's "Madrigal (2)".

> Tu vientre sabe más que tu cabeza
> y tanto como tus muslos.
> Esa
> es la fuerte gracia negra
> de tu cuerpo desnudo.

> Your womb knows more than your head,
> and as much as your thighs.
> That
> is the strong black grace
> of your naked body.[33]

Pérez Firmat's comment that Guillén "[grounds] grace in the uterine knowledge of a robust black body" does little to rescue this supposed celebration of black womanhood from its racially inflected sexist biases. Indeed, Pérez Firmat applauds those biases as "the founding myth of Guillén's poetic practice. *Sóngoro cosongo* is the sort of uterine utterance that the new woman knows. When you think with your thighs, you speak *sóngoro cosongo*. These are the tropical fruits of her womb, the unpublished words that she vouchsafes to her poet."³⁴ More to the point, when you think with your thighs, as it were, you *don't speak*. And there is really no good reason, other than perhaps arrogance, why that silence, which is actually a silencing, ought to be interpreted as woman's vouchsafing her "unpublished words" for the benefit of a male Cuban poet, no matter what his color.

But there is more to the antiapocalyptic vision Benítez Rojo encodes in the phrase "in a certain way" which, as he proceeds in his Introduction, takes on a theoretical life of its own so that the initial signifier, the old black women, becomes expendable. Their erasure enables Benítez Rojo, as it did other Cuban writers before him, to formulate an abstract idea of black femininity that comes to be associated with carnival. As "the great Caribbean *fiesta*," carnival is a sort of meta-performance that subsumes all other semiotic systems, "music, song, dance, myth, language, food, dress, bodily expression, etc." And, most tellingly:

There is *something strongly feminine* [*algo poderosamente feminino*] in this extraordinary *fiesta*: its flux, its diffuse sensuality, its generative force, its capacity to nourish and conserve (juices, spring, pollen, rain, *seed,* shoot, ritual sacrifice—these are words that come to stay). Think of the dancing flourishes, the rhythms of the conga, the samba, the masks, the hoods, *the men dressed and painted as women* [*los hombres vestidos y pintados como mujeres*], the bottles of rum, the sweets, . . . the figure of a centipede that comes together and then breaks up, that winds and stretches beneath the ritual's rhythm, that flees the rhythm without escaping it, putting off its defeat, stealing off and hiding itself, imbedding itself finally in the rhythm, always in the rhythm, the beat of the chaos of the island.³⁵

My purpose in punctuating Benítez Rojo's text with added emphases is to bring out its disposition toward gender (for race is completely elided here). Obviously, there are no representations of women anywhere in the lines I have quoted (and in those I have omitted). It would appear that women are the scapegoats in this sacrificial ritual, whose powerful feminine qualities refer us not to women but, ultimately, to "men dressed and painted as women." Given the allusions in this passage to Afro-Cuban comparsas and the colonial celebrations of the "Día de Reyes," one of the favorite subjects among nineteenth-century painters and lithographers such as Landaluze and especially Mialhe, the phrase would have to be revised to read: "men of various ethnicities dressed and painted as women of color." What Benítez Rojo appropriates here, for his own and his nation's imaginative purposes, is the female reproductive function combined with nonreproductive, and thus nonthreatening, black sexuality. The racist belief in the mulata's supposed sterility, a myth perpetuated in Cuba's national cult of the Virgin of Charity on the one hand and in the stylized erotic commodification of the nonwhite woman on the other, hides a male homosocial, indeed homoerotic, subtext. In that subtext the concrete social threat that uncontrolled interracial reproduction poses to masculine power is sublimated in the fantasy that all blacks, like all whites, are, or at any rate should be, male.[36] Of course, for white and black men openly to eroticize the black male body would have wreaked ideological havoc with the institution of paternalistic heterosexuality that guaranteed the sociosexual subordination of all women. Far from being contradictory or incompatible, heterosexuality, homosociality, and homoeroticism are mutually sustaining in this scenario.[37] The male desire for the racial Other who is also of the same gender is played out in the (dis)guise of heterosexuality. Even Miguel Barnet's *Biografía de un cimarrón* (*Autobiography of a Runaway Slave*) (1966), a homoerotically inflected interracial collaboration between Barnet, the white ethnographer/novelist, and his mulato informant Esteban Montejo, sustain this sexual masquerade.

It stands to reason that the mulata would be the preferred site for the displacement of male homoerotic desire, since her mixed racial origins grant access to both black and white "grandfathers." The incestuous aspect of the desire for these "(grand)fathers" is hardly incidental; it is a safe desire to the extent that it does not involve even the possibility of sexual reproduction. *Mestizaje*, then, represents the birth of a new race of *men*. Palés Matos's "Mulata-Antilla," for instance, offers a variation on the theme of Guillén's "Balada de los dos abuelos" in the line "en tu vientre conjugan *mis* dos razas" (in your womb *my* two races come together).[38] Though somewhat less explicitly homoerotic than Guillén's male-oriented vision in "Balada"—"in me they meet"—"Mulata-Antilla" negotiates its poetic authority through black femininity. It is helpful here to recall Sedgwick who notes, "that a woman is present is not to say that her point of view is expressed, that we are in position to know anything about her, or that she is a subject of consciousness."[39]

Eduardo González has fittingly described *mulatez,* or *mestizaje,* as "*maleness* sublime." In the case of *poesía mulata,* the "inescapable" rhythms of Afro-Cuban popular music played a major role in the construction of that sublime, which, González argues, "led to the exorcism of the demons of race."[40] Always the rhythm, as Benítez Rojo would have it. *Poesía mulata's* peculiarity resides in the debt it owes to the percussive rhythms of specific Afro-Cuban musical forms, most frequently to the *son* and the rumba.[41] The most obvious vehicle for this kind of musicality is so-called *jitanjáfora,* presumably nonsensical words and syllables employed as phonic signifiers of "blackness." Many of Palés's early poems, for instance, use certain words for their supposed "black" sound.[42] It is, however, a common (and convenient) misconception that *jitanjáfora* is mere playful onomatopoeia and to that extent nonrepresentational.[43] That convenience reveals itself to be ideologically functional at the point where words of actual and possible African origin, such as Guillén's "sóngoro cosongo," are dismissed as *jitanjáfora* rather than being recognized as elements of languages with their own discrete histories.[44] Linguistic constructs such as "Repique, repique, pique,/repique, repique, pó," from Guillén's "Secuestro de la mujer de Antonio," and "¡Mayombe, bombe, mayombé!," from his "Sensemayá: Canto para matar una culebra" (Sensemayá: Chant for Killing a Snake), do infuse written language with the sounds of different percussive instruments such as drums, claves, or maracas. The effects of this may very well be musical, and indeed a number of *poemas mulatos,* especially Guillén's, were set to music.[45] But even music is representational. The very notion of *jitanjáfora,* particularly as it has been applied to *poesía mulata,* is symptomatic of a formalism that seeks to disguise political choices as purely aesthetic ones. With the increasing denial of the social and political significance of race and color in Cuban society, "blackness" emerged as a "style" that had aesthetic currency only. How else could Guillén have called Ballagas's "Elegía de María Belén Chacón" a "little masterpiece"? Ballagas's own separation of stylistics from politics, on which I remarked in the previous chapter, is another case in point.

Pérez Firmat's reading of Guillén's "El abuelo" further complicates and confuses the issue. "The loud point of 'El abuelo,'" argues Pérez Firmat, "is that visual appearances may deceive, but phonic realities do not."[46] In other words, sound—or better still, certain kinds of sounds—becomes a privileged index of cultural authenticity, one presumed to be more reliable than sight. However, this claim does not take into account that *poesía mulata's* phonic patterns and rhythmic signatures are, in the end, no less stereotypical than more familiar physiognomic signifiers of blackness such as skin tone and hair texture. Is this not what is also implicit in the negative responses to Guillén's use of Afro-Cuban vernacular in *Motivos de son?* It may well be argued that the *Motivos* were not stylized enough, not far enough removed from their black Cuban referents. Besides, if visual appearances are (potentially) deceptive, then why not phonic ones?[47] According to Pérez Firmat's logic, all those white Cuban men who wrote *poesía negra/ mulata* must have been, much like Guillén's angelic lady, of (albeit unacknowledged) African extraction, because their poetry, for all intents and purposes, "sounds black." Since this would theoretically be true of all Cubans, the uncomfortable question arises why, historically, some Cubans were subject to racial oppression while others were not.

While *poesía mulata,* to the extent that it privileges phonic appearances, does pose certain questions about the adequacy of representational models or theories based on visual analogues, those questions are far from unproblematic in a historical setting where attempts at collective racial self-representation had been systematically squelched for fear that they would harm the national body politic and rupture the official ideology of *mestizaje.*[48] Afro-Cubanism's privileging of black musical sound as a reliable index of national authenticity had the effect of further denying the practice of social discrimination based on visual markers and thus of making the political representation of Cuba's mostly lower-class black population a nonissue. This disacknowledgment of the social significance of race and color had concrete consequences in the realm of political representation. The *Ley Morúa,* for one, held that visual analogues as signifiers of race were indeed an inadequate basis for the political representation of black Cubans in the form of a separate party. In Cuba, poetics and politics, it seems, converged only when it came to resisting the cultural effects of U.S. American imperialism, not in the troubled realm of domestic affairs. If the negative reception of Guillén's *Motivos* by Havana's mulato professionals was any indication, Cuban society was deeply fraught with racism, even at times when there were no public protests or race riots.

What is at issue in *poesía mulata,* then, is the aesthetic commodification of blackness and the depersonalization of race and of racist social practices. Represented as pure rhythm, blackness could easily be appropriated by Cuba's literati and, at a distance from the squalor of Havana's ill-famed "Afro-Cuban underworld" and similar urban ghettos, be assimilated into a poetics of *mestizaje.* One of the most striking absences in Felipe Pichardo Moya's "La comparsa" (The carnival procession), published in *Gráfico* in 1916 and often cited as one of the first poems to explore the literary possibilities of Afro-Cuban music, are direct references to skin color or other familiar racial markers. While it may be tempting to attribute this absence to the fact that Pichardo was himself of partly African ancestry, it is important to realize that it was quite unnecessary for him to resort to physical description to identify the dancers in the poem as Afro-Cuban. Here are some lines from the poem that, ironically enough, was written and published at a time when actual comparsas were banned in Cuba.

> Por la calleja solitaria
> se arrastra la comparsa como una culebra colosal.
> . . . . .
> Entre dos filas de mujeres
> que *se contorsionan* nerviosas como mordidas de Satán,
> va un alto anciano *tembloroso* en cuyos ojos luce el fuego
> de una mirada casi irreal.
> Lleva un cetro entre las manos y murmura con voz opaca
> un misterioso sortilegio que sólo él puede rezar.
> . . . . .
> y los cuerpos *se descoyuntan* en una furia demoníaca
> al impulsar irresistible de los palitos y el timbal.

Through the deserted narrow alleys
the carnival procession creeps like a colossal snake.
· · · · ·
Out of the midst of two rows of women,
who are nervously *contorting* their bodies as if possessed by the
    devil,
emerges an old man, *trembling,* his eyes livid with the fire
of an almost unreal gaze.
He holds a scepter in his hands and, in a low voice, murmurs
a mysterious spell only he can recite.
· · · · ·
and the bodies are *twisting and bending* with demonic fury
at the irresistible pulse of the staffs and the timbal.[49]

Even though these lines recall Federico Mialhe's famous engraving *Día de Reyes,* they also show that Pichardo's interest is not
in the kind of "realistic" detail that characterizes that lithograph's
painstaking reproduction of the dancers' ritualistic garb. Instead,
"La comparsa" focuses on the way in which "the hoarse, monotonous music" inscribes the dancers' bodies that tremble, shake,
whirl, zigzag, twist themselves out of shape, convulse as if caught
in epileptic fits. The pathological undertones of Pichardo's verbs
uncomfortably recall Muñoz del Monte's "La mulata." What racially marks these bodies, male and female, are the musical
rhythms their dancing translates into sight. They are visually displaced and dismembered by these rhythms, which the poem itself
attempts to reproduce through different uses of repetition. Pichardo's perspective, by contrast, remains that of an unmoved observer of a cultural event that seems to have neither emotional nor
political resonances for him. That "La comparsa" is dedicated to
"el Dr. Fernando Ortiz" comes as little surprise. The poem can
indeed be read as a miniature ethnographic study of *la mala vida
habanera* (the seedy side of Havana), inspired, much like Guillén's
"Sensemayá," by Ortiz's not-so-scientific accounts of Afro-Cuban
religious practices in *Los negros brujos.* But unlike in Guillén's
"Sensamayá," which completely forgoes any description of dancing and becomes itself a "song for killing a snake," there is no
sense in "La comparsa" that such performances were highly politi-
cized events rather than exotic spectacles.[50] The sole value "La

comparsa" attaches to Afro-Cuban music, never mind its religious significance, is its presumed ability to transcend politics. Always the rhythm.

Similar assumptions are operative in the technically more sophisticated "Elegía de María Belén Chacón" by Ballagas, which opens with the following lines:

> María Belén, María Belén, María Belén,
> María Belén Chacón, María Belén Chacón, María Belén Chacón.
> con tus nalgas en vaivén,
> de Camagüey a Santiago, de Santiago a Camagüey.
>
> En el cielo de la rumba,
> ya nunca habrá de alumbrar
> tu constelación de curvas.

> María Belén, María Belén, María Belén,
> María Belén Chacón, María Belén Chacón, María Belén Chacón.
> with your buttocks swinging back and forth,
> from Camgüey to Santiago, from Santiago to Camagüey.
>
> Never again will
> the constellation of your curves
> set ablaze the rumba heaven.[51]

Ballagas's main interest is in the rhythmic properties of the name María Belén (Chacón). The entire poem is a formal improvisation based on the 2/4–time measure embedded in the phrase "María Belén," which represents the rhythm normally used to accompany the *son* and the rumba. Like "Rita Barranco" from "Nombres negros en el son," "María Belén Chacón" has significance only as a metric construct that corresponds to a specific musical measure. She is nothing more than the "hot and pretty" name whose rhythm she embodies: "nalgas en vaivén" not only rhymes with "María Belén"; it identifies her. Unlike the mulata herself,[52] who is but an eclipsed star in "rumba heaven" and whose violent death the poet laments in his "Elegy," the *son* has a distinctive identity and a historical origin to which the poem alludes by situating its rhythms geographically in Cuba's eastern provinces, Camagüey and especially Oriente, from where the *son* is believed to have come to Havana.[53] Federico García Lorca's "Son de los negros en Cuba" contains a similar reference to Santiago de Cuba in Oriente Province. So does Alfonso Camín's "Danzón de María Belén," which resembles Ballagas's poem.

> De Santiago a Caimanera,
> de la Habana a Caibarién,
> todo es cintura y cadera
> si baila María Belén.

> From Santiago to Caimanera,
> from Havana to Caibarién,
> all is waist and hips
> when María Belén dances.[54]

To comment more fully on the mythic origin these poems invoke, and to add another dimension to the representational issues *poesía mulata* both raises and conceals, I would like to call attention to a particular aspect of the "Son de la Ma Teodora" (*Son* of the Ma Teodora). This mother, as it were, of the Cuban *son* is frequently cited as an important source for Guillén's musical *poemas-son* and other, similar poetic ventures. The call-and-response lyrics open with a question, variations on which recur throughout: "¿Dónde está la Ma Teodora?/. . ./¿Dónde está que *no la veo?*" (Where is Ma Teodora?/. . ./Where is she that *I can't see* her?; my emphasis). The response—namely that "she's splitting logs" or, to use a more recognizable though somewhat inappropriate English idiom, cutting a rug—provides the reason why we do not see her: because she is dancing.[55] It is her dancing that defines her as an absence; she does not exist outside of the syncretic *son* that supposedly originated with her. Because of Ma Teodora's conspicuous textual invisibility, it is relevant to note that there has been serious doubt among musicologists about the actual origins of this prototypical Cuban dance, which has been linked with and named after the black Dominican dancer Teodora Ginés. Some even suspect that the "Son de la Ma Teodora" was neither a product of the late sixteenth century nor performed by Teodora Ginés, but a nineteenth-century invention. Most readings of this "Son," however, have remained untroubled by such doubts.[56] In what is the most extensive literary commentary on the "Son de la Ma Teodora" Roberto González Echevarría identifies Ma Teodora as an embodiment of tradition, as "memory incarnate." "The jubilation at the end," he adds," is a recovery of tradition, an immersion in a rhythm that is primordial."[57] But whose tradition? Who is that seeing I/Eye in pursuit of the elusive figure of Ma Teodora, who herself can neither see nor be seen? Her sole shapes are the cross-cultural rhythms of the *son,* presumably the earliest known product of Cuba's *mestizaje.* Indeed, the perpetual quest for tradition in this *son* is premised on her (textual) displacement.

That Cuba's cultural tradition can be recovered only by absenting or displacing the black mother figure is perhaps the most significant lesson of the "Son de la Ma Teodora." This is also why the actual historical existence of a Ma Teodora is quite irrelevant to the masculine structures of cultural memory that the rhythms of the *son* have come to represent; the feminine myth suffices. The erasure of the nonwhite woman from the scene of cultural (re)production is precisely what is at the origin of the Cuban *son.* It is what constitutes the silent (or silenced) legacy and liability of this musical sound.

Like their mythic female ancestor, none of the women in Ballagas's above poems have any existence or significance beyond the timed gyrations of their forever formidable hips and buttocks, the parts to which their bodies in motion are invariably reduced. Arrom is one critic who almost cheerfully admits to not being scandalized by such "natural" images. Relying on the "authority" of Fernando Ortiz's study of the steatopygia of African women, Arrom endorses racial stereotypes by attributing the reductive eroticism of these representations to the "black perspective" operative in *poesía negra/mulata*: "for the Negro, and for good reason, the female of the species is a compound of shoulders and buttocks joined by a navel in continuous circling motion."[58] For Arrom, it seems, nonwhite women, in fact all persons of African extraction, are barely human; his use of *hembra* (female) instead of *mujer* (woman) animalizes them even more than the above poems do. Indeed, few *poemas mulatos* are as overtly sexist and racist as Arrom's remarks are.

"Copla mulata" (1929) by the Puerto Rican Luis Llorens Torres is a notable exception. In this poem, the "criolla pelinegra y ojinegra" (black-haired and black-eyed creole woman) becomes a "caliente potranca" (hot-blooded filly) who is "digna de ensangrentar en sus ijares/mis espuelas de plata" (worthy of bloodying my silver spurs in her flanks).[59] Ballagas's "Elegía" may not be as crude, but it also leaves little doubt about the poet's interest in María Belén and the reasons for his elegiac lament: "Ya no veré mis instintos/en los espejos redondos y alegres de tus dos nalgas" (I shall no longer see my instincts/reflected in the round and joyous mirrors of your two buttocks.)[60]

The specular imagery in these lines would seem inconsistent with *poesía mulata's* purported erotic investment in sound if it were not for the fact that the poet's nostalgia for the "mirrors" of the mulata's buttocks masks a desire for something (or someone) the poem does not represent. It is important in this respect that the conduit for white male sexuality in this instance is not a living woman's body but the poem's own disembodied constellation of feminine curves that celebrates the death (or simply nonbeing) of the nonwhite woman and the construction of black femininity her demise makes possible. Underlying the shift from sight to sound in this poem is an aesthetics of violence: The knife that perforates the mulata's lungs is the poet's pen. As Ballagas puts it in "Nombres negros en el son": "¡Por ti repica mi canto lo mismo que un atabal!" (Through you I play my song in the same way as an *atabal* drum!). The difference between "por ti" (through you) and "para ti" (for you) is a subtle, but significant indicator of the poet's instrumental use of the mulata, who becomes what Evaristo Ribera Chevremont calls "la morena rítmica y *perfecta*" (the rhythmic and *perfect* brown-skinned woman; my emphasis). Her stereotypical image also reappears in Marcelino Arozarena's "Liturgia etiópica".

> Lasciva, rugiente, se ríe Mersé,
> y mientras la mulata su cuerpo menea,
> tonante toque en tumulto
> tam tam tamborilea
> sobre la liturgia pura del etiópico ancestral.
>
> Lascivious, roaring, Mersé laughs,
> and while the mulata shakes her body,

thundering, tumultuous beat,
tam tam drumming
upon the pure liturgy of the ancestral Ethiopian.[61]

The stylized opening lines of Arozarena's "Amalia" similarly recall the rhythmic counterpoint of female hips inscribed in "Rita Barranco, sí/Rita Barranco, no" from Ballagas's "Nombres negros en el son":

Amalia baila temblando.
—Sí, señor.
Amalia tiembla bailando.
—Cómo no.

Amalia dances, shaking it.
—Yessir.
Amalia shakes it, dancing.
—Indeed.[62]

Guillén's "Secuestro de la mujer de Antonio," in its turn, thematizes the all-consuming eroticism that produces such poetic rhythms.

Te voy a beber de un trago,
como una copa de ron;
te voy a echar en la copa
de un son,
prieta, quemada en ti misma,
cintura de mi canción.

I am going to drink you down in one gulp,
like a glass of rum;
I am going to drown you in the cup
of a *son,*
mulata, burning within yourself,
waist of my song.[63]

Guillén's title is tellingly self-referential: It is the poet who "abducts" Antonio's woman, that "mulata, mora, morena," in an appropriative gesture reminiscent of the Dominican Manuel de Cabral's "Trópico suelto," where the poet savors the mulata's "fantasy flesh" like a "café con leche."[64] Yet, there is a significant difference between these two acts of (sexual) appropriation. In

"Secuestro," the poet cuckolds another man, which makes it possible to read the act of making the mulata the "waist of *my* song"
(my emphasis) as a homosocial transaction parading as heterosexual desire.[65] Chevremont's "Morena" aptly summarizes the position of all these poets: "Y yo, que soy guardián de tus riquezas/de
carne y hueso, avaramente guardo,/. . . tu silueta" (And I, who am
the guardian of the riches/of your flesh and bone, greedily guard/
. . . your silhouette).[66]

By far the best-known self-appointed "guardian" of the mulata's "riches" is Luis Palés Matos. His "Mulata-Antilla" is, as the
title already suggests, a "mujer-isla" (woman-island),[67] a figure
that represents the Antilles as a whole. As *poesía mulata,* however,
Palés's poem is rather atypical to the extent that it has no overt
investment in the percussive aspects of Afro-Antillean music, especially when compared to a poem like "Plena de menéalo," from
which I took the epigraph for the second part of chapter 5. As
befits the grand pan-Caribbean scheme of "Mulata-Antilla," as
well as its Eurocentrism, the poem's dominant musical trope is
symphony, not syncopation. The poem's opening line, which recurs at the beginning of the next stanza for emphasis, places the
poet, not inside the mulata's head, but actually inside her womb's
darkness, where reason ("la luz," light or enlightenment) is held
in abeyance.

> En ti ahora, mulata,
> me acojo al tibio mar de las Antillas,
> agua sensual y lenta de melaza,
> puerto de azúcar, cálida bahía,
> con la luz en reposo.

> In you now, mulata,
> I take refuge in the warm sea of the Antilles,
> sensual water, flowing slowly as molasses,
> sugar port, warm bay,
> with the light in repose.[68]

In the third stanza, the poet is reborn from that warm, sugary
sea to a spectacular "symphony" of colors. But unlike Her-
maphroditus in Ovid's *Metamorphoses,* Palés's poet reemerges

from his plunge into the Antillean waters with his maleness fully intact. As in the case of Ballagas and Guillén, heterosexual encounters serve as a strategy for obtaining instrumental use of the mulata's "offerings."

¡Oh despertar glorioso en las Antillas!
Bravo color que el do de pecho alcanza,
música al rojo vivo de alegría,
y calientes cantáridas de aroma
—limón, tabaco, piña—
zumbando a los sentidos
sus embriagadas voces de delicia.

Eres ahora, mulata,
todo el mar y la tierra de mis islas,
sinfonía frutal cuyas escalas
rompen furiosamente en tu catinga.
He aquí en su traje verde de guanábana
con sus finas y blandas pantaletas
de muselina; he aquí el caimito
con su leche infantil; he aquí la piña
con sus corona de soprano. . . . Todos
los frutos ¡oh mulata! tú me brindas
en la clara bahía de tu cuerpo
por los soles del trópico bruñida.

Oh glorious awakening in the Antilles!
Bold color that the high C reaches,
music to the lively red of joy,
and hot cantharides of aroma
—lemon, tobacco, pineapple—
make the senses buzz
with their intoxicated, delicious voices.

You are now, mulata,
all the water and earth of my islands,
fruity symphony whose scales
rip furiously in your *catinga* dance.
Here I have the green garment of the guanabana,
with its delicate and soft pantalets
of muslin; here is the star apple
with its mother's milk; here is the pineapple

with its soprano crown. . . . All these
fruits, oh mulata, you offer me
in the clear bay of your body
burnt by the tropical suns.[69]

This polychromatic vision seeks to bridge the gap between color and music. For Palés, the mulata is not a "woman of color" but a woman of colors, all blended together in this "symphonic" representation of Antilles' "fiery, lyrical lands." The mulata, in short, represents everything but herself, all colors except her own. In fact, all that is left of her here is an empty shell of femininity in which the poet has comfortably taken up residence to hurl a "gilded artillery" of plantains and coconuts "al barco transeúnte que nos deja/su rubio contrabando de turistas" (at the transient ship that leave us/with its blond contraband of tourists). One cannot help but wonder if these are among the lines Frederick Habibe and other critics have in mind when they insist that Palés's Afro-Antillean poems are based on historical realities.[70]

What is at issue, however, is not Palés's interest in history. Rather, the question is whose historical realities his poems represent. A good example here is "Majestad negra" (Black majesty) with its references to the Puerto Rican sugar economy.

Culipandeando la Reina avanza,
Y de su inmensa grupa resbalan
Meneos cachondos que el gongo cuaja
En ríos de azúcar y de melaza.
Prieto trapiche de sensual zafra,
El caderamen, masa con masa,
Exprime ritmos, suda que sangra,
Y la molienda culmina en danza.

Swaying her hips the Queen advances,
and from her immense buttocks flow
salacious movements the drums curdle
into rivers of sugar and molasses.
Dark sugarmill of a sensuous harvest,
her thighs, mass against mass,
squeeze out rhythms, sweat till they bleed,
and the grinding culminates in dance.[71]

It is useful to situate this stanza, which resonates with portions of Guillén's "Secuestro de la mujer de Antonio,"[72] in the context of Moreno Fraginals's comments on the myths of black sexuality that historically evolved in Cuba and other plantation societies. His remarks also constitute a response of sorts to the misguided beliefs of a critic like Arrom. Fraginals points out that

Certain dances and songs of African origin, which either had no sexual connotations to begin with or in which those connotations had been sublimated, acquired under slavery an almost lascivious meaning. It is therefore no coincidence that a good part of the Cuban . . . sexual lexicon originated on the sugar plantations. In sum: the pathological obsession with sex that stained the world of the American blacks was not produced by physiological or cultural conditions in Africa, but originated in the subhuman way of life on the plantation. . . . Slavery distorted the slaves' sexuality, and the racists justified such distortions by inventing the myth of the sadistic sexuality of the black man, the immorality of the black woman, and the promiscuity of the mulata.[73]

Throughout this book, I have pointed to the frequency with which nineteenth-century Cuban literary and visual texts establish discursive links between sugar production and black female sexual pathology. The epigraph to the second part of this chapter, from Alfonso Camín's "La mulata Candelaria," serves as a reminder of the continuation of this discursive practice in early-to-mid-twentieth-century Afro-Antillean poetry, a practice exemplified by both "Majestad negra" and, to a lesser extent, "Mulata-Antilla." Aníbal González's commentary on "Majestad negra" is instructive.

Following the Cuban historian Ramiro Guerra y Sánchez's observations in *Sugar and Society in the Caribbean* (1927) (as well as Fernando Ortiz's idea of cultural fusion in *Los negros brujos*), Palés sees the sugarmill and the process of sugar production as the common ground for the meeting and melding of cultures. In the sugarmill, the white man's secularized notion of temporality as linear progression is transformed into a cyclical one, bound to the rhythms of sugar production, and closer to a black sense of time which, Palés, like Spengler, considers to be inherently circular or cyclical. . . . For Palés, the privileged cultural expression of such a synthesis, of such a meshing of cycles and rhythms, lies in music and dance; music marks the beat of the liturgical, sacred time of the black, while dance mimics in its gestures the movement of the body at work in the process of sugar production.[74]

Much like the opening chapter of Carpentier's *¡Ecue Yamba-O!* Palés's poem suggests a compatibility between the production cycles of the sugar plantation and the rhythms of black music, which come to represent an entire cosmology. Aside from the fact that González's remarks are in no way attentive to the almost invariably female gender of the dark bodies in which sugar production is so lyrically fused with dance, what goes entirely unmentioned, both in the poem and in its attendant critical commentary, is that this compatibility, or fusion, of technology with "natural" religion is, first and foremost, the result of slavery. The (false) analogy between the *enslaved* "body at work" on the sugar mill and black religious or secular dance is significantly founded on a denial of the distorting, dehumanizing effects of slavery and technology combined. For a slave, working on the sugar plantation was hardly as benign an activity as dancing; and it most certainly was not erotic, or only to a sadistic imagination for which the kind of violence inscribed in "suda que sangra" (sweat till they bleed) would enhance sexual pleasure. A sobering contrast here is the lexicon of physical tortures for disobedient slaves that Morúa links with sugar production in *Sofía*. What Moreno Fraginals neglects to mention is that slavery in the context of a plantation society such as Cuba distorted not just *black* sexuality.

One of few poems that even attempts to explore the nexus of rhythm, sexuality, and sugar from a different perspective is Felipe Pichardo Moya's "Filosofía del bronce" (Bronze philosophy). This poem, which first appeared in his *La ciudad los espejos* (The city of the mirrors) (1925) and then became part 4 of *El poema de los cañaverales* (The poem of the cane fields) (1926), will serve as a contrast to Palés's "Majestad negra" in particular and, by extension, to all of the *poemas mulatos* on which I have commented in this chapter with varying degrees of detail. Unlike most of those poems, "Filosofía" is not exactly a text whose plurimetric organization is noticeably indebted to Afro-Cuban rhythms. If anything, Pichardo's use of cross-rhymed quartets in five of the six stanzas makes this poem resemble a redondilla, that sixteenth-century poetic form whose presumed origin is an old Spanish dance. Of course, "Filosofía" is not, strictly speaking, a cross-rhymed redondilla for it does not employ alternating lines of eight and four syllables. But Pichardo, it seems, compensates for the poem's metric irregularities by alternating quartets and octaves. The exception to all this is the final, eleven-line stanza, to which I shall return. It is safe to suggest, then, that the relation between poetry and Afro-Cuban percussive music is still at issue in "Filosofía," though in a way that is rather different from later "mulata poems." Unlike Ballagas's María Belén Chacón, for instance, Pichardo's mulata is not a fiery *rumbera;* hers is a slower, meditative pace that is more in keeping with the poem's title.

> ¡Tendrás de tus antepasados
> sabe Dios cuanta gente!
> !Cuántos pedrigrées ignorados
> que forman tu modo presente!
>
> ¡Sangre bárbara y sangre nuestra
> bajo el sol cómplice mezcladas
> por bendición de la siniestra
> mano, son luz en tus miradas!
> La caravana de ignominia
> de los tratantes, desenroscará su serpiente,
> y en los caminos que van a Angola y a Abisinia
> aún el sol quema las osamentas de tu gente. . . .
>
> Quizás tuviste un ascendiente
> que fue de sangre real,
> y en el negrero algún marino, bajo el puente
> unió a su sangre el porte rubio de boreal.

> God knows how many people
> you have for ancestors!
> How many are the unknown pedigrees
> that make up your present being!
>
> Barbaric blood mixed with our blood,
> under the complicitous sun
> with the blessing of the sinister
> hand, is in your luminous gaze.

> The ignominious caravan
> of the slavers will uncoil its serpent,
> and on the paths from Angola and to Abyssinia
> the sun still bleaches your people's bones. . . .
>
> Perhaps you had an ancestor
> who was of royal blood,
> and on the slave ship a sailor, under the bridge,
> fused to her blood the blondness of the North.[75]

Rather than eroticizing and commodifying the mulata, "Filosofía" meditates on the history of economic and sexual enslavement that produced her. Underscored by the absence of physical description in these opening stanzas, the withholding of the addressee's female identity until the final stanza effectively counteracts an aesthetics of masculine voyeurism. Similarly, the sexual symbolism of the serpent, along with its carnivalesque references, is turned entirely on its head in "Filosofía." It is not the mulata's body (and thus her moral fiber) that is compared to a winding serpent but the "ignominious caravan" of captured Africans to the West African coast, where those who had survived the ordeal of the journey would be loaded onto slave ships bound for New World ports. This image recurs elsewhere in *El poema de los cañaverales* with the transformation of the serpent into a "Cadena viva que a la costa/se arrastra desde el interior" (living chain that drags itself/from the coast to the interior) and a "negro rosario del dolor" (black rosary of suffering).[76] What we *see*, in the mulata's eyes that are "luminous" with her history, are bleached bones along trails of blood that link Africa with the Americas. That these serpentine trails are also bloodlines that lead to unknown or absent ancestors makes this poem a search for origins comparable to those dramatized in several of Guillén's poems, most notably in this context his "Balada de los dos abuelos" and "El abuelo." Even though formally "Filosofía," like Guillén's two poems, is (deceptively?) indebted to European poetic conventions—in this case the redondilla which Lope de Vega recommended particularly for matters of the heart—even a cursory comparison of these three poems reveals major differences in Pichardo's approach to the topic of racial mixing.

Unlike Guillén, whose lyric preoccupation with black and white grandfathers in both poems conspicuously preempts any female participation in the poetic "performance" of racial mixing, Pichardo insists on representing the mulata's possibly "royal" African ancestry as a woman. Her body and blood were "fused" with that of some blond sailor, whose active status as subject of this sentence implies violence. Though "su" is an equivocal pronoun, the context of the stanza requires a feminine referent for this violent union to yield the *re*productive connotations implicit in "sangre," blood. The following stanzas, which replay the act while shifting the setting from the slave ships of the Middle Passage to the cane fields of Cuba, are more explicit about the nature of this interracial "union."

> ¡O el abuelo noble y español,
> cedió al impulso que le daba,
> en una siesta ebria de sol,
> la carne negra de la esclava!
> Idilio monstruo entre los cortes de las cañas,
> concepción contra las leyes . . .
> ¡Visiones de cosas extrañas
> exacerbando las nostalgias de los bueyes!
>
> ¡Y en una copia de los horrores del infierno
> que nunca tendrá igual,
> sintió sobre el torso materno
> los latigazos quizás, tu germen paternal!

Oh the noble Spanish grandfather,
during a siesta inebriated with sun,
yielded to the temptation
of the slave woman's black flesh!
Monstrous idyll amidst canebrakes,
conception against the laws. . . .
Visions of foreign things
nourish the nostalgia of the oxen.

And in an imitation of hell's horrors
that know no equal,
she felt on the maternal chest
the whiplashes, your paternal seed!

This encounter is dramatically different from the fraternal embrace of Don Federico and Taita Facundo in the final stanza of Guillén's "Balada." The apostrophe, which suspends rather than sustains the poem's previous mode of direct address, is now a sign of accusation rather than adulation. This irony is underscored by the Spaniard's deflated nobility. But even though the sense of violence and violation, as well as of indignation on the poet's part, is much stronger here than in the previous stanza, the responsibility for this "monstrous" act is also indirectly (that is, grammatically) attributed to the slave woman, a temptress by virtue of her black skin. This sudden return to a symbolic system effectively dismissed in the previous stanza is irritating, yet neither unconscious nor without purpose.

In an argument consistent with Moreno Fraginals's above comments, the stanza proceeds to situate slavery and sugar production at the root of the mulata's imputed sexual pathology. Pichardo's vision of Cuba's cane fields as a "monstrous idyll" explodes rather than nourishes nostalgic sentiment. The adjective "monstruo" is of interest not only as a figure for the mulata's "conception against the laws" of racial purity. It also defines her as the product of "unnatural" acts of a different kind: rape. The welts on the "maternal body" in the following stanza can leave no doubt in the reader's mind about the black woman's resistance to the Spanish grandfather's ignoble desires. The earlier image of the black woman as temptress now clearly assumes the status of a pathological fiction designed to diffuse the issue of white men's sexual violence toward African women. A product of that violence, the mulata is indeed the "supreme flower of injustice," a trope that renders explicit what was latent, nearly eighty years earlier, in Plácido's hybrid.

> ¡Y así llegaste hasta nosotros,
> hermana nuestra y de los otros,
> suprema flor de la injusticia,
> que conviertes en bravos potros
> las palomas de la caricia
> en un anhelo vengativo
> que tu grupa conserva vivo,
> porque tu impulso pasional
> eleva, sobre los abrazos,

el furor de los latigazos
del inclemente mayoral!

And so you arrived among us,
sister who is ours and other,
supreme flower of injustice,
who transforms into wild colts
the dovelike caresses
through a desire for vengeance
that your rump keeps alive,
because your passionate impulse
raises, beyond the embraces,
the fury of the whiplashes
of the merciless overseer!

Much more overtly than Plácido's "La flor de la caña," "Filosofía del bronce" divests the discourses of sugar and *mestizaje* of all mythic sweetness. Rather than eroticizing the mulata's body and making it a vehicle for masculinist visions of interracial reconciliation, Pichardo turns this Cuban icon into a living testimony to her African mother's violation. Beyond the passionate embrace lies the "fury" of the overseer's whip, as ineradicable a mark on the mulata's memory as the welts on the black slave woman's "maternal" body. The sensuous gyrations of the mulata's "rump" do not transcend, and thus conceal, slavery's and sugar's violence; if anything, they reveal it and raise it to a higher pitch. Even though "Filosofía" is not exactly a poetic masterpiece, its perspective on the origins of Cuban culture and society troubles the synthetic fiction of *mestizaje* like few other poems do. Maybe those *poemas negros/mulatos* that are regarded as poetic feats, notably Guillén's, are valued precisely because they are less troublesome, that is, they cover their ideological tracks with a sustained literary elegance that escapes Pichardo's poem.

The emphasis on the link between sexual violence and the discourse of sugar makes "Filosofía del bronce" resonate with Morúa Delgado's *Sofía* in some rather obvious ways. At this stage in my argument, even the titles themselves have acquired certain resonances. It would by no means be inappropriate to read "Filo/sofía" as a trope in which the memory of Filomena/Filomela is partially restored to Sofía. In this trope the lexis of sexual exploitation, that "darker" side of love, is already and necessarily part of the culture—and of the kind of cultural wisdom—represented by the figure of the mulata and sublimated in the masculine construct of *mestizaje*. In Pichardo's poem, as in Morúa's novel, the "shadow" attached to the mulata is not that of a heroic black man, such as Silvestre de Balboa's Salvador Galomón in the *Espejo de paciencia* or Guillén's *cimarrón* in "El abuelo." It is the faint outline of a perhaps not-so-glamorous black woman who probably was not even of royal blood, but whose image, however ephemeral, ruptures the discursive simulacrum that is *mestizaje* just long enough for us to glimpse a withered black breast—before it is hastily covered with a gleaming coat of ivory paint.[77]

Notes

Select Bibliography

Index

Notes

Introduction

1. Alejo Carpentier, *The Lost Steps*, 81 [147]. Page references provided hereafter in parentheses in the text are to this edition; bracketed page numbers here and in the subsequent textual parentheses refer to *Los pasos perdidos* (1985).

2. Paul Julian Smith, *The Body Hispanic: Gender and Sexuality in Spanish and Spanish American Literature*, 2–3.

3. The 1964 edition of the *Pequeño Larousse ilustrado* offers *adulterar*, to commit adultery, as the primary definition of the verb *mestizar*, even before mentioning racial mixing (*cruzar las razas*). The 1984 bilingual *Larousse: Gran diccionario moderno* translates *mestizaje* as crossbreeding and mestization, a word that does not appear to exist in English or American usage. The *Oxford English Dictionary*, defining miscegenation as "mixture of races; *esp.* the sexual union of whites with negroes," traces the American usage of the term *miscegenation* to 1864. See also Joel Williamson, *The Crucible of Race: Black-White Relations in the American South since Emancipation*, 40, and George M. Frederickson, *The Black Image in the White Mind: The Debate on Afro-American Character and Destiny, 1817–1914*.

4. I am using Stuart Hall's broad definition of *ideologies* as "concepts, ideas, and images which provide frameworks of interpretation and meaning for social and political thought" (Hall and Donald James, eds., *Politics and Ideology: A Reader*, 36).

5. My focus on the Hispanic Caribbean, and on Cuba in particular, should not be misconstrued as a subscription to the Balkanization of Caribbean literary and social history. It would clearly be deceptively simple to deem Cuba representative of the Caribbean—Hispanic and otherwise—or of Hispanic America, or both. But it would be no less misleading to regard Cuba as an isolated case, especially once the extreme fluidity of cultural, though not political, boundaries in (and beyond) the Caribbean and South and Central America is acknowledged. In order to

suggest that, particularly in the twentieth century, the nationalist concepts of *cubanidad/cubanía*, which I discuss in chapter 5, are only provisionally separable from transnational ideas of Caribbeanness, for instance, Edouard Glissant's *antillanité* and Wilson Harris's "cross-cultural imagination," one does not at the same time have to deny Cuban nationalist discourse its local historical specificity. See Glissant, *Caribbean Discourse*, and Harris, *The Womb of Space: The Cross-Cultural Imagination*. For a useful summary of this Balkanization debate among Caribbeanists see A. James Arnold's "Caribbean Literature/Comparative Literature," 39–46. For a recent assessment of nationalism see Homi K. Bhabha, ed., *Nation and Narration*.

6. See note 19 to chapter 3 and note 33 to chapter 4.

7. Cuba's anxiety over its perceived loss of national cultural homogeneity is reminiscent of the late-nineteenth-century United States. Compare Martha Banta's comments on the latter situation: "It was an anxiety over how to determine the identity of things in a society where there were no commonly accepted patterns to guarantee confident recognition. For how could knowing what was real be accomplished in a country where many were announcing their belief that cultural homogeneity had been lost?" (*Imaging American Women: Idea and Ideals in Cultural History*, 6). Of course, the issue in each case in not a "loss" of homogeneity but the increasing inability of respective national ideologies to contain social divisions.

8. Despite campaign promises from both the Moderate and the Liberal parties, not a single black politician came into office in 1908. The PIC was outlawed in 1910 with the posthumous passage of what is known as the *Ley Morúa*, named after Martín Morúa Delgado, one of Cuba's foremost "colored" politicians at the time.

9. See Edward Kamau Brathwaite, *Contradictory Omens: Cultural Diversity and Integration in the Caribbean*, and his "The African Presence in Caribbean Literature"; Glissant, *Caribbean Discourse*; Judith Berzon, *Neither White nor Black: The Mulatto Character in American Fiction*; Kutzinski, *Against the American Grain*; and Sneja Gunew, "Denaturalizing Cultural Nationalisms: Multicultural Readings of 'Australia,'" in Homi K. Bhabha, ed., *Nation and Narration*, 99–120. Wilson Harris's *The Womb of Space* has by far the most expansive range, including U.S. American, Caribbean, Hispanic American, and Australian writing.

10. José Martí, *The America of José Martí*, 144; *Nuestra América*, 85.

11. Martí, *The America of José Martí*, 141, 150; *Nuestra América*, 82, 90.

12. Martí, *The America of José Martí,* 308–12; *Cuba,* 515–18.

13. In strict usage, a *mestizo/a* is defined as the offspring of American Indian and white parents, while a *mulato/a* is of black and white parentage. However, the two are frequently used as synonyms (see, for instance, the *Pequeño Larousse ilustrado*). Similarly, the OED notes that the term *mulatto/a* is "also used loosely for any half-breed resembling a mulatto," presumably in skin color. This kind of conflation and confusion suggests the difficulty in conclusively determining the exact origins of racially mixed persons: the mulata is a third term, whose tenuous and exceedingly problematic relation to historical realities and social practices is itself a major point of discussion in this study. My use of the term *mulata* throughout this book refers to female figures of racially mixed or uncertain, at least partially African, origin. To avoid confusion between the different systems of racial classification in English-, French-, and Spanish-speaking Caribbean countries, I have retained the Spanish spelling, mulata, without italics, to denote a Hispanic American cultural context. The reasoning behind this decision is similar to Eduardo González's remarks about the difference between the Cuban *mulata* and the American *mulatta* (see his "American Theriomorphia: The Presence of *Mulatez* in Cirilo Villaverde and Beyond," in Gustavo Pérez Firmat, ed., *Do the Americas Have a Common Literature?* 182).

14. See Benedict Anderson, *Imagined Communities: Reflections on the Origin and Spread of Nationalism.*

15. See note 29 to chapter 5.

16. Ralph Ellison makes a similar point in his novel *Invisible Man* (1952).

17. Reinaldo Arenas, *Graveyard of the Angels,* 4; my emphasis. This novel, originally titled *La loma del angel,* has thus far been published only in an English translation.

18. See Roy Wagner's argument in *The Invention of Culture.*

19. The term discourse of sugar is Antonio Benítez Rojo's. See his "Nicolás Guillén and Sugar" and "Azúcar/poder/literatura." Versions of both articles are included in his *The Repeating Island: The Caribbean and the Postmodern Perspective* (*La isla que se repite: El Caribe y la perspectiva posmoderna*).

20. The other major plantation crop in Cuba was coffee, but coffee's impact on the island's culture and society was nothing like sugar's.

21. The possible English equivalents of *poesía negra* and *poesía mulata*—"black poetry" and "mulatto poetry"—are misleading because, unlike the Spanish terms, they imply the author's race. *Poesía negra/mulata,* on the other hand, signifies poetry about "blacks," or poetry for

which "black" culture serves as a reference point. It does not specify authorship. To avoid confusion, I will use the terms *poesía negra/mulata* and/or *poemas negros/mulatos* (and some variations such as *poesía negrista* or *poesía de lo negro*) throughout; no English translation would accurately render them. For a discussion of *poesía negra/mulata*, see chapter 5.

22. "Caramel Candy For Sale"—"Caramelo Vendo," which literally translates as "I sell candy"—is the title of a song that the mulato tailor-by-day, musician-by-night José Dolores Pimienta dedicates to Cecilia (Cirilo Villaverde, *Cecilia Valdés, o la loma del angel: Novela de costumbres cubanas*, 74).

23. See, for instance, Wilfred Cartey, *Black Images;* Ben Coleman, "Black Themes in the Literature of the Caribbean"; Richard L. Jackson, *Black Writers in Latin America*, and his "Literary Blackness and Literary Americanism: Toward an Afro Model for Latin American Literature"; as well as Marvin A. Lewis's *Afro-Hispanic Poetry, 1940–1980: From Slavery to "Negritud" in South American Verse*. Such revisionary procedures may yield an Afro-Hispanic American literary canon or even something akin to a "black aesthetic" in Hispanic America, but they do not bring us any closer to an understanding of the ways in which highly ambivalent social and literary attitudes toward race have functioned and continue to function within the nationalist discourses in these countries.

24. Arguments that acknowledge such complexities have of late been made with respects to early-twentieth-century texts by African-American writers in the United States. See particularly Houston A. Baker, *Modernism and the Harlem Renaissance*, and Gloria T. Hull, *Color, Sex, and Poetry: Three Women Writers of the Harlem Renaissance*.

25. See my *Against the American Grain*, part 3.

26. For a discussion of this issue see Frederick Hendrick Habibe, *El compromiso en la poesía afroantillana de Cuba y Puerto Rico*, especially his introduction, "Poesía afroantillana: Definiciones hasta la fecha."

27. Stuart Hall, "The Whites of Their Eyes: Racist Ideologies and the Media," 36.

28. There are significant numbers of texts by African-American authors both from the United States and from Hispanic America that worry the category "black literature" just as much as do the *poemas negros/mulatos* written by the likes of Ballagas, Guirao, Carpentier, and Palés Matos or, for that matter, the allegedly white poetry penned by Plácido and Manzano. Examples of such texts, which do not overtly expound "black themes," range from the "traditional" sonnets of Paul Laurence

Dunbar, much of the lesser-known poetry written (frequently by African-American women) during the Harlem Renaissance years, and the largely unpublished post-*Cane* (1923) writings of Jean Toomer to various poems by Robert Hayden and Jay Wright, as well as novels such as Richard Wright's *Savage Holiday* (1954) and James Baldwin's *Giovanni's Room* (1956). An assortment of texts by non-white writers from various parts of Hispanic America may be added to this list, including novels by the Colombian Manuel Zapata Olivella (*Detrás del rostro* [Behind the face], 1963), the Ecuadorian Adalberto Ortiz (*El espejo y la ventana* [The mirror and the window], 1967), the Peruvian Nelson Estupiñán Bass (*Bajo el cielo nublado* [Under the cloudy sky], 1981) and the Costa Rican Quince Duncan (*Final de calle* [End of the street], 1979). This is not even to mention much of Guillén's postrevolutionary poetry.

29. See Richard L. Jackson, "'Mestizaje' vs. Black Identity: The Color Crisis in Latin America," and his *The Black Image in Latin American Literature*, chapter 1: "Backdrop to Literature: Racism, *Mestizaje*, and the Crisis of Black Identity." Also relevant is Benítez Rojo, *The Repeating Island*, 26 [*Isla*, xxxiv]. The concept of lynching in this context further obfuscates gender by making nonwhite women, like La Malinche in Octavio Paz's Mexico, the bearers of the "original sins" of Cuban/Caribbean founding fathers (see Octavio Paz, *The Labyrinth of Solitude*, 65–88, as well as Lemuel Johnson's suggestive discussion of La Malinche/*la chingada* in his "A-beng: (Re)Calling the Body In(to) Question," in Carole Boyce Davies and Elaine Savory Fido, eds., *Out of the Kumbla: Caribbean Women and Literature*, 127–28). The rhetorical maneuvers through which *mestizaje* turns into "ethnic lynching" are indeed remarkable in their dislocation of historical (ir)responsibility and blame. They construe nonwhite female bodies as sites (and implicitly as agents) not of their own historical violation but of a different form of violence—lynching, we recall, is a form of social discipline often, though not exclusively, reserved for black men presumably accused of (eye)raping white women, and is possibly the most perverse of homosocial rituals (James Baldwin's 1965 short story "Going to Meet the Man" is a particularly striking example of what I am talking about). Of course, white men were not penalized in this way, if at all, for raping women of whatever color or race. All that defining *mestizaje* as "ethnic lynching" accomplishes, then, is to perpetuate the discursive erasure of all women as historical subjects from the realm of Hispanic Caribbean culture. In this respect, the notion of "ethnic lynching" is curiously complicitous with the very discourse it purports to criticize.

30. See Rafael Conte and José M. Capmany, *Guerra de razas: Negros contra blancos en Cuba*; also William Luis, ed., *Literary Bondage: Slavery in Cuban Narrative*, 19–23.

31. I take it that this is also what Sidney W. Mintz means when he refers to the need for decoding the process of codification, not merely the code itself (*Sweetness and Power: The Place of Sugar in Modern History*, 14). What I am calling Afro-Hispanic criticism's thematic bias reveals the burden of literary realism (and thus an attachment to the kind of historical accuracy abolitionists demanded of nineteenth-century slave narratives) that continues to be imposed on Afro-Hispanic American literature. For details on early African-American slave narratives see William Andrews, *To Tell a Free Story: The First Century of Afro-American Autobiography, 1760–1865*.

32. See Homi K. Bhabha, "The Other Question," 18–19, and Edward Said, *Orientalism*, 21. See also, Gloria Anzaldúa, *Borderlands/La Frontera: The New Mestiza*, esp. chapter 7.

33. See Adrienne Rich, "Disloyal to Civilization: Feminism, Racism, Gynephobia." Teresa De Lauretis's comments on "dis-identification" were also useful to me ("Eccentric Subjects: Feminist Theory and Historical Consciousness," 138).

34. Nancy Morejón's study *Nación y mestizaje en Nicolás Guillén* unfortunately does not consider gender and sexuality in any detail.

35. To reduce racial and color differences in the Caribbean to class differences is, according to Sidney Mintz, wishful thinking (*Caribbean Transformations*, 318). Somewhat in keeping with this, Elaine Savory Fido contends that "the perception of literature or of writers from the Caribbean as being able to be confined to large simplicities of race, nationality, color, class or gender is simply a very misguided one" ("Textures of Third World Reality in the Poetry of Four African-Caribbean Women," in Davies and Fido, eds., *Out of the Kumbla*, 30). Such indirect criticisms of the often-crude Marxist methodologies that have been applied to the study of Caribbean, especially Cuban, literatures should not, however, be taken to mean that class is an utterly negligible factor in a Caribbean context. My own discussion touches upon class issues, but they are not a major focus in this book.

36. "If the problems of gender and sexuality have not been solved by theorists in Europe, they have rarely been raised by the diverse Marxisms in Latin American" (Smith, *The Body Hispanic*, 140–41).

37. Among such critical studies are: Jean Franco, "Trends and Priorities for Research in Latin American Literature" (1983), and her *Plotting Women: Gender and Representation in Mexico* (1989); Beth Miller, ed.,

Women in Hispanic Literature: Icon and Fallen Idols (1983); Sharon Magnarelli, *The Lost Rib: Female Characters in the Spanish-American Novel* (1985); Carmelo Virgillo and Naomi Linstrom, eds., *Woman as Myth and Metaphor in Latin American Literature* (1985); Evelyn Picon Garfield, *Women's Voices from Latin America: Interviews with Six Contemporary Authors* (1985); Lucía Guerra Cunningham, ed., *Splintering Darkness: Latin American Women Writers in Search of Themselves* (1990); Selwyn R. Cudjoe, ed., *Caribbean Women Writers: Essays from the First International Conference* (1989); and Pamela Mordecai and Betty Wilson, eds., *Her True-True Name: An Anthology of Women's Writing from the Caribbean* (1990). Jeniphier R. Carnegie's "Select Bibliography" in Davies and Fido, eds., *Out of the Kumbla* (373–94), "the first real forum for a dialogue about the meaning and direction of feminist thought in Caribbean literary history and cultural criticism" (Kathleen M. Balutansky, "Naming Caribbean Women Writers," 540), provides further references. See also Sylvia Wynter's "Beyond Miranda's Meanings: Un/silencing the 'Demonic Ground' of Caliban's 'Woman,'" (in Davies and Fido, eds., *Out of the Kumbla,* 355–72) for a discussion of the "paradoxical" relations between feminisms and the Caribbean women intelligentsia (in *Out of the Kumbla,* 355–57). Notable in the context of Cuban studies are Hilda Perera's *Idapo: El sincretismo en los cuentos negros de Lydia Cabrera* (1971); Reinaldo Sánchez and José A. Madrigal, eds., *Homenaje a Lydia Cabrera* (1977); Gladys B. Zaldívar and Rosa Martínez de Cabrera's *Homenaje a Gertrudis Gómez de Avellaneda* (1981); and Jill Ann Netchinsky's "Engendering a Cuban Literature: Nineteenth-Century Antislavery Narrative (Manzano, Suárez y Romero, Gómez de Avellandea, A. Zambrana)" (1985).

   38. Race is a category almost completely ignored in the 1974 *Revista/Review Interamericana* special issue on "The Latin American Woman: Image and Reality." Wynter's "Beyond Miranda's Meanings" is possibly the most provocative recent contribution to Caribbean feminist/womanist studies. In addition, there are a substantial number of articles on the image of the black woman in Hispanic-American writing, the earliest of which is Gabriel R. Coulthard's chapter on "The Coloured Woman in Caribbean Poetry" in his *Race and Colour in Caribbean Literature* (1958). Other studies include Kay Boulware's "Women and Nature in *Negrismo*" (1977), Mónica Mansour's *La poesía negrista* (1973), Ann Venture Young's "The Black Woman in Afro-Caribbean Poetry" (in Miriam DeCosta, ed., *Blacks in Hispanic Literature,* 1977) and her "Black Women in Hispanic American Poetry: Glorification, Deification, and Humanization" (1982), Janet Jones Hampton's "The Image of the Black

Woman in the Spanish-American Novel: A Study of Characterization in Select Spanish-American Novels," Ineke Phaf's "Caribbean Imagination and Nation Building in Antillean and Surinamese Literature" (1988), Claudette May Williams's "Images of Black and Mulatto Women in Spanish Caribbean Poetry: Discourse and Ideology" (1986), and Roberta L. Salper's "Gender and Ideology in Caribbean Narratives" (1991).

39. Since I focus in this book on the invisibility of racial politics, it seems rather inappropriate to use a more common label such as "women of color," especially in light of the incisive questions Hazel V. Carby has recently raised about that phrase. "I know we are all supposed to be familiar with who is being evoked by this term," Carby writes, "but do we honestly believe that some people lack color? What does it mean, socially, politically, and culturally, not to have color? Are those without color not implicated in a society structured in dominance by race? Are those without color outside of the hierarchy of social relations and not racialized?" ("The Multicultural Wars," 13).

40. But, as Sandra Messinger Cypess stresses in her discussion of Puerto Rican literature, there is "a discrepancy between the real literary contributions of [for example] Puerto Rican women and the value assigned them in critical analyses. . . . Let us put aside, then," she rightly urges, "the quantitative element in regard to [literary] tradition" ("Tradition and Innovation in the Writings of Puerto Rican Women," in Davies and Fido, eds., *Out of the Kumbla,* 78).

41. Roberta Salper confirms that "in the textualization of the female mestizo experience in postcolonial and revolutionary Cuba, the *mulata* speaking as a *mulata* has remained voiceless. She has not yet articulated her own text" ("Gender and Ideology in Caribbean Narratives," 174,). Paul Julian Smith's analogy is interesting but too general: "The case of woman under patriarchy is rather similar in theoretical terms to that of the dependency of Latin America on a dominant First World. Like woman, Latin America has no language of her own" (*The Body Hispanic,* 29). In this formulation, the unqualified term *woman* is merely a theoretical substitute for the figure of Caliban as conceived most notably by Roberto Fernández Retamar (see his *Caliban* and my brief discussion of it in chapter 6). The result is a familiar obfuscation of race and gender issues.

42. In a recent interview, Nancy Morejón remarks on what she calls a present "boom" in Cuba of women writers, especially poets, many of whom are black (see Elaine Savory Fido, "A Womanist Vision of the Caribbean: An Interview," in Davis and Fido, eds., *Out of the Kumbla,* 268–69).

43. Wynter, "Beyond Miranda's Meanings," 356; my emphasis. It is unfortunate that Wynter's phrase "'native' woman," even though it suspends the adjective in quotation marks, contributes further to the marginalization of race implicit in labels such as "women of color" (see note 39, above).

44. Edward Said, *Orientalism*, 6. Toni Morrison writes: "The scholarship that looks into the mind, imagination, and behavior of slaves is valuable. But equally valuable is a serious intellectual effort to see what racial ideology does to the mind, imagination, and behavior of masters" (*Playing in the Dark: Whiteness and the Literary Imagination*, 10–12).

Chapter 1

Note on the epigraph

The lyrics from an anonymous nineteenth-century guaracha that appear in the epigraphs to this and subsequent chapters are included in *Guarachas cubanas*, 64. For further details see also Juan José Arrom, *Certidumbre de América: Estudios de letras, folklore y cultura*, especially "Presencia del negro en la poesía folklórica americana."

1. Instituto de Literatura y Lingüística de la Academia de Ciencias de Cuba, eds., *Perfil histórico de las letras cubanas*, 226. For a detailed account of that period in Cuban history see Robert L. Paquette, *Sugar Is Made with Blood: The Conspiracy of La Escalera and the Conflict between Empires over Slavery in Cuba*, 29–130.

2. Steam engines were used in the grinding process as early as 1820, and the building of railroads began in 1837. With respect to the slaves' changed working conditions, Villaverde writes in *Cecilia Valdés*: "It is . . . an odd coincidence that so many blacks have rebelled at the same time and on the same plantations that recently modernized their systems of grinding sugarcane. Could it be that these stupid creatures have got the notion that their work will be increased because the steam engine has replaced oxen or mules in the grinding process?" (433).

3. See Manuel Moreno Fraginals, *El ingenio: Complejo económico social cubano del azúcar*, 1:271–72.

4. See José Antonio Saco's monumental *Historia de la esclavitud de la raza africana on el Nuevo Mundo* (1879).

5. One of the most prominent members of the Real Sociedad Económica de Amigos del Pais, Del Monte encouraged and sponsored abolitionist literature, often at the request of Richard R. Madden, the British

Consul in Havana and one of Del Monte's close friends. Del Monte was also a son-in-law of Domingo Aldama Arechaga, the island's most powerful saccharocrat and partner in one of the five largest slave-trading companies in Cuba. Richard Jackson compares Del Monte to Harlem Renaissance patron Carl Van Vechten ("Slavery, Racism, and Autobiography in Two Early Black Writers: Juan Francisco Manzano and Martín Morúa Delgado," in William Luis, ed., *Voices from Under: Black Narrative in Latin America and the Caribbean,* 56). For further details on Del Monte and early Cuban antislavery narrative, see Salvador Bueno, *Las ideas literarias de Domingo Del Monte;* Ilena Rodríguez, "Romanticismo literario y liberalismo reformista: El grupo de Domingo Del Monte"; Jill Netchinsky, "Engendering a Cuban Literature"; and Luis, *Literary Bondage,* chapter 1. Arguably the "most cultured" member of the saccharocracy, Del Monte was in many ways an exceptional personality, though it was by no means unusual at the time for sugar mill owners, retired or not, to speak out against slavery. The best case in point is that of Francisco de Arango y Parreño, the most influential spokesman of the Havana sugar oligarchy, who began to write and translate works opposing slavery and the slave trade in the twenties. See his *Informes al Rey sobre la condición de los esclavos en la isla de Cuba, y urgente necesidad de la supresión de la trata* (1828 and 1832). For further information on Arango y Parreño see Paquette, *Sugar Is Made with Blood,* 83–85.

6. The term *romantic abolitionism* is Pedro Barredas's (*The Black Protagonist in the Cuban Novel*). Barreda divides the nineteenth-century Cuban novel into two periods, both linked by similar sentimental and idealistic approaches to their subject matter. The first period is characterized by a mixture of Enlightenment ideas and costumbrismo.

7. Gómez de Avellaneda was among those Cubans who moved their families to Spain to protect them from the consequences of possible slave rebellions. For commentaries on *Sab* see Netchinsky, "Engendering a Cuban Literature," chapter 4, and Doris Sommer, *Foundational Fictions: The National Romances of Latin America,* chapter 4.

8. See Netchinsky, "Engendering a Cuban Literature," 94–95, and Luis, *Literary Bondage,* 82–100.

9. The second novel, which Tanco y Bosmoniel apparently did complete, was entitled *Hombre misterioso;* the third one, which he described in a letter to Del Monte, *Historia de Francisco.* Both are lost.

10. For an excellent discussion of Del Monte's relations with his protégés, notably Manzano and Suárez y Romero, see Netchinsky, "Engendering a Cuban Literature," chapters 2 and 3.

11. The short story "Cecilia Valdés" and the first part of the novel were both published in 1839, but, as Luis argues, neither text can be called antislavery (*Literary Bondage,* 100–101). Netchinsky, who does not include *Cecilia Valdés* in her study, argues that, unlike other white antislavery writers, notably Suárez y Romero, Villaverde text lacks "the immediacy of . . . poetic identification" ("Engendering a Cuban Literature," 17; see also 18–23).

12. See the *Diccionario provincial casi razondado de voces y frases cubanas* (1836), as quoted in Verena Martínez-Alier, *Marriage, Class, and Color in Nineteenth-Century Cuba: A Study of Racial Attitudes and Sexual Values in a Slave Society,* 72; see also xiii.

13. Martínez-Alier, *Marriage, Class, and Colour,* xiii. For a discussion of the compensation of racial status by economic performance, see 24–25.

14. From a confidential circular letter dispatched by the Captain-General of Cuba in 1866, quoted ibid., 31.

15. See ibid., 26.

16. On the "tragic mulatto" figure in United States literature, see Werner Sollors, "'Never Was Born': The Mulatto, an American Tragedy?"; Judith Berzon, *Neither White Nor Black;* and Hazel V. Carby, *Reconstructing Womanhood,* 89ff. For a recent study of the mulatta in the literature of the U.S. American South see Anna Shannon Elfenbein, *Women on the Color Line: Evolving Stereotypes and the Writings of George Washington Cable, Grace King, Kate Chopin.*

17. Villaverde, *Cecilia Valdés,* 48; see also 358.

18. Netchinsky, "Engendering a Cuban Literature," 76.

19. Eduardo González, "American Theriomorphia: The Presence of Mulatez in Cirilo Villaverde and Beyond," in Pérez Firmat, ed., *Do the Americas Have a Common Literature?* 181, 187.

20. Netchinsky effectively contrasts Gómez de Avellaneda's articles on "La mujer" in *El Album* to Villaverde's dedication ("Engendering a Cuban Literature," 206n. 11).

21. Elfenbein notes that the "tragic mulatta," "the North's favorite emblem of slavery," became the rage in abolitionist fiction (*Women on the Color Line,* 3).

22. Ibid., 12.

23. Villaverde, *Cecilia Valdés,* 33–34. Compare this to Villaverde's description of Cecilia's mother, Rosario (27).

24. Hortensia Ruiz del Vizo, ed., *Poesía negra del Caribe y otra areas,* 13.

25. Chapters 2 and 3 of the 1882 edition of Villaverde's novel coincide with chapters 1 and 2 of the first version and with the short story (see Luis, *Literary Bondage,* 108–9).

26. Dixon's trilogy included *The Leopard's Spots: A Romance of the White Man's Burden* (1902); *The Clansman: An Historical Romance of the Ku Klux Klan* (1905); and *The Traitor: A Story of the Fall of the Invisible Empire* (1907).

27. Nechinsky sees the figure of the absent or powerless father as a common feature of the antislavery plot ("Engendering a Cuban Literature," 130).

28. Enrique Noble, ed., *Literatura afro-hispanoamericana: Poesía y prosa de ficción,* 74. See also Sandra M. Gilbert and Susan Gubar, *The Madwoman in the Attic: The Woman Writer and the Nineteenth-Century Literary Imagination,* 28, 30, 66, and Sander L. Gilman, "Black Bodies, White Bodies: Toward an Iconography of Female Sexuality in Late Nineteenth-Century Art, Medicine, and Literature."

29. While it may be worth noting that Muñoz was not Cuban but Dominican, the fact that his poem was published in Cuba is what is important here.

30. Francisco Muñoz del Monte, "La mulata," in Jorge Luis Morales, ed., *Poesía afroantillana y negrista (Puerto Rico, República Dominica, Cuba),* 195–200. Quotations from this poem that follow are from the same source.

31. Williams, "Images of Black and Mulatto Women in Spanish Caribbean Poetry," 136. The earlier statement is that "the speaker [in the same poem] demonstrates his awareness of the need to modify its [Western culture's] traditional images in order to differentiate the Caribbean subject" (99).

32. The distinction was a familiar one at the time (see, for instance, Villaverde, *Cecilia Valdés,* 100, 397). The slave cargo was generally referred to as *sacos de carbón* (sacks of coal). See also Homi Bhabha, "The Other Question," 30.

33. Villaverde, *Cecilia Valdés,* 62, 398.

34. See Kate Chopin's 1893 short story "Desirée's Baby" which is discussed in Elfenbein, *Women on the Color Line,* 126–31.

35. An interesting and telling contrast to the high public visibility of the mulata in Hispanic Caribbean literature is the fact that the preferred dwelling places for mulatto women in U.S. African-American literature until well into the twentieth century are secluded cabins, hiding places with distinctly extrasocietal attributes (see, for instance, William Wells Brown's *Clotel; or, The President's Daughter* [1853]; James Weldon John-

son's *The Autobiography of an Ex-Coloured Man* [1912]; and Jean Toomer's *Cane* [1923]). In light of that, the Cuban mulata's overt, public sexuality may surprise, but one also has to bear in mind that her social and racial illegitimacy define that sexuality as residing outside of societal norms and standards. In this sense, female sexuality comes to signify not only transgression of but also exile from social conventions: The mulata's illicit sexuality is situated as much on the margins of society as the secluded spaces in which Brown and Johnson project their racially mixed female characters.

36. See Williams, "Images of Black and Mulatto Women," 123. Her claim that "the attitude of the speaker is underlain by the commonly held view in nineteenth-century Cuba that racial mixing was morally wrong" (124) is an inaccurate historical simplification.

37. Karen Newman, "And Wash the Ethiop White": Femininity and the Monstrous in *Othello*," 152.

38. Villaverde, *Cecilia Valdés*, 399. Sydney Gest's translation is as usual rather restrained. He writes: "But to fall head over heels in love with her [Isabel]—impossible." (*Cecilia Valdés, or Angel's Hill*, 347). See also Landaluze's painting of a slave kissing a bust (fig. 9), which I discuss in chapter 2.

39. See Edward Said's comments on Edward William Lane in *Orientalism*, 164.

40. To commend Muñoz del Monte for creating a "proud" mulata without "inferiority complexes," as Mónica Mansour does in her discussion of this poem, seems to me to miss the point entirely (*La poesía negrista*, 78–80). Even if this mulata shows no sense of inferiority, she, not unlike the Amazon figure in the *Iliad*, remains very much a figment of masculine imagination and as such subject to the subliminal mechanisms of social control operative within Cuban culture at the time (see Christine Froula, "The Daughter's Seduction: Sexual Violence and Literary History," 625–26). Williams's suggestion that Muñoz's is a "more complex racial image" is no less confused. Though she admits that the mulata's "superiority has a dubious character," due to the fact that the "controlling consciousness of the poem is that of the speaker and not that of the mulata," she does not consider that representational strategies are not just a matter of individual consciousness but are part of a larger, historically specific discursive setting ("Images of Black and Mulatto Women," 63–68).

41. Among the runaway slaves from the Gamboa estate appears a certain Cleto gangá (Villaverde, *Cecilia Valdés*, 432), possibly an allusion to Crespo's "black" incarnation. *Gangá* is not a proper last name but

indicates the *nación* or cultural affiliation, like Kalabar, Kongo, Mandinga, etc. For further details see Fernando Ortiz's "Los cabildos afrocubanos" in Miguel Barnet and Angel L. Fernández, eds., *Ensayos etnográficos*, 11–40, as well as the reproduction of Landaluze's painting of a "Diablito gangá" (fig. 17 in that edition).

42. It remains unclear who this second "escritor bozal" actually was. For details see Mary Cruz, *Creto Gangá*, 157–68.

43. Crespo's poems, especially "La mulata" and "El canto de bodas" (The wedding song), are frequently included in anthologies of *poesía negra* or *negrista* such as Emilio Ballagas's *Mapa de la poesía negra americana* (1946). See also Cruz, *Creto Gangá*, 16–17; Mónica Mansour, *La poesía negrista*, 80–82; and Williams, "Images of Black and Mulatto Women," 97–98. Noble even goes so far as to call Creto's poems precursors of Guillén's vernacular poetry in *Motivos de son* (*Literatura afrohispanoamericana*, 81).

44. "Crespo y Borbón was to Cuban letters as Landaluze was to painting" (Cruz, *Creto Gangá*, 16). It should be added that, perhaps ironically, neither Crespo nor Landaluze were separatists in their respective political orientations.

45. Bartolomé José Crespo y Borbón, "La mulata," in Morales, ed., *Poesía afroantillana y negrista*, 310–11. Quotations from this poem that follow in text are from the same source.

46. See Cruz, *Creto Gangá*, 80.

47. *Guarachas cubanas*, 65.

48. Villaverde, *Cecilia Valdés*, 367.

49. See especially Creto Gangá's "La serenata del negro Pascual a Francisca" (The black Pascual's serenade to Francisca), which anticipated the *décimas* of *Laborintos y trifucas de Canava* (1845), subtitled, in a style reminiscent of the North American slave narratives, "verarero hitória en vesa de lo que pasa en la macara yo Creto Gangá y negrita mio Frasica lucumí, cuento po yo memo" (true history of what happened to me, Creto Gangá, and my little Negress Francisca Lucumí, told by myself). See Cruz, *Creto Gangá*, 32–35.

50. This, however, has not prevented anthologizers from conflating the two. In Morales's *Poesía afroantillana y negrista*, for instance, "La mulata" is attributed to Creto Gangá in the same breath as the "Canto de bodas" from *Un ajiaco*.

51. Mansour, at the same time she points to the great similarity between the speech of Creto's characters and that of Spanish Golden Age playwrights such as Quevedo and Lope, commends him for interpreting blacks "from within" (*La poesía negrista*, 80, 82).

52. See Arrom, *Historia de la literatura dramática cubana*, 61. Though a relatively sketchy survey, this study includes a useful detailed bibliography.

53. Torroella's play *El mulato* was performed in 1870 in Mexico City (see Arrom, *Historio de la literatura dramática cubana*, 64).

54. See Robert C. Toll, *Blacking Up: The Minstrel Show in Nineteenth-Century America*, 65, 86.

55. Berndt Ostendorf, *Black Literature in White America*, 67.

56. See Robyn Wiegman, "Economies of the Body: Gendered Sites in *Robinson Crusoe* and *Roxanna*," 34.

Chapter 2

1. *Ajiaco*, a term later adopted by Fernando Ortiz as a "culinary emblem of Cuba," combines "the African name of an Amerindian condiment, the *ají* or green pepper, with a Spanish suffix *-aco*" (see Gustavo Pérez Firmat, *The Cuban Condition: Translation and Identity in Modern Cuba*, 24; also 25, 27–28). Pérez Firmat does not mention Creto Gangá's play in the context of his comments on Ortiz's use of *ajiaco* as an alternative to *crisol* (melting pot).

2. See Cruz, *Creto Gangá*, 62. On Cuban "vernacular theater" see also Odilio Urfé, "Music and Dance in Cuba," in Manuel Moreno Fraginals, ed., *Africa in Latin America*, 187–88. For an overview of blacks in nineteenth- and twentieth-century Cuban theater see Joseph R. Pereira, "The Black Presence in Cuban Theatre."

3. See the description of the character Malanga/Polanco in Villaverde, *Cecilia Valdés*, 454. See also Fernando Ortiz, "Los negros curros," in *Ensayos etnográficos*, 79–162. The same edition includes reproductions of several paintings and lithographs by Landaluze of Havana's *negros curros* and *mulatas curras* (see figs. 12, 12A, 12B, 12C, 13, 14). Moreno Fraginals notes that while Cuban slave owners systematically cultivated ethnic rivalries on the plantations, "in urban centers these ethnic differences were institutionalized. In Cuba . . . the colonial government . . . sponsored and legalized the formation of *cabildos* (lodge-type mutual aid associations on a strictly regional or tribal basis, with religious, social, and cultural overtones) where slaves could get together. With the same care displayed by plantation owners, urban authorities encouraged *cabildos* of various ethnic groups to form, making sure that none was sufficiently powerful to overshadow the rest. The urban *ca-*

bildos permitted the survival, with a relatively high degree of purity, of certain aspects of African culture, including language, which acquired ritual significance. In this respect, the Spanish slave policy differed radically from British colonialism in the Caribbean, which persecuted all African cultural manifestations" ("Cultural Contributions and Deculturation," in his *Africa in Latin America*, 8).

4. Unless otherwise indicated, page numbers cited in parentheses to Núñez Jiménez throughout this chapter refer to his 1985 volume, *Cuba en las marquillas cigarreras del siglo XIX*.

5. Adelaida De Juan notes that the Real Litografía (Royal Lithography Press) in Spain was not established until 1826 (*Pintura y grabado colonial cubano*, 28).

6. See Villaverde, *Cecilia Valdés*, 13.

7. See De Juan, *Pintura y grabado colonial cubano*, 29.

8. A distinction must be drawn between the lavishly designed cigar-box labels and the cigarette *marquillas*. The former, which tended to consist only of the *emblema*, or brand label, were intended specifically for export, whereas the latter, on which the *emblema* has been moved to the right to make room for the *escenas*, or topical prints, were for the domestic market (see De Juan, *Pintura cubana: Temas y variaciones* [1978], 29–30; also Ortiz, *Cuban Counterpoint: Tobacco and Sugar*, 44). It is also worth noting that in 1844 Cuba exported 1,934,899 boxes of cigars (at fifty cigars per box); in 1861, 8.8 million (see Núñez Jiménez, *Marquillas cigarreras cubanas*, 32). Núñez Jiménez provides no figures for domestic sales.

9. See also the section on "Las fábricas de tabaco y sus emblemas" in Núñez Jiménez, *Marquillas cigarreras cubanas* (133–36). There was even a *cigarrería* called La Africana, owned by Eduardo González and Son, whose *emblema* was the face of a mulatta. One label from La Africana is reproduced in the above volume (120).

10. See Núñez Jiménez, *Marquillas cigarreras cubanas*, for details on the different series.

11. See Antonio Benítez Rojo, "Nicolás Guillén and Sugar," 329–32, and *The Repeating Island*, 105–10. Núñez Jiménez claims that Luis Marquier's press began operations in 1874, which appears to be a typographical error (*Marquillas cigarreras cubanas*, 34). For a recent reproduction of some of Laplante's lithographs see *Los ingenios de Cuba*, ed. Leví Marrero.

12. See Dawn Ades et al., *Art In Latin America: The Modern Era, 1820–1980*, 66–67.

13. The Beinecke Rare Book Library at Yale University has a copy of *Isla de Cuba pintoresca,* but no publication date is indicated.

14. Relevant here is also Banta's "Images For Sale" in her *Imaging American Women,* 593–671.

15. ABC's *20/20* aired a segment on Cuba's tourist effort, produced by Janet Klein, on July 26, 1991. It included a relatively lengthy interview with Julio G. Oliveras, president of the Cuban Chamber of Commerce. Other televised reports on Cuba's courting European and American tourists have since followed.

16. Ortiz, *Cuban Counterpoint,* 44; Benítez Rojo, *The Repeating Island,* 114 [*Isla,* 108].

17. La Honradez had its own printing press (see Núñez Jiménez, 31–49).

18. See Moreno Fraginals, *El ingenio,* 1:57.

19. Ortiz, *Cuban Counterpoint,* 61, 46.

20. Ortiz first used this contrast in a 1936 essay entitled "Contraste económico del azúcar y el tabaco" (Ortiz quoted in Pérez Firmat, *The Cuban Condition,* 163n. 1).

21. Ibid. 17; Benítez Rojo, *The Repeating Island,* 157 [*Isla,* 158–59].

22. Ortiz, *Cuban Counterpoint,* 58, 23, 46, 22. By the second half of the nineteenth century, free blacks and mulatos far outnumbered whites in occupations such as tobacco farming. See also, for instance, the image of a nineteenth-century tobacco farm (with black workers) in Núñez Jiménez, 21.

23. Núñez Jiménez, 78–79, 81, and *Marquillas cigarreras cubanas,* 86–87.

24. Sidney Mintz, *Sweetness and Power,* 59.

25. Clive Bush's remark that "for Americans of the post-revolutionary period, machines of all kinds were felt to be better indications of national character than the conservative arts of literature and painting" is certainly relevant here, though with obvious qualifications, since the Cuban situation is by no means strictly analogous to that of the United States (*The Dream of Reason: American Consciousness and Cultural Achievement from Independence to the Civil War,* 83).

26. Villaverde, *Cecilia Valdés,* 416; my emphasis.

27. Compare Laplante's lithographs, especially his interiors of boiler houses, to those by W. Clark (*Ten Views of Antigua,* 1823) and R. Bridgens, which are reproduced in Mintz, *Sweetness and Power,* inserted between pages 78 and 79.

28. Villaverde, *Cecilia Valdés,* 423.

29. Ortiz, *Cuban Counterpoint,* 98.

30. Mintz notes that "the highly developed industrial character of the plantation system meant a curious 'modernization' or 'westernization' for the slaves—an aspect of their acculturation that has too often been missed because of the *deceptively rural, agrarian, and pseudo-manorial quality of slave-based plantation production* (*Caribbean Transformations,* 9; my emphasis).

31. Bush, *The Dream of Reason,* 303.

32. For a contrast see Landaluze's painting *La mulata* (fig. 8), which I discuss later in this chapter.

33. Margaret R. Miles, "The Virgin's One Bare Breast: Female Nudity and Religious Meaning in Tuscan Early Renaissance Culture" (in Susan Rubin Suleiman, *The Female Body in Western Culture,* 193–203), reads variations on the nursing Virgin as attempts to balance erotic with religious/moral messages.

34. See Roland Barthes, *Mythologies.*

35. See Naomi Schorr, *Reading in Detail: Aesthetics and the Feminine,* and Bush, *The Dream of Reason,* 109–11, 325, 344.

36. Two relevant reference points here are Dutch genre painting and its depiction of domestic, not heroic, subjects, as well as Hogarthian caricature (see Bush, *The Dream of Reason,* 95–109).

37. The translations of these particular captions are not mine, but are included in Núñez Jiménez's 1985 volume. This edition includes some rather perplexing English and French translations, especially of the captions. For instance, the specific reference in the phrase "Samba la culebra" to the ritual of killing a snake associated with the "Día de Reyes" is completely lost in the translation. It is also interesting that the background of this particular print shows a somewhat blurred but still recognizable image of the Virgin Mary. For details about the "Día de Reyes" see Fernando Ortiz, *La antigua fiesta afrocubana del "Día de Reyes,"* and Kutzinski, *Against the American Grain,* part 3.

38. Villaverde, *Cecilia Valdés,* trans. Sydney Gest, 50 [56]. See also Villaverde's remarks on the significance of the minuet at "colored balls" 57 [66].

39. See Toll, *Blacking Up,* chap. 1.

40. These three series are also reproduced in Núñez Jiménez, *Marquillas cigarreras cubanas* (53–57), with a special commentary devoted to them (42–43).

41. The first time we encounter the child Cecilia in Villaverde's novel, we are told that her life in the streets aroused suspicion, fear, and pity (see Villaverde, *Cecilia Valdés,* 34).

42. My discussion that follows is indebted to De Juan's "El negro en la pintura cubana del siglo XIX" (in her *Pintura cubana* [1978], 21–30). The 1978 and 1980 editions of her *Pintura cubana* are not identical; for one thing, the illustrations are different. For a discussion of the broader Hispanic American context see Ades, *Art in Latin America*, chapter 2: "Academies and History Painting in Latin America" (which, incidentally, does not even mention Cuba).

43. De Juan delineates two trends in nineteenth-century Cuban painting that dominated the scene from the founding of the Escuela de San Alejandro de La Habana in 1815 to the first quarter of the twentieth century: (*a*) costumbrista painting and its romantic representation of the Cuban landscape (for instance, Esteban Chartrand [1840–83], Valentín Sanz Carta [1850–98], and José Joaquín Tejada [1867–1943]); (*b*) the canonical "academic" painters of the French-Italian school, such as Juan Jorge Peoli (1825–93), Miguel Melero (1836–1907), Guillermo Collazo (1850–96), Armando Menocal (1861–1942), and Leopoldo Romañach (1862–1951). Something of an exception among the early canonical painters were Vicente Escobar (1757–1834), who is mentioned in *Cecilia Valdés*, and Nicolás de Escalera (1734–1804). Commissioned in the 1760s by the Catholic church to produce the paintings to be hung in the Santa María del Rosario Church, Escalera included a black slave in his homage to the count of Casa Bayona, clearly an accessory figure who mediates a social hierarchy. This was also the first and last time that such a figure appeared in his work. Another glimpse of such a figure, in this case female, is offered in José María Romero's *J. M. Ximeno con su criada y un carnerito*. (See *Pintura cubana* [1978], 20ff.)

44. Bush, *The Dream of Reason*, 107.

45. See Said's comments on nineteenth-century French and British travelers to the Orient and compare them to Benítez Rojo's remarks on travel narratives (*Orientalism*, chap. 2, pts. 3 and 4, and *The Repeating Island*, chap. 5). Although Said, unlike Roland Barthes, is not mentioned anywhere in Benítez Rojo's chapter on travelers in the Caribbean, some of Benítez Rojo's comments (and procedures) are undoubtedly indebted to *Orientalism* (compare especially *The Repeating Island*, 186–87, and *Orientalism*, 158).

46. Also worth mentioning here are Frederika Bremer, George W. Carleton, and James Gay Sawkins. Almost all of the "academic" painters were Cubans, while the major engravers were Europeans (see De Juan, *Pintura y grabado colonial cubano*, 49). See, for example, Garneray's *Vista de la Plaza de Armas*, a detail of which is reproduced in De Juan, *Pintura cubana* (1980), plate 8; and Sawkins's *Volante de La Habana*.

The most influential of these nineteenth-century traveler-artists were Jean Baptiste Debret, who traveled in Brazil from 1816 to 1824 (see his *Voyage pittoresque et historique au Brésil*, published in Paris between 1834 and 1839), and the Bavarian Johann Moritz Rugendas, who traveled in South American and Mexico from 1821 to 1847 (see, for instance, his *Voyage pittoresque dans le Brésil*, Paris, 1835). For further details see Ades, *Art in Latin America*, especially Stanton L. Catlin's "Traveller-Reporter Artists and the Empirical Tradition in Post-Independence Latin America."

47. The Ades volume notes that the style of the traveler-artists in Hispanic America was perhaps indebted to seventeenth-century Dutch genre painting (*Art in Latin America*, 47). It also points to the connection between traditions of caricature in Hispanic America and the costumbrismo in the work of Landaluze and others (85).

48. See De Juan, *Pintura y grabado colonial cubano*, 51–53.

49. Ortiz, "Dos 'diablitos' de Landaluze," n.p.

50. Bush, *The Dream of Reason*, 291–92. Landaluze's paintings and engravings are comparable, in many ways, to the work of Debret and Rugendas.

51. Bush, *The Dream of Reason*, 79. The Spanish physician and horticulturalist José Celestino Mutis was one of the most prominent disciples of Linnaeus at the time. He headed the Expedición Botánica of Nueva Granada (today's Colombia), which began in 1784. During the thirty-three years of this project, nearly 5,300 detailed studies of previously unknown species of flora were produced, which remained unpublished until 1950 (see Ades, *Art in Latin America*, 43–45).

52. Carol Armstrong, "Edgar Degas and the Representation of the Female Body," in Suleiman, ed., *The Female Body in Western Culture*, 229. On male participation in the representation of the female body see also John Berger, *Ways of Seeing*, 64ff.

53. Octavio Uzanne points out that "When a woman out walking meets one of her aspirants, and lets her Fan fall, it is an invitation. If she adds to it a glance of her eye, it is the first step in advance" (*The Fan*, 82–83). See also MacIver Percival, *The Fan Book*, chap. 9: "The Fan in Literature and History."

54. See the description of Josefa in Villaverde, *Cecilia Valdés*, 44.

55. De Juan, *Pintura y grabado colonial cubana*, 46.

56. Examples of similar paintings are those of Jean Domingue Ingres (*Odalisque with a Slave*, 1839), Jean Courbet (*Baigneuses*, 1853), and Edouard Manet (*Olympia*, 1863, and *Nana*, 1877), which are cited and reproduced in Sander L. Gilman, "Black Bodies, White Bodies: Toward

an Iconography of Female Sexuality in Late Nineteenth-Century Art, Medicine, and Literature."

57. See Gilman, "Black Bodies, White Bodies," 209.

58. Villaverde, *Cecilia Valdés,* 34; my emphases.

59. Richard Jackson comments briefly on Villaverde's preoccupation with physical description (*The Black Image in Latin American Literature,* 27–30). See also Luis, who claims that "*Cecilia Valdés* represents a rejection of the Romanticism and *Costumbrismo* . . . of his early works in favor of a more realistic expression of Cuban problems" (*Literary Bondage,* 103–4). Luis takes Villaverde's prologue and the fact that many of the characters in *Cecilia Valdés* are in fact historical personalities as evidence of the novel's "accuracy" without examining the concept of nineteenth-century literary realism more closely.

60. Villaverde, *Cecilia Valdés,* 33. Gest translates "voluptuosidad" more positively (or neutrally?) as "creative instinct" (28).

61. See Gilman's comments on the 1810 London exhibition of Sarah Bartman, the so-called Hottentot Venus, in his "Black Bodies, White Bodies." Also useful are Helena Michie's comments on the representational dressing of women's bodies in *The Flesh Made Word: Female Figures and Women's Bodies,* 76–78, which follow Roland Barthes's notion that clothing makes the human body "significant" in the sense of making it "a sign or carrier of signs" ("Encore le corps," 647). In contrast to Barthes, Julia Kristeva contends that "significance is inherent in the human body" (*The Power and the Horror,* 10).

62. See Gilman, "Black Bodies, White Bodies," 226.

63. Relevant here is also the work of two Frenchmen, Etienne and Isidore Saint-Hilaire, on teratology, which Said calls a form of "Romantic biology." In their works, *Philosophie anatomique: Des monstruosités humaines* (Paris, 1822) and *Histoire générale et particulière des anomalies de l'organisation chez l'homme et les animaux* . . . (Paris, 1832–36), they see physiological aberrations as the result of internal species degradation (see Said, *Orientalism,* 144, 339 n. 54. The mulata's skin color and other "negroid" features are similarly classified as aberrations or anomalies.

64. Henry Hughes, a major apologist for slavery in the antebellum North American South, quoted in Mary Dearborn, *Pocahontas's Daughters,* 150.

65. All quotations from Ezponda are from De Juan, *Pintura y grabado colonial cubana,* 58–59. I was unable to locate a copy of Ezponda's text itself anywhere in the United States. Compare also the description of the mulata Camila in Antonio Zambrana's *El negro Francisco,* 47.

66. Villaverde, *Cecilia Valdés,* 62.

67. De Juan notes that the only exceptions to the former are Landa-luze's depictions of the mayoral, or overseer, and the cimarrón, or run-away slave (see *Pintura y grabado colonial cubana,* 46, 20). Bush remarks that the depiction of people at leisure and not at work is a "desire inher-ent in an essentially commercial world" (*The Dream of Reason,* 348).

68. Compare *La mulata* to the painting *El costeño* (The coast dweller) by the Mexican Manuel Arrieta, which is reproduced in Ades, *Art in Latin America,* 89 (figure 3.88).

69. Several variations on this topic—the black man's mythic desire for white women—appear on the *marquillas,* most notably in the allegor-ical drawings that frame the lithographs in La Honradez's "Prophetic Al-manac for the Year 1866" (see fig. 3). They alternate between images of two half-naked, savage-looking black men with spears and a bottle of rum, chasing after a buxom black woman who mocks their failure to catch her by making faces at them, and a scene in which a half-clad male slave, again with exaggerated negroid, even animalistic, features, is shown standing on the shoulders of another, deviously grinning, black. The former's head is stuck through an opening in a brick wall that pro-tects an idyllic setting in which four fair-skinned maidens lounge around a swan pond. In the background on the upper left corner of this frame we see the sketchy figure of the master or overseer running toward his disobedient slaves, ready to give them a lick with his raised stick. See also the black vendor in "Dulce con dulce, dulce de aquello" (Sweets, any-one?) (Núñez Jiménez, 50–60, 88).

70. Compare Sylvia Molloy's incisive comments on the ex-slave Manzano's descriptions of his life as a house slave ("From Serf to Self: The Autobiography of Juan Francisco Manzano," 408–9). It is also worth mentioning that Villaverde in fact employs a similar strategy when he compares the "nappy" hair of the mulato tailor Uribe to Medusa's snakes (*Cecilia Valdés,* 166).

71. Villaverde, *Cecilia Valdés,* 174.

72. Landaluze's portrait was part of a *marquilla* series by González y Llaguno (formerly Llaguno y Compañía) entitled "Galería literaria," where he appears in the company of José Fornaris, Victoriano Betan-court, and other Cuban writers (Núñez Jiménez, 128).

73. See De Juan, *Pintura cubana,* 34; also 29–30, esp. n. 3, in the 1974 edition. Núñez Jiménez (or more accurately, Alberto Arraiza and Francisco Gutiérrez Contreras, who produced the texts in *Marquillas ci-garreras cubanas*) identifies Landaluze but mentions nothing about the history of this *emblema* (134).

74. The reference here is presumably to the readers employed in the tobacco factories to divert the workers.

75. A familiar synecdoche for degeneracy, the drinking of alcohol appears most notably in the July print of La Honradez's "Prophetic Almanac for the Year 1866" (56) and in print 10 ("Noche buena") from "Vida y muerte de la mulata" (14).

76. Some of Villaverde's characters show a similar predilection for such pearls of popular wisdom as "por donde salta la madre salta la hija" (like mother like daughter) (*Cecilia Valdés*, 398), which is a variation on the Cuban proverb "no hay tamarindo dulce ni mulata señorita" (there is no more a sweet tamarind fruit than there is a virgin mulata), quoted in Martínez-Alier, *Marriage, Class, and Colour in Nineteenth-Century Cuba* (xv).

77. The black female servant appears in an even more familiar role in another La Honradez series, titled "El campo de Cuba" (61–64), as well as in the print "Naranja de China bueno" from one of the Guilló *marquillas* (101).

78. Prints 8 and 10 would aptly illustrate Villaverde's descriptions of Mercedes Ayala's party (*Cecilia Valdés*, part 1, chapters 5 and 6).

79. The different frames would suggest that these prints were part of different series, but there is no evidence that Para Usted ran more than one series under the same title.

80. Villaverde, *Cecilia Valdés*, 129.

81. See Michel Foucault, *Discipline and Punish: The Birth of the Prison*.

82. See Karen Newman's comments on blackness as disease in "And Wash the Ethiop White": Femininity and the Monstrous in *Othello*," 146–47 and 159 n. 19.

83. Paul Brown, "'This thing of darkness I acknowledge mine': *The Tempest* and the Discourse of Colonialism," 59.

84. Villaverde, *Cecilia Valdés*, 507. Luis reads María de Regla as a reference to the black Virgen de Regla (see *Literary Bondage*, 116).

Chapter 3

1. Villaverde, *Cecilia Valdés*, 365. Gest renders "educación" as "good breeding" (316).

2. Seven of the nine figures Villaverde mentions in this passage, including the tailor Francisco Uribe, Plácido, and Manzano, were actually

implicated in La Escalera. Villaverde gets ahead of the chronology of his novel here: *Cecilia Valdés,* as William Luis points out, is set between 1812, the year of Cecilia's birth and also the year of the Aponte Conspiracy, and 1832 (see *Literary Bondage,* 100, 112–15).

3. Villaverde, *Cecilia Valdés,* 365–66. Plácido is mentioned once before in the novel (129). See also Gest's translation, 175 n. 5.

4. See Paquette, *Sugar Is Made with Blood,* 234.

5. Sylvia Molloy, in her discussion of "the nodules of resistance in Manzano's story," points out that this self-presentation, as well as other passages relating directly to Manzano's person, were carefully suppressed in Madden's translation (1840). Criticizing the "notion that the impure text [Manzano's] must be replaced by a clean (white?) version for it to be readable," Molloy also comments on Ivan Schulman's modernized Spanish edition of Manzano's text (1975) and on Edward Mullen's reproduction of Madden's translation (1981) ("From Serf to Self," 404–5, 407, 414, 417). Like Molloy, Netchinsky is critical especially of the "sanitized" Schulman edition (see "Engendering a Cuban Literature"). See also, Luis, *Literary Bondage,* 90–100.

6. Molloy, "From Serf to Self," 414–15. See also González Echevarría's comments on "exaggerated similarity" (*Alejo Carpentier: The Pilgrim at Home,* 30).

7. Juan Francisco Manzano, "La música," in Ramón Guirao, ed., *Orbita de la poesía afrocubana, 1928–37,* 47–48; my emphasis.

8. Manzano, "Ilusiones," in Guirao, ed., *Orbita,* 38. Guirao includes this poem, along with several others by Manzano, as a "precursor" text of Afro-Cubanism.

9. While Williams's argument that this passage "demonstrates [Manzano's] complete submission to the hegemony of the dominant mode of perception" is plausible, her reading of this figure as "evidently a white woman" seems to me unsubstantiated. The woman in question here is Delia, who is elsewhere (for instance, in "La música") identified as a *parda* or brown-skinned woman (see "Images of Black and Mulatto Women in Spanish Caribbean Poetry," 59).

10. Manzano, "La musica," in Guirao, ed., *Orbita,* 47.

11. See Molloy, "From Serf to Self," 409, as well as her remarks there on the opening of Manzano's *Autobiografía* (393–94).

12. See Richard Jackson's disparaging comments on the work of other nineteenth-century black and mulato poets in Hispanic America in his *The Black Image in Latin American Literature.* Mintz perceptively comments that some cross-cultural formations have obviously been re-

garded as more interesting than others (*Caribbean Transformations*, 227).

13. At the height of his literary career (1836 to 1844), Plácido was also employed as official poet by the daily *La Aurora de Matanzas* as well as contributing regularly to the triweekly *El Eco de Villa-Clara*. At the same time, he was much in demand as a writer of occasional verse, to him a distasteful chore that brought him under attack for prostituting his poetic talent. For further details, see Frederick S. Stimson, *Cuba's Romantic Poet: The Story of Plácido*, 60–69.

14. Plácido's execution quickly became a cause célèbre not only in Hispanic America but also in Europe and the United States (see Stimson, *Cuba's Romantic Poet*, 89–102). For further information see García Garófala Mesa, *Plácido, poeta y mártir* (1938); Leopoldo Horrego Estuch, *Plácido, el poeta infortunado* (1960); Jorge Casals, *Plácido como poeta cubano* (1944); and José Antonio Portuondo, "Miseria y soledad de Plácido, el mulato" (1981). Attempts at making Plácido either into a symbol of black liberation or into a heroic martyr for Cuban sedition appear in many of the early biographical sketches, both in English and in Spanish, as well as in two fictionalized works: Joaquín de Lemoine's novel *El mulato Plácido* (Santiago de Chile, 1875) and Diego Vicente Tejera's one-act play *La muerte de Plácido* (Plácido's Death) (New York, 1875). Cirilo Villaverde's melodramatic novel *La peineta calada* (The pierced comb), which was serialized in *El Faro Industrial de la Habana* in February–March 1843, is based on Plácido's life only to the extent that its protagonist Andrés is a combmaker. In the United States, Martin R. Delaney fictionalized the arguments in favor of Plácido's revolutionary activities in his 1861 novel *Blake; or The Huts of America*.

15. Salvador Bueno, among others, has called Plácido "a superficial poet who lacks inner concentration, who cannot express his own individuality" (*Historia de la literatura cubana*, 104). Pedro Barreda, like most other critics, argues that a "black point of view" is present only in the "Epigrama satírico" (*The Black Protagonist in the Cuban Novel*, 17). Others have acknowledged Plácido as a precursor of the Afro-Antillean movement (see Instituto de Literatura y Lingüística de la Academia de Ciencias de Cuba, eds., *Perfil histórico de las letras cubanas*, 213–14; Ben Fredric Carruthers, "The Life, Work, and Death of Plácido," 14; and Richard Jackson, *Black Writers in Latin America*, 36–44).

16. James Weldon Johnson, *The Book of American Negro Poetry*, 37.

17. Ibid., 39–40.

18. The best known among Plácido's "prison poems" are: "Plegaria a Dios" (Prayer to God), "A la fatalidad" (To fate), "Despedida a mi madre" (Farewell to my Mother), "A la justicia" (To justice), and "Adios a mi lira" (Farewell to my lyre), all first published in Madrid in 1844. "Plegaria a Dios," whose authorship has been disputed, and "Despedida a mi madre" are the two poems most frequently translated into English (see Stimson, *Cuba's Romantic Poet*, 126–38). On translations into English and French see also Itzhak Bar-Lewaw, *Plácido: Vida y obra*, 152–67). Stimson and others have argued that Plácido was not a political poet but "foremost . . . a poet of occasion and of the exotic and fanciful," whose "originality and inherent genius" is most evident in the "blossom poems," "La flor de la piña" (The pineapple flower), "La flor del café" (The coffee flower), "La flor de la cera" (The wax flower), and, of course, "La flor de la caña" (The sugarcane blossom) (see Stimson, *Cuba's Romantic Poet*, 116, 143–45; also Stimson and Humberto E. Robles, eds., *Los poemas más representativos de Plácido*, 21–23). Casals (*Plácido como poeta cubano*, 37) and Bar-Lewaw (*Plácido*, 105–9) also praise the "blossom poems."

19. See, for instance, Sebastián Alfredo de Morales, ed., *Plácido, Poesías completas*, xxxii, and Antonio Bachiller y Morales, "Plácido." See also Instituto de Literatura y Lingüística . . . , eds., *Perfil histórico de las letras cubanas*, 211, and Bar-Lewaw, *Plácido*, 70–87. Carruthers argues that Plácido was probably not guilty of conspiracy but was certainly a sympathizer, and Stimson concludes, all historical evidence notwithstanding, that since Plácido was reputed not to have been a man of action, his involvement in this or any other conspiracy must be considered unlikely. For additional details and other opinions see José de Jesús Márquez, *Plácido y los conspiradores de 1844* (1894); Vidal Morales y Morales, *Iniciadores y primeros mártires de la Revolución cubana* (1901), 147–77; Casals, *Plácido como poeta cubano*. The most thorough research into the Escalera Conspiracy to date has been conducted by Paquette, who surveys the various theories concerning Plácido's revolutionary activities, or lack thereof, in his introduction to *Sugar Is Made with Blood* (3–26). Paquette argues persuasively that La Escalera "was not one 'Conspiracy' but several conspiracies, each many years in gestation; each was volatile, each had its own distinct character, but they converged" (248–49). Finding the evidence of Plácido's relation to La Escalera inconclusive, he nevertheless suggests that "Plácido may not have led the Conspiracy of La Escalera or any other project, but between the two extremes are numerous other possibilities" (257).

20. The *siboneístas* glorified Cuba's extinct native populations. Jorge

Castellanos, although he sees Plácido as "a representative of agrarian utopianism, steeped in Rousseau," also shows quite convincingly that Plácido, though not exactly a sociologist, was an astute observer of social processes and that, in essence, he was a poet "profoundly preoccupied with politics" (see *Plácido: Poeta social y político,* especially chapters 1 and 2).

21. Accounts vary, but it seems that Plácido was first arrested in Havana in 1834 for "La sombra de Padilla," again in 1840 and 1843 for being suspected of antislavery activities because of his frequent trips from Matanzas to Villa Clara (now Santa Clara)—at the time one of the centers of sugar production with a large slave population—and finally in January of 1844 (see Castellanos, *Plácido,* 97).

22. De Morales, ed., *Plácido, Poesías completas,* 482. This is as complete an edition as exists to date. "Que se lo cuente a su abuela" is not included in the first substantial collection of Plácido's poems, F. J. Vingut's third edition of *Poesías de Plácido* (1857).

23. See also Villaverde, *Cecilia Valdés,* 174. More contemporary literary versions of this topic are the poem "¿Y tu agüela, a'onde ejtá?" ("And your grandma, where is she"?) by the Puerto Rican poet Fortunato Vizcarrondo (from *Dinga y mandinga* [1942], 77), as well as the plays *Vejigantes* (Masquerades) (1958) and *La carreta* (The cart) by his fellow-countrymen Francisco Arriví and René Marqués, respectively. The illusion of a "pure" Hispanic genealogy is an explicit target in the Afro-Panamanian writer Cubena's novel *Chombo* (1981). By far the most vicious parody of the theme of the hidden black grandmother is included in Reinaldo Arenas's *Graveyard of the Angels,* chapter 19.

24. Martínez-Alier, *Marriage, Class, and Colour in Nineteenth-Century Cuba,* 74.

25. According to Savaldor Arias, "La flor de la caña" was first published in 1847 (*Poesías escogidas,* ed. Aries, 137). The "authoritative" version of this poem is believed to be the one printed in the De Morales edition, *Plácido: Poesías completas* (430–32). It appears, however, that the most frequently reprinted version of the poem appeared in Vingut's edition, *Poesías de Plácido* (1854–57). I am quoting from the third (1957) Vingut edition here and subsequently in the text. (1:40–44). See also the modernized version in Stimson and Robles, eds., *Los poemas más representativos de Plácido,* which gives some textual variations (36–39).

26. Williams argues that "the race of the woman whose eyes inspire the poet's creation is not clearly identifiable," but she does not pursue this point ("Images of Black and Mulatto Women," 59). Hector Pedro

Blomberg is the only one who calls the female figure in "La flor de la caña" a mulata ("La negra y la mulata en la poesía americana," 9). The only anthology of Afro-Antillean poetry that includes "Los ojos de mi morena" is Morales's *Poesía afroantillana y negrista*, 308–9.

27. Another *trigueña* appears in Plácido's "La flor del café." For historical definitions and usage of the term *trigueño/a* (translatable as wheat-brown, darkish, tawny), see Jack D. Forbes, *Black Africans and Native Americans: Color, Race, and Caste in the Evolution of Red-Black Peoples* (1988), 104, 106. Forbes also notes that modern Portuguese dictionaries often define a *mulato* as a person of "trigueiro" color (170). See also Julia De Burgos's "Ay, ay, ay de la grifa negra" (The lament of the nappy-haired black woman), which uses *trigueña* instead of *mulata*: "que a mi negra raza huye/y con la blanca corre a ser trigueña" (if only I could flee from my black race/and run together with the white race to become a *trigueña*) (in Morales, *Poesía afroantillana y negrista*, 160), and Martínez-Alier, *Marriage, Class, and Color*, 72.

28. Low economic and/or occupational status played a significant role in this (see Martínez-Alier, *Marriage, Class, and Colour*, 24).

29. Villaverde, *Cecilia Valdés*, 414, 421.

30. *Aphrodite* also has the same Greek root as *Africa* (see Benítez Rojo, *The Repeating Island*, 15–16 [*Isla*, xx-xxi]. On the cult of the Virgin Mary, who is part of Benítez Rojo's "supersyncretism," see Julia Kristeva, "Stabat Mater," in Suleiman, ed., *The Female Body in Western Culture*.

31. See Ortiz, *Cuban Counterpoint*, 91. The tobacco flower would come to be associated with precolonial freedom on the one hand and free (white) labor on the other.

32. Moreno Fraginals, *El ingenio*, 3:137. See also my comments on the classification of colored women in terms of different grades of refined sugar in chapter 2. Mintz comments on whiteness as evidence of the refined sugar's purity: "The idea that the finest and purest sucrose would also be the whitest is probably a symbolically potent aspect of sugar's early European history; but the fact that sucrose can be prepared in many usable forms [and many colors] is also significant" (*Sweetness and Power*, 22).

33. See Moreno Fraginals, *El ingenio*, 1:60–61.

34. The importance of sugar as the primary economic foundation of Cuban (and Caribbean) culture and society is well known and has been studied in detail by historians such as Ramiro Guerra (*Azúcar y población en las Antillas*, 1927), Moreno Fraginals (*El ingenio*), and Mintz (*Sweetness and Power*). Not so well known are the "scientific" works on

sugar production, among others those by José Ricardo O'Farrill (1793), Antonio Morejón y Gato (1797), José Martínez de Campos (1797), and, most notably, Francisco de Arango y Parreño's *Discurso sobre la agricultura de La Habana y medios de fomentarla* (Discourse on Havana's agriculture and on ways of developing it) (1792). In 1795 Fray José María Peñalver proposed to the Sociedad Patriótica his project of a *Diccionario provincial de voces cubanas* that would include the new technical terminology. The founding of *El Papel Periodico de La Habana* was yet another by-product of this overwhelming interest in sugar that promoted by the first "dance of the millions" in the 1790s, also occasioned a fascinating reinterpretation of the past: Everything prior to the British occupation of Havana (1761–63), which was synonymous with free trade, was suddenly regarded as *tiempos primitivos,* as pre-historical. Cuban history became the history of sugar and of free trade. That history began with an interruption of Spanish colonial rule that, though temporary, had lasting economic and ideological effects: It was a symbolic cutting of the umbilical cord, which amounted to nothing less than a denial of the island's connections with Spain. For details see Moreno Fraginals, *El ingenio,* 1:73, 77, 127; Benítez Rojo, "Azúcar/poder/literatura" and *The Repeating Island.*

35. Being sent to the sugar mill was a familiar punishment for disobedient slaves. See, for instance, José Luciano Franco, ed., *Autobiografía, cartas y versos de Juan Fco. Manzano,* 55.

36. Benítez Rojo argues that since "all order, all power, implies by necessity a form of *resistance,*" the evolving discourse of sugar was "accompanied by a discourse that resists being enunciated or reported by it. This discourse begins to organize itself, at the end of the eighteenth century, in the form of a series of legal-economic texts attempting to limit or weaken the dense concentration of power accumulated by the Havana saccharocracy" ("Nicolás Guillén and Sugar," 333; see also *The Repeating Island,* 116). The first significant instance of this counterdiscourse is the 1805 *Informe* (Report) written by the Camagüeyan Ignacio Zarragoitia y Jauregui to the Royal Consulate: "The people of the island of Cuba are not represented, nor are they made up of, the residents of and around Havana, Trinidad, or Matanzas. The Cuban people are composed of all of the island's inhabitants, and these same people made up of all the inhabitants ought not but to form a single family, and among the members of that family ought to be distributed the good and the bad, without distinction or privilege" (quoted in Moreno Fraginals, *El ingenio,* 1:147). Moreno Fraginals claims that this is the first document to voice the concept of Cubanness, and of a national identity in conflict with

the parochial interests of the sugar industry (*El ingenio,* 1:147; see also Benítez Rojo, "Azúcar/poder/literatura," 198–200). It is perhaps ironic that those economic interests contributed crucially to the unification of the island that, until the end of the eighteenth century, had consisted of distinct, autonomous social and political nuclei. According to Moreno Fraginals, the single most important factor in the development of a concrete notion of national unity was railroad construction, for which large numbers of blacks, especially recaptured cimarrones, were employed (see *El ingenio,* 1:148, 289). In contrast to Ortiz, Moreno Fraginals argues that it was railroads, not the steam engine, that drastically altered the conditions of sugar production in Cuba and marked the beginning of an industrial revolution (see *Cuban Counterpoint,* 49, and *El ingenio,* 1:151).

37. Nicolás Guillén, "Mi patria," in his *Obra poética, 1920–1972,* 1:225.

38. Ortiz, *Cuban Counterpoint,* 58.

39. See Sherry Ortner's provocative and problematic essay "Is Female to Male as Nature Is to Culture?" in Michele Zimbalist Rosaldo and Louise Lamphere, eds., *Woman, Culture, and Society,* and the various responses to it in Carol P. MacCormack and Marilyn Strathern, eds., *Nature, Culture, and Gender.* See also, Roy Wagner, *The Invention of Culture,* chapter 6.

40. Or, as Villaverde put it, "they crystallized the sugarcane juice with the blood of millions of slaves" (*Cecilia Valdés,* 408). See also Moreno Fraginals, *El ingenio,* 1:95.

41. Agustín Acosta, *La zafra: Poema de combate,* 103. Moreno Fraginals explains this "tragic" contradiction in the saccharocracy's ideology as follows: Since sugar required slave labor, it preempted the development of a genuine bourgeois concept of liberty in nineteenth-century Cuba; emancipation would have meant the decline of sugar and of the social class connected with it. The first of the great ideological documents of the sugar industry, *La representación de la ciudad de La Habana a las cortes españoles* (The representation of the city of Havana in the Spanish courts) (1791), already signaled a severe crisis in this class's political values, stemming from the economic need to renounce all liberties within the realm of sugar production. This amounted to sacrificing the nation to the plantation. The uneasy compromise resulting from this crisis was the "reformismo con esclavitud" (reformism with slavery) that characterizes most of the period's antislavery treatises (*El ingenio,* 1:128–30).

42. Villaverde, *Cecilia Valdés,* 413; my emphasis.

43. *Petaca,* or in this case the diminutive *petaquilla,* means both to-

bacco case and cigar or cigarette case. Netchinsky notes in her discussion of Gómez de Avellaneda's *Sab* that the trope of concealment, of wrapping, is of course archetypically feminine ("Engendering a Cuban Literature," 241–42).

44. See Netchinsky's comments on Sab's letter as a cult object ("Engendering a Cuban Literature," 246–47).

45. See, for instance, Villaverde, *Cecilia Valdés,* 355.

Chapter 4

1. See Pedro Barreda, *The Black Protagonist in the Cuban Novel.* Other examples of this "humanistic" approach to *poesía negra* on the one hand and to Afro-Hispanic American fiction on the other are Williams's "Images of Black and Mulatto Women in Spanish Caribbean Poetry," Richard Jackson's *Black Literature and Humanism in Latin América,* and Shirley M. Jackson, *La novela negrista en Hispanoamérica.*

2. Barreda, who discusses all three novels, criticizes the "flatness" and "falseness" of Sofía's character (*The Black Protagonist in the Cuban Novel,* 112–13).

3. *Sofía* is the first volume of "Cosas de mi tierra" (My country's affairs), the projected series of which Morúa completed only one other novel, *La familia Unzúazu* (1901), before his death in 1910.

4. Morúa's mother, Inés, was a slave of the Delgado family, who later freed her; his father, Francisco, was from Bizcaya (see Alvarez García's introduction to *Sofía,* viii). In 1879 Morúa founded the journal *El Pueblo* in his native Matanzas and also wrote for *La Luz.* In Havana, he contributed regularly to the black paper *El Ciudadano,* which was edited by Manuel García Albuquerque (also known as El Mandinga—Siriaco Mandinga?). For further biographical information see Horrego Estuch, *Martín Morúa Delgado, vida y mensaje,* and Aleyda T. Portuondo, *Vigencia política y literaria de Martín Morúa Delgado.*

5. Martín Morúa Delgado, "Las novelas del Sr. Villaverde," in *Obras completas,* vol. 5: *Impresiones literarias y otras páginas,* 30, 42.

6. Ibid., 25, 32, 36, 49. Morúa extends some of his charges beyond the specifics of *Cecilia Valdés.* For instance, he writes that "because it is opposed to the perfection of art, I detest this literary aberration called 'the historical novel'—an ambiguous, amphibious creation that ends up being neither novel nor history, and at the most, in its preciosity, serves only as a transparent screen that half obscures the insufficient imagination of those who write it" (30–31). On Morúa's own no-less-problem-

atic representations of Afro-Cuban vernacular see Onyria Herrera McElroy, "Martín Morúa Delgado, precursor del afro-cubanismo," 21–22.

7. Morúa Delgado, "Las novelas," 25, 32–33.

8. For details on Morúa's changing political beliefs and affiliations, see Luis, *Literary Bondage,* 150, 155–59; the text of the bill itself is quoted on 159. For further details see Richard Jackson, *Black Writers in Latin America,* 45–46.

9. See Richard Jackson, "Slavery, Racism, and Autobiography in Two Early Black Writers: Juan Francisco Manzano and Martín Morúa Delgado," in Luis, ed., *Voices from Under,* 61. For other discussions of Villaverde and Morúa see Luis, *Literary Bondage,* 141–48, and Herrera McElroy, "Martín Morúa Delgado," 19–20. Luis does not mention Morúa's ideological objections to *Cecilia Valdés.*

10. Morúa Delgado, *Sofía,* 4. All subsequent page references to this edition will appear in textual parentheses.

11. Luis comments on Morúa's critical attitude toward his black characters in *Sofía* (see *Literary Bondage,* 148).

12. See Richard Jackson, "Slavery, Racism, and Autobiography," in Luis, *Voices from Under,* 61, and Luis, *Literary Bondage,* 150–51, 159–61.

13. Jackson, *Black Writers in Latin America,* 47. In "Slavery, Racism, and Autobiography," Jackson refers to the "literary blackness" of Morúa's novels (in Luis, *Voices from Under,* 62). See also Herrera McElroy, "Martín Morúa Delgado," 21, and chapter 5. Herrera McElroy's view of Morúa as a precursor of Afro-Cubanism, which is based largely on the material about the religious organization of the ñáñigos included in *La familia Unzúazu,* is debatable. For a different reading see Luis, *Literary Bondage,* 160.

14. It appears to be a common misconception that, in the case of black characters, "psychological complexity" equals "sympathetic" portrayal. Along those lines, it could easily be argued, for instance, that Villaverde's nonwhite characters are more "sympathetic" than Morúa's (though Morúa himself would clearly have disagreed with this assessment). Worth considering in this context is Luis's categorical statement that "*Any* sympathetic presentation of blacks in nineteenth-century Cuban literature represents a counter-discourse to power and is subversive to a Western form of rule" (*Literary Bondage,* 2).

15. Morúa Delgado, "Las novelas," 40.

16. Compare this to George Washington Cable's *The Flower of the Chapdelaines* (1918), which features the character Fortune, a white girl

mistakenly sold into slavery. Like Sofía, Fortune assumes that she has black blood.

17. Barreda, *The Black Protagonist in the Cuban Novel,* 110–11.

18. Morúa's comments on the extent to which racial bias is internalized even by its victims prefigures the argument that was presented much later by O. Mannoni in *Prospero and Caliban: The Psychology of Colonization* (1950), the book that so infuriated Frantz Fanon.

19. Barreda calls Morúa "the most modern in the strict sense of the term, for he introduces the narrative techniques of the naturalist school" (*The Black Protagonist in the Cuban Novel,* 85). See also Jackson, *Black Writers in Latin America,* 47. Barreda further suggests that *Sofía* is indebted to Zola's *Les Rougeon-Macquart* (1871), which, interestingly enough, is conspicuously missing from among the novels Morúa himself mentions in "Las novelas." What Morúa admires about Zola is "the rigorous method with which he dissects and distributes everything, *putting each thing in its place.* . . . But he displays everything in an exaggerated nakedness, accumulating all the microcosmic morbidities of Parisian society, wresting from his characters the protective cloaks in order to expose the putrefaction of all systems in their most vile manifestations. And he devotes the same minute attention to the most notable artifacts and the most insignificant gadgets alike" ("Las novelas," 20).

20. Morúa was born in Matanzas in 1857.

21. Barreda on the other hand reads *trigueña* as an unambiguous racial signifier (*The Black Protagonist in the Cuban Novel,* 112).

22. Unlike Cecilia Valdés, for instance, or "la china" Teodora—*china* refers to her Afro-Asian descent—Sofía refuses invitations to colored dances: the "bachitas" or "jaranitas de arroz con frijoles" frequented by Federico (4, 87). She does not, in other words, attempt to attract a white lover who would buy her freedom, perhaps even marry her "in secret." Morúa chides Villaverde for using *cuna* instead of *bacha* when referring to those dances (see "Las novelas," 39–40).

23. The illiteracy rate among Cuba's nonwhite population was 72 percent in 1899. It was probably even higher in the early 1890s (see Aguilar's Introduction to *Sofía,* 23). *Sofía*'s publication was financially supported by a white patron, Raimundo Cabrera, who also sponsored Morúa's membership in the famous Sociedad Económica de Amigos del País (see Aleyda Portuondo, *Vigencia política y literaria de Martín Morúa Delgado,* 12).

24. The same character is earlier named Leonardo Bonanza, most likely in reference to Villaverde's Leonardo Gamboa.

25. Hortense Spillers's comments, though referring to a slightly different context, are relevant here: "The denied genetic link becomes the chief strategy of an undenied ownership, as if the interrogation into the father's identity—the blank space where his proper name will fit—were answered by the fact, *de jure* of a material possession. 'And this is done,' [Frederick] Douglass asserts, 'too obviously to administer to the [masters'] own lusts, and make a gratification of their wicked desires profitable as well as pleasurable" ("Mama's Baby, Papa's Maybe: An American Grammar Book," 76).

26. Spillers writes that "the term 'mulatto/a'. . . . becomes a displacement for a proper name, an instance of the 'paradox of the negative'" ("Notes on an Alternative Model—Neither/Nor," 169).

27. Criticizing Sofía's "external dramatization," Barreda claims, to my mind erroneously, that "it is as if the author assumed the view of her that the other characters have" (*The Black Protagonist in the Cuban Novel*, 113).

28. "The deceits of a culture are mirrored on the mulatto/a's face," Spillers comments, though only with reference to the problem of paternity ("Notes on an Alternative Model," 167).

29. Paul Brown, "'This thing of darkness I acknowledge mine,'" 59.

30. This particular scene most decisively belies Barreda's contention that Morúa "reduced the imaginative element to a minimum, giving great importance to observation" (*The Black Protagonist in the Cuban Novel*, 110). This is also a curious claim to make in light of the fact that Morúa accuses Villaverde of a lack of imagination!

31. Morúa Delgado, "Las novelas," 44. Morúa introduces Federico as a character whose "stay at the Spanish Court and in the 'capital of the world' had added to his title of lawyer a mental illness that manifested itself in the form of the most ridiculous pretentions and of the most inflated opinion about his intellectual abilities and political ideas" (31).

32. Though he mentions Morúa's "scientistic writing," his "naturalist proclivity," in connection with the character of Federico and the snippets of medical discourse offered in the context of Sofía's complicated pregnancy, Barreda makes no reference to this important passage (see *The Black Protagonist in the Cuban Novel*, 110, 115).

33. The conspiracy of La Escalera derived its name from this notorious practice.

34. See also Acosta's poetic version of these tortures in "Los ingenios antiguos."

Después las curas en la enfermería:
sal y vinagre sobre las heridas;
fricciones mercuriales en las úlceras viejas,
y un poco de alimento; el necesario
para salvar la vida desde el punto
de vista utilitario; porque el negro
era una cosa propiedad del amo,
y una pérdida real si aquel moría . . .

Afterwards the cures in the infirmary:
salt and vinegar on the wounds;
mercurial throbbing in the old ulcers,
and a bit of food; just enough
to save the life from a practical
standpoint; because the black
is a piece of property for the master,
and a real loss if it were to die . . .

(La zafra, 66)

35. For a translation of the Spanish Slave Code of 1842 see Appendix 1 in Robert L. Paquette's *Sugar Is Made with Blood,* 267–72.

36. Compare this to Carpentier's mention of the *boca-abajo* in *¡Ecue Yamba-O!* (93). See also Paquette, *Sugar Is Made with Blood,* 66–67.

37. One of Morúa's major complaints about *Cecilia Valdés* was that Villaverde did not create a single "really interesting type." Isabel Ilincheta comes closest to what Morúa perceives as a "sympathetic character," and he promptly chides Villaverde for making her so physically unattractive ("Las novelas," 43, 46).

38. Morua was jailed for conspiracy in 1880, and when freed, he left Cuba for the United States until 1890. *Sofía* was written between 1888 and 1890, during Morúa's exile. In the United States, he became a member of the Comité Patriótico de Nueva York and later went to Key West, where he founded the *Revista Popular.* In 1890, he returned to Cuba and launched the journal *La Nueva Era.* His earlier journalistic activities and interests inform the lengthy debates in *Sofía* about the purpose of black periodicals in Cuba (72ff.). See Luis for further details (*Literary Bondage,* 151–55).

39. Here, Morúa takes yet another swipe at *Cecilia Valdés* by correcting what appeared to him a thoroughly ludicrous situation: María de la Regla's trusting confession to her mistress's daughters. See Morúa, "Las novelas," 36–37.

40. Spillers, "Mama's Baby," 76.

41. See Spillers, "Toward an Alternative Model," 173.

42. Spillers, "Mama's Baby," 66.

43. See Michel Foucault, *The History of Sexuality,* 1:107.

44. Spillers, "Mama's Baby," 77.

45. Morúa Delgado, "Las novelas," 40. One of Morúa's main criticism's of Villaverde's plot is that everybody, except for Leonardo and Cecilia, seem to know that they are siblings, which makes the incest all the more incredible.

46. See the emphasis on Sofia's "barriga" (paunch) (90).

47. In this context it is well worth noting that, at least in the United States, slaves were also used for experimental medical research (see Spillers, "Mama's Baby," 68).

48. Sofía first meets her mother because the latter is looking to purchase a young mulata to add to her stable (107–10).

49. Luis, somewhat too optimistically, takes Leonardo's death to signal "an end to the historical exploitation of black and mulatto women by white men" (*Literary Bondage,* 117).

50. Luis acknowledges the possibility that "the Gonzaga of the first novel is not the same character of the second novel" (*Literary Bondage,* 153).

51. Gonzaga is Morúa's "sympathetic character" who is supposed to fill the gap Villaverde left in *Cecilia Valdés.* Somewhat in keeping with Morúa's criticism of Villaverde, Netchinsky argues that the absence of Villaverde's voice in any of his novel's major characters "raises the issue of his authority" ("Engendering a Cuban Literature," 10). Gonzaga's presence in *Sofía* also is consistent with Morúa's modified naturalism, evident from his preference for Daudet over Zola because the former balances sordid detail with "dignified characters," "noble, edifying scenes," dramatic situations, and humorous interludes: "Daudet is more spontaneous, more humane, more refined. Both [Zola and Daudet] are artists of the first order, but Daudet is also a poet, and a very elegant one at that" ("Las novelas," 20). And he adds later on, "I do not believe that any writer always looks at society from its worst side" (43). For additional comments on Gonzaga see Luis, *Literary Bondage,* 152–55.

52. At the time of the novel's publication, Martí was in exile in the United States. A few months after the founding of the Partido Revolutionario Cubano in 1892, Máximo Gómez, Antonio Maceo, and other *autonomistas* joined Martí in Florida to prepare for the War of Independence. Martí was assassinated in Cuba on May 19, 1895. It is telling that Morúa chose to assign the role of Martí to another white character,

a patron of sorts, instead of creating an earlier version of the mulato Fidelio from *La familia Unzúazu*.

Chapter 5

1. The 1896 sugar harvest dropped to barely over 200,000 tons, the lowest figures in fifty years. The production figures I am using in this section are taken from Ramiro Guerra, *Azúcar y población en las Antillas* (1944), 227–30 (appendix 3).

2. See Louis A. Pérez, Jr., *Cuba under the Platt Amendment*, 26.

3. The omission of Cuba from this formulation was indeed portentous. It was not until 1947 that the Spanish-American War was properly renamed the Spanish-Cuban-American War.

4. Pérez, *Cuba under the Platt Amendment*, 3.

5. See Guerra, *Azúcar y población*, 78.

6. Pérez, *Cuba under the Platt Amendment*, 11–12; see also Jules R. Benjamin, *The United States and the Origins of the Cuban Revolution*, 20–21.

7. Benjamin, *The United States and The Origins of the Cuban Revolution*, 69n. 37. He adds: "Washington had sweetened the pill of the Platt Amendment [1901] by the trade treaty that gave Cuban sugar privileged access to the North American market. The Cubans had made such access one of their principal requests, even though Washington obtained in return the practical elimination of Cuban barriers to the entry of U.S. goods. . . . By the 1920s, Cuba was the sixth largest market for U.S. goods. The flood of products from large-scale enterprises in North America prevented the creation of a strong Cuban manufacturing sector. Cuban governments could not effectively protect domestic producers because the entry of U.S. goods was tied to access to the North American sugar market" (68–69). The tobacco industry, which declined sharply in the 1890s when unemployment forced thousands of cigar makers to emigrate to Florida, is a case in point (see Pérez, *Cuba under the Platt Amendment*, 8). For purposes of comparison, consider that in 1896 only 10 percent of the total Cuban sugar production came from U.S.-owned mills.

8. Guerra, *Azúcar y población*, 125, 91.

9. See ibid., 132–33, 135.

10. Ibid., 145–46.

11. Pérez, *Cuba under the Platt Amendment*, 116–17.

12. Benjamin, *The United States and the Origins of the Cuban Revolution,* 99.

13. Ibid., 16; see also 8–10, 17–19, 74.

14. Free-Soiler James Shepherd Pike quoted ibid., 16.

15. Ibid., 27–28.

16. Figures vary substantially. According to Rafael Fermoselle-López, black soldiers made up about 70 percent of the revolutionary army ("Black Politics in Cuba: The Race War of 1912," 1). See also Miguel Barnet, *Biografía de un cimarrón* (*The Autobiography of a Runaway Slave*), part 3.

17. Benjamin, *The United States and the Origins of the Cuban Revolution,* 53. Benjamin elaborates:

> The prevailing racial perspective in North America also helped to define the meaning of "pacification." Before the war, both moral and imperial expansionists had kept a decent distance from the race issue because Spain used the specter of "Africanization" to prevent U.S. support for the rebels and because the inferiority and unassimilability of "backward" peoples were an influential argument of the anti-imperialists. After the defeat of Spain, imperialists and expansionists rediscovered the black component of the island's population. Many of them now argued that the inferiority of that race made necessary continued U.S. rule over the island [the "white man's burden" argument]. . . . The changed attitude toward Cuba appeared in magazine illustrations and political cartoons as well. Prior to the war, the principal pictorial image of Cuba had been that of a helpless maiden (often Lady Liberty herself) in mortal danger. After 1899 the most common image of the Cuban was that of an ignorant or unruly brat. Miss Liberty had been white and graceful; the brat was black and ungainly. (54–58)

18. See Fermoselle-López, "Black Politics in Cuba," 10–15, 132.

19. Fifty thousand Spanish workers immigrated to Cuba during the term of Estrada Palma's administration (1902–6) (see Fermoselle-López, "Black Politics in Cuba," 28), augmenting the ranks of those who had arrived during the 1880s and 1890s, when emigration was encouraged by the Spanish colonial government. See also Luis E. Aguilar, *Cuba 1933: Prologue to Revolution,* 36–37. Aguilar downplays the significance of racial conflict in Cuba (22–24). On Cuban race relations and the treatment of this topic in contemporary historiography see Frederick Hen-

drick Habibe, *El compromiso en la poesía afroantillana de Cuba y Puerto Rico,* 11–14.

20. See Fermoselle-López, "Black Politics in Cuba," 105ff.

21. See ibid., 114ff.

22. According to Fermoselle-López, rumors that foreign black workers participated in this rebellion remained unconfirmed (ibid., 177).

23. Lino Novás Calvo's *Pedro Blanco, el Negrero* (1937) is usually ignored. Exceptions to this rule are José Antonio Fernández de Castro, "La literatura negra actual de Cuba (1902–1934)," which praises Carpentier's first novel, and Enrique Noble, ed., *Literatura afro-hispanoamericana.* See also Luis, *Literary Bondage,* chap. 4.

24. Carpentier, *¡Ecue Yamba-O!* 119.

25. Ibid., 13.

26. See Rita Gnutzman, "La evolución de un tema: El negro en la obra de Alejo Carpentier," and Shirley Jackson, *La novela negrista en Hispanoamérica.*

27. Carpentier, *¡Ecue Yamba-O!* 203.

28. Writes René Depestre: "*negrismo* in art and in literature was never a well-structured movement but a changing spiritual state and sensibility with regard to the historical destiny . . . of the peoples [of sub-Saharan Africa] displaced to the Americas" (*Buenas días y adiós a la negritud,* 20).

29. See Pérez Firmat for details on Ortiz's refashioning of *cubanidad* (Cubanness) as *cubanía* (Cubanity) (*The Cuban Condition,* chap. 1). See also, Jorge Mañach, "La crisis de la alta cultura en Cuba," a lecture delivered before the Sociedad Económica de Amigos del País in 1925.

30. Ramón Guirao, ed., *Orbita de la poesía afrocubana, 1928–37 (Antología),* xii-xvi; my emphases.

31. See Alain Locke, ed., *The New Negro,* 145. These resonances are neither extraneous nor coincidental: "I Too" (Yo también) was one of three of Langston Hughes's early poems to be printed in the *Diario de la Marina*'s "Ideales de una raza" page in April 1930, in translations by José Antonio Fernández de Castro. The other two poems were "Los blancos" (The white men) and "Soledad: Retrato de una cubana" (Solitude: portrait of a Cuban woman). Translations of Hughes's poems by Fernández de Castro had already appeared in *Social* in 1928.

32. José Jacinto Milanés in a letter to Domingo Del Monte, quoted in Instituto de Literatura y Lingüística de la Academia de Ciencias de Cuba, ed. *Perfil histórico de las letras cubanas,* 233. Another letter to Del Monte, written by Félix Tanco in 1836, puts the matter somewhat

differently: "Cuba's blacks are our poetry, and it cannot be otherwise; but not the blacks alone, but the blacks with the whites, all joined together, form the pictures, the scenes (quoted in Angel Augier, *Nicolás Guillén: Notas para un estudio biográfico-crítico*, 98).

33. See, for instance, Ortiz's "La reforma pentitenciara en Cuba" (*Revista Bimestre Cubana*, 1911), as well as the series of articles by Israel Castellanos in the same journal in 1914. Castellanos, author of *La manibula criminal* (Havana, 1914), also translated substantial portions of the work of the Frenchman Henri Dumont for the *Revista Bimestre* (1915 and 1916). See also the review of Felix Plaut's *El negro en Cuba* (Berlin, 1926), a study in comparative psychiatry, in *Revista Bimestre* (1927). Ortiz had also founded the Society for the Study of Cuban Folklore, with *Archivos del Folklore Cubano* (1924) as its official organ. It is of interest here that Ortiz used early antislavery narratives as sources of information for his later work (see Luis, *Literary Bondage*, 7).

34. The official organ of this organization was the short-lived journal *Estudios Afrocubanos*. For a roster of founding members and associates see volume 1, number 1 (1937).

35. Depestre, *Buenas días y adiós a la negritud*, 10.

36. The notice in the form of a letter is reproduced in Habibe, *El compromiso en la poesía afroantillana*, 34. The Library of Congress has an almost complete run of *El Diario de la Marina* on microfilm.

37. See the Sunday Literary Supplements for February 12, 1928; March 17, 1929; June 23, 1929; and January 5, 1930. García Caturla had made a name for himself in Europe with "Danza lucumí" (Yoruba-Cuban dance), "Danza del tambor" (Dance of the drum) and Carpentier's "Liturgia" (Liturgy). The first to compose symphonies with Afro-Cuban themes and rhythms (many inspired by ñáñigo ceremonies) and to incorporate on a regular basis typical Cuban percussion instruments in their performance, Roldán had collaborated with Carpentier on two ballets/suites, *La rebambaramba* (1928) and *El milagro de Anaquillé* (The miracle of Anaquillé) (1929). Both earned him an international reputation: *La rebambaramba*, for one, was performed in Mexico, Paris, Berlin, and California in the early thirties. He had also written the music for Luis Palés Matos's "Danza negra" (Black dance) (1928, 1929). It is quite possible that Roldán's early pieces, especially *Tres pequeños poemas* (Three little poems) (1926), partly inspired the poetic use of Afro-Cuban rhythms. For further information see Zoila Gómez, *Amadeo Roldán*; Adolfo Salazar, "El movimiento africanista en la música de arte cubana"; and Habibe, *El compromiso en la poesía afroantillana*, 19–20.

38. In June 1928, the Supplement was reduced to a single page. From

August to November 1929, its appearance became sporadic and its topics exceedingly safe (the article on Mrs. Coolidge is from this period). The same thing happened again in mid-1930, right after the Supplement had briefly been expanded to three pages, one of which was devoted specifically to "Temas hispanoamericanas."

39. See April 11 and 18, 1926; June 19 and November 20, 1927; April 8, May 13, and September 2, 1928; and throughout March and October 1929.

40. Del Valle's story "La Majagua nueva" appeared in the "Ideales" section on March 31, 1929, with an illustration by Valls. See also June 12 and November 20, 1927; January 29 and April 8, 1928.

41. *El Diario de la Marina,* November 25, 1928.

42. Along similar lines see also Herminio Portell Vilá, "La población negra norteamericana como factor de la vida nacional" (1937), and "Conflictos de población y de razas en los Estados Unidos: Resultantes sociales y problemas del futuro" (1938). At the time that he wrote these articles, Portell Vilá was Professor of Civilization at Black Mountain College.

43. Even before the convergence of ethnographic, aesthetic, and political concerns gave rise to *negrismo* in the Hispanic Caribbean, black intellectuals in the French Antilles such as Atenor Firmin, author of *De l'égalite des races humaines* (1855), and Hannibal Price, who published *De la réhabilitation de la race noire par le peuple d'Haiti* in 1900, as well as W. E. B. Du Bois in the United States (*The Souls of Black Folk* [1903]), had initiated image renovations that, combined with the advent of Garveyism (1915), culminated in the Harlem Renaissance and negritude movements. It is also worth noting that René Maran's prizewinning novel *Batouala* (1921), an important precursor of French West Indian Negritude, appeared in Spanish the same year it was first published. Ortiz reviewed another one of Du Bois's books in 1939 (see bibliography). In that review, he is exceedingly critical of what he calls Du Bois's lack of precise knowledge of Hispanic American history. For instance, he takes Du Bois to task for not mentioning Máximo Gómez in connection with Cuba's War of Independence and for misspelling Guillén's name.

44. Both poems are from Pereda Valdés's *Raza negra* (1929). His earlier volume of poetry, *La guitarra de los negros* (1926), was reviewed in the *Revista Bimestre Cubana* that same year (see bibliography). *La guitarra* includes a total of five poems with thematic or formal references to African-American culture: "La guitarra de los negros," "Los tambores de los negros" (The drums of the blacks), "Música de la selva" (Jungle music), "Candombe," and "La canción bruja" (The sorcery song).

45. Tomás Blanco notes that in Puerto Rico, Palés's "fase negra" (black phase) was received with relative indifference. An exception to this was Tomás Carrión Maduro, "a writer of color," who credited Palés with "a privileged imagination," and Urrutia, who called the Puerto Rican "a white man and an admirable black poet" (see Blanco, "Escorzos de un poeta antillano [Luis Palés Matos]").

46. Both "Africa" and "Danza negra" first appeared in *La Democracia* on March 18 and October 9, 1926. A third poem by Palés, "Danza canibal" (Cannibal dance) followed in *Poliedro* on March 5, 1927. See Ortiz's "Más acerca de la poesía mulata: Escorzos para su estudio" for an early commentary on "Pueblo negro." Afro-Cubanism/Antilleanism's immediate literary antecedents in Hispanic America were poems such as Diego Vicente Tejera's "Dos niños" (Two children) (1876), Rubén Darío's "La negra Dominga" (The black woman Dominga) (1892), Llorens Torres's "El negro" (1914), and Pichardo Moya's "La comparsa" (The carnival procession) (1916). Although these and other poems attempted to portray blacks sympathetically, they nevertheless perpetuated the representational conventions of a discursive tradition that ranges from the slave traders' travelogues and the Enlightenment's exotic "noble savages" to the romantic paternalism of the nineteenth-century antislavery novels and pseudoscientific theories of race. For further details on this tradition see Depestre, *Buenos días y adiós a la negritud,* 20–21.

47. For additional details see Habibe, *El compromiso en la poesía afroantillana,* chap. 5.

48. See, for instance, Cendrars's *Anthologie nègre* (1921) and his *Voyage au Congo* (1927), as well as Apollinaire's collection of African religious motifs (1917). For further details see Depestre, *Buenos días y adiós a la negritud,* 20–25.

49. *Revista Bimestre Cubana* 21 (1926): 310. For further details on the impact of Spengler's work in the Hispanic Caribbean see González Echevarría, *Alejo Carpentier,* and Aníbal González Pérez, "Ballad of the Two Poets: Nicolás Guillén and Luis Palés Matos."

50. Although the political situation in Puerto Rico had been little different from that in Cuba since the Paris Treaty and the U.S. Congress's ratification of the Foraker Law in 1900, there was much less opposition to North American ventures. In fact, between 1920 and 1930, all of Puerto Rico's political parties (including the Socialists!) were in favor of Americanization.

51. See Kenneth Ramchand, "West Indian Literary History: Literariness, Orality, and Periodization"; Ian I. Smart, *Central American Writers*

of West Indian Origin: A New Hispanic Literature; and A. James Arnold, "Caribbean Literature/Comparative Literature," 42.

52. See especially Martha K. Cobb, *Harlem, Haiti, and Havana: A Comparative Critical Study of Langston Hughes, Jacques Roumain, and Nicolás Guillén.* Of interest also is Melvin Dixon, "Rivers Remembering Their Source: Comparative Studies in Black Literary History—Langston Hughes, Jacques Roumain, and Negritude."

53. Guillén, "Conversación con Langston Hughes," *El Diario de la Marina,* March 9, 1930. For further details see Arnold Rampersad, *The Life of Langston Hughes,* 1:177–81, 201–3.

54. See Langston Hughes and Ben Frederic Carruthers, eds. and trans., *Cuba Libre: Poems by Nicolás Guillén* (1948).

55. Some critics have been all too eager to cast the relationship of Hughes and Guillén in the mold of literary influence (see, for instance, Martha K. Cobb, *Harlem, Haiti, and Havana*). Regino Boti considers their literary relationship a "falso parentesco" (false parentage) (see his "La poesía cubana de Nicolás Guillén").

56. See José Piedra, "Through Blues," in Pérez Firmat, ed., *Do the Americas Have a Common Literature?* 107–29.

57. See *El Diario de la Marina,* April 27 and May 11, 1930. One of the few exceptions was Ramón Vasconcelos. See also Boti, who praises *Sóngoro cosongo* over *Motivos* ("La poesía cubana de Nicolás Guillén"), and Richard L. Jackson, *Black Writers in Latin America,* 80–92.

58. For details on the history of the Cuban *son* see Eduardo Sánchez de Fuentes, *Influencia de los ritmos africanos en nuestro cancionero (Conferencia),* and Natalio Galán, *Cuba y sus sones.*

59. Grenet's most popular *son* was "Papa Montero," while Matamoros was known primarily for "Son de la loma" (*Son* of the hills) and "La mujer de Antonio" (Antonio's woman).

60. The *son* is a syncretic blend of Spanish, African, and taíno/Arawak musical ingredients. For further details see González Echevarría, "Literature of the Hispanic Caribbean," and his "Guillén as Baroque: Meaning in *Motivos de son.*"

61. Guillén, *The Daily Daily,* 5. The very mixed reception of *Motivos,* its succès de scandale, bears comparison to the controversy surrounding the practice of so-called dialect poetry among the New Negro writers in the United States. This controversy dates back at least as far as the publication of Dunbar's *Lyrics of Lowly Life* (1901) and William Dean Howells's praise for their "'authenticity." See Countee Cullen, ed., *Caroling Dusk: An Anthology of Verse by Negro Poets* (1927), xiv; and

James Weldon Johnson's introduction to the first edition of his *Book of American Negro Poetry* (1921).

62. Many important anthologies of "black" poetry and prose fiction did not appear until decades later. The majority of them were published in the seventies: Rosa E. Valdés-Cruz's *La poesía negroide en América* (1970); Hortensia Ruiz del Vizo's *Poesía negra del Caribe y otra areas* (1972) and her *Black Poetry of the Americas* (1972); Enrique Noble's *Literatura afro-hispanoamericana* (1972); Stanley Cyrus's *El cuento negrista sudamericano: Antología* (1972); Morales's *Poesía afroantillana y negrista* (1976 and 1981); Armando González Pérez's *Poesía afrocubana última* (1976); and José Luis González and Mónica Mansour's *Poesía negra de América* (1976). In the same decade, a number of publishing houses, among them Casa de las Américas in Cuba and Ediciones Universal in Miami, started to reprint "classic" twentieth-century Afro-Hispanic texts: Morúa Delgado's *Sofía* (Havana, 1972) and *La familia Unzúazu* (Havana, 1975), Juan Francisco Manzano's *Autobiografía de un esclavo* (Madrid, 1975), Guillén's *Motivos de son* (Havana, 1980), Marcelino Arozarena's *Canción negra sin color* (Havana, 1983), Regino Pedrozo's *Poesías* (Havana, 1984), and the complete works of Alejo Carpentier, whose first volume (Mexico, 1983) includes all of his Afro-Cuban texts.

63. The usual suspect is Guillén's *Motivos*. For a different reading see González Echevarría, "Guillén as Baroque."

64. Poems by white North Americans regularly included in anthologies of *poesía negra americana* are Henry Wadsworth Longfellow's "The Slave's Dream" and "The Quadroon Girl"; John Greenleaf Whittier's "The Farewell"; Herman Melville's "Formerly a Slave"; Walt Whitman's "The Runaway Slave," "The Drayman," and "Ethiopia Saluting the Colors"; Vachel Lindsay's "The Congo" (which Palés admired for its musicality); and Hart Crane's "Black Tambourine."

65. See the introduction to the revised edition of Johnson's *Book of American Negro Poetry* (1931).

66. Ballagas, *Mapa de la poesía negra americana*, 33. Subsequent page references to this volume will appear with a short title in parentheses in the text.

67. See also Ballagas, *Antología*, 14.

68. Letter to Ballagas, quoted in Argyll Pryor Rice, *Emilio Ballagas: poeta y poesía*, 228.

69. Ballagas, *Antología*, 180–82. Guirao's *Orbita* somewhat more systematically divides contributors into "raza blanca," "raza negra," and "mestizo. Cruce afroespañol" (Afrohispanic mix or cross) Guillén and Arozarena are the only ones in the latter category.

70. Guirao, ed., *Orbita de la poesía afrocubana,* xviii. Susequent page references to this edition will appear with a short title in parentheses in the text.

71. For *jitanjáfóra* see chap. 6.

72. These passages are culled from an earlier essay, "Poetas negros y mestizos de la época esclavista" (1934).

73. Ballagas, "Situación de la poesía afroamericana," 53–54. The nonwhite Cuban poets whose work is included in Ballagas's *Antología* are Guillén, Arozarena, Ignacio Villa, and Regino Pedrozo; *Mapa* adds Plácido and Pichardo Moya. Guirao mentions Francisco Calcagno's anthology *Poetas de color* (1878) as the only register of black and mulato poets available at the time. He adds to Calcagno's list the names of Juan Bautista Estrada and Vicente Silvera (*Orbita,* xxxii).

74. Gustavo Urrutia, quoted in Tomás Blanco, "Escorzos de un poeta antillano (Luis Palés Matos)," 232. See also Ortiz's discussion of Vicente Gómez Kemp's *Acento negro: Poemas* (Havana, 1934) in "Los últimos versos mulatos," as well as his "Más acerca de la poesía mulata" and Gilberto González Contreras, "La poesía negra."

75. See note 57, above, and related text.

Chapter 6

1. Ballagas's "Elegía de María Belén Chacón" was first printed in the *Revista de Avance* in 1930, while "Nombres de negros en el son" appeared in the *Gaceta Literaria* (Madrid) in September 1931. Arozarena's "Caridá" was published in *El Mundo* (Havana) on March 26, 1933; "Mulata rumbera" was written in the thirties but not published prior to its inclusion in *Canción negra sin color* (Black song without color) (1966). "Amalia" first appeared in Janheinz Jahn's anthology *Rumba Macumba* (1957).

2. By contrast, poetic portraits of mulatas are fairly rare in the United States, especially during the Harlem Renaissance years. During that period, there are a number of poems devoted to black women, for example, Claude McKay's "Harlem Dancer" and, to a lesser extent, his "Harlem Shadows" and "America"; Ray Garfield Dandridge's "Zalka Peetruza"; Otto Leland Bohanan's "The Washer Woman"; Helene Johnson's "Poem"; Clarissa Scott Delany's "The Mask"; Gwendolyn Bennet's "To a Dark Girl"; and George Leonard Allen's "Portrait" (these being the only examples from James Weldon Johnson's *The Book of American Negro Poetry* and Countee Cullen's *Caroling Dusk.* Later, there are several

poems by Hughes, some of them included in Alain Locke's *The New Negro*. A notable exception is Toomer's *Cane* (1923).

3. De Lauretis, "Eccentric Subjects," 115.

4. Johnson, "A-beng," in Davies and Fido, eds., *Out of the Kumbla*, 131–32. Johnson adds parenthetically: "It is most ironic, of course, that this should be the product of a consciousness which wants, so it tells itself, 'a geography without myth.'"

5. Ibid., 126.

6. González Echevarría, *Alejo Carpentier*, 26.

7. Julie Ellison, *Delicate Subjects: Romanticism, Gender, and the Ethics of Understanding*, 11; De Lauretis, *Technologies of Gender*, 26.

8. Eve Kosofsky Sedgwick notes that male heterosexual desire can be homosocial to the extent that it is "a desire to consolidate partnerships with authoritative males in and through the bodies of females" (*Between Men: English Literature and Male Homosocial Desire*, 38).

9. González Echevarría points out that natural conceptions in the novel are either fictional or nonexistent but does not pursue this point (see *Alejo Carpentier*, 172).

10. Carpentier, *The Lost Steps*, 81–82 [147].

11. This scenario, for one, illustrates Michael Warner's point that gender is not "our only access to alterity" ("Homo-Narcissism; or, Heterosexuality," 200).

12. See Marta E. Sánchez, "Caliban: The New Latin-American Protagonist of *The Tempest*," and Emir Rodríguez Monegal, "The Metamorphoses of Caliban." Miguel Barnet's testimonial narrative *Biografía de un cimarrón* (*Autobiography of a Runaway Slave*) (1966) can be read as another instance of this male homosocial paradigm. See Kutzinski, "Parallel Caribbean Universes: Sexuality and Power/Androgyny and Seduction in Miguel Barnet and Wilson Harris."

13. See José David Saldívar, *The Dialectics of Our America: Genealogy, Cultural Critique, and Literary History*, chap. 6: "The School of Caliban." The homoerotic standoff between Prospero and Caliban at the end of Césaire's play—"Moi-toi" (Me-you)—is suggestive of the constructions "Marnet and Bontejo," or, alternatively, "Montenet and Bartejo" in two of the best-known readings of Barnet's *Biografía de un cimarrón*. See also González Echevarría, *The Voice of the Masters: Writing and Authority in Modern Latin American Literature*, 123, and Luis, *Literary Bondage*, 217n. 33.

14. In keeping with the quotation from a speech delivered by Che Guevara at the University of Las Villas on December 28, 1959, in which he enjoins students and faculty alike to "become black, become mulatto,

a worker, a peasant; go down among the people," Fernández Retamar as Ariel "seeks from Caliban the honor of a place in his rebellious and glorious ranks" (Fernández Retamar, *Caliban,* 45). It is also worth mentioning that Fernández Retamar takes Caliban as representative not so much of Cuba's African population but primarily of the island's pre-Columbian inhabitants, the (conveniently) extinct Caribs. (The substitution of the descendants of African slaves and their distinctive expressive culture for that of, by then, the long-extinct indigenous populations began in the nineteenth century and was consolidated during the years of the Afro-Antillean movement, when Africans became the Caribbean's living "natives.") Fernández Retamar's essay enacts a paradigmatic quest for otherness whose links to the genre of the chivalric romance are ideologically revealing: "in those few instances where the errant knight . . . does find a form of otherness that he prefers to the realm of the same from which he came, this otherness is interpreted . . . as the realm of the dead, for it is ideologically inconceivable that there should exist an otherness of the same ontological status as the same, without there being immediately mounted an effort at its appropriation" (Michel de Certeau, *Heterologies,* xiii). While Fernández Retamar is no Lohengrin, he still chooses not to take this opportunity to make racial otherness an issue in the realm of the living.

15. Nicolás Guillén, "Balada de los dos abuelos," in Guillén, *Obra poética,* 1:139; my emphasis.

16. See also Smith, *The Body Hispanic,* 148, 169.

17. Johnson points out that "The Mother-figure in the literature [of the Caribbean] . . . suffers a curious displacement. She is more a medium than full representation as such" ("A-beng," 138).

18. Guillén, "El abuelo," in his *Obra poética,* 1:149; my emphasis. My translation is reprinted from *Callaloo* 10 (1987): 191.

19. Pérez Firmat, *The Cuban Condition,* 67–79.

20. Guillén, "La canción del bongó," in his *Obra poética,* 1:117.

21. Guillén, "Mulata," in his *Obra poética,* 1:104. The translation is mine. See Langston Hughes and Ben Frederic Carruthers's "High Brown" for an earlier translation (in *Cuba Libre*).

22. See Clarisse Zimra's incisive comments on Frantz Fanon's and Edouard Glissant's views of the black woman as complicitous whore ("Righting the Calabash: Writing History in the Female Francophone Narrative," in Davies and Fido, eds., *Out of the Kumbla,* 149–50).

23. Guillén, "Mujer nueva," in his *Obra poética,* 1:120. My translation is reprinted from *Callaloo* 10 (1987), 341.

24. Pérez Firmat, *The Cuban Condition,* 90.

25. Ibid., 90–91.

26. Benítez Rojo, *The Repeating Island*, 26 [*Isla*, xxxiv]. I do not fully agree with Benítez Rojo that "*mestizaje* is not a synthesis, but rather the opposite." My point is that the icons through which the discourse of *mestizaje* seeks to represent itself, icons such as the "Virgen mulata" that Benítez Rojo so brilliantly discusses in his Introduction, are syncretic and thus unstable, while the masculinist theory of *mestizaje* itself is not. Its "tragic" problem is precisely that it does not admit its own instability.

27. See Michie, *The Flesh Made Word*, 7, and Bhabha, "The Other Question," 30.

28. Wynter, "Beyond Miranda's Meanings," in Davies and Fido, eds., *Out of the Kumbla*, 360.

29. See Selwyn Cudjoe, ed., *Caribbean Women Writers*, 15.

30. Benítez Rojo, *The Repeating Island*, 10–11 [*Isla*, xiii–xv].

31. Benítez Rojo, "The Repeating Island," trans. James Maraniss, in Pérez Firmat, ed., *Do the Americas Have a Common Literature?* 92. This translation is reprinted from the *New England Review and Bread Loaf Quarterly* 7 (1985): 430–52.

32. Ibid., 94.

33. Guillén, "Madrigal (2)," in his *Obra poética*, 1:121.

34. Pérez Firmat, *The Cuban Condition*, 90–91.

35. Benítez Rojo, *The Repeating Island*, 29 [*Isla*, xxxviii], my emphases.

36. See Eduardo González, "American Theriomorphia," in Pérez Firmat, ed., *Do the Americas Have a Common Literature?* 185.

37. Wayne Koestenbaum's claim that "within male texts of all varieties lurks a homosexual desire which, far from reinforcing patriarchy, undermines it and offers a way out" (*Double Talk: The Erotics of Male Literary Collaboration*, 5) does not seem to apply here.

38. Luis Palés Matos, "Mulata-Antilla," in *Tuntún pasa y griféria*, 1:109.

39. Sedgwick, *Between Men*, 36.

40. González, "American Theriomorphia," 188, 193.

41. Mónica Mansour is suspicious of *poesía negra's* links with African or African-American music. Her own analyses seek to demonstrate that the basic rhythm of the *son* and of other Afro-Antillean musical forms is the same as that of the traditional Spanish ballad. On the basis of those similarities, she claims that "the 'Afro-American' musical rhythms are nothing more than accentual variations on a traditional European rhythm." This, according to Mansour, confirms once again "the

idea that the poets of the *negrista* movement had recourse to the models of popular Spanish lyrics, and not to the analysis and application of African music or the inclusion of Afro-American music." She regards the rise of the Afro-Antillean movement as parallel to the "neopopularismo" of the Generation of '27, a point also made by González Echevarría (see his "Guillén as Baroque"). Finally, she notes that African music is not only percussion but also melody, something Carpentier emphasized, and that *negrista* poetry does not use or recreate that melodic element (*La poesía negrista*, 146–53).

42. Mansour claims that Palés Matos was the first to use "African toponyms" and not just words invented to produce rhythmic effects (*La poesía negrista*, 162).

43. Fernández Retamar, for one, writes that "Those words are to *poesía negra* what onomatopoeia is to pure poetry: mere verbal play, sound liberated from the bonds of meaning" (*La poesía contemporánea en Cuba (1927–1953)*, 52).

44. For an alternative reading of "sóngoro cosongo" see González Echevarría, "Guillén as Baroque." See also J. Bekunuru Kubayanda, "The Linguistic Core of Afro-Hispanic Poetry," and José Piedra's at times rather fanciful "etymologies" in his "Through Blues," in Pérez Firmat, ed., *Do the Americas Have a Common Literature?*

45. García Caturla completed the music for two of Guillén's *Motivos de son*. The whole of *Motivos* was set to music by Amadeo Roldán in 1933 and was first performed in New York in 1934. Two pieces were performed in Havana in 1937, but the whole set was not heard until 1959. The fiftieth anniversary edition of *Motivos* includes the musical scores (see bibliography).

46. Pérez Firmat, *The Cuban Condition*, 107.

47. See Henry Louis Gates, Jr., "'Authenticity,' or the Lesson of Little Tree," 1.

48. Mansour, for one, argues that the use of black themes was more a form of social than of racial criticism (*La poesía negrista*, 137).

49. Felipe Pichardo Moya, "La comparsa," in Morales, ed. *Poesía afroantillana y negrista*, 324; my emphases.

50. For different readings of Guillén's "Sensemayá" see Kutzinski, *Against the American Grain*, 136–46, and Ian Isidore Smart, *Nicolás Guillén: The Caribbean's Popular Poet*, 36–39.

51. Ballagas, "Elegía de María Belén Chacón," in his *Cuaderno de poesía negra*, n.p. The poem is reprinted in Guiaro, *Orbita*, 107.

52. Pereda Valdés notes that María Belén was probably a mulata (*Lo negro y lo mulato en la poesía cubana*, 27).

53. See González Echevarría, "Where the Singers Come From: Fragments."

54. Alfonso Camín, "Danzón de María Belén," in his *Maracás y otros poemas*, 45.

55. José Piedra reads "rayando la leña está" as an allusion to the "unnamed Wild," the mythic Afro-Cuban space of el Monte, in which, he argues, Ma Teodora "'hides' defensively, along with her secrets" ("Through Blues," in Pérez Firmat, ed., *Do the Americas Have a Common Literature?* 117).

56. See Odilio Urfé, "Factores que integran la música cubana," and Alberto Muguercia Muguercia, "Teodora Ginés ¿mito o realidad histórica?" González Echevarría mentions both articles in "Guillén as Baroque," but does not find them relevant to his discussion, which "focuses more on this 'Son' as a mythic origin of Cuban culture" (317 n. 28).

57. González Echevarría, "Literature of the Hispanic Caribbean," 8.

58. José Juan Arrom, "La poesía afrocubana," 399–400. See also Ortiz, "Los últimos versos mulatos," 326–29.

59. Luis Llorens Torres, "Copla mulata," in Morales, ed., *Poesía afroantillana y negrista*, 42–43.

60. Compare the following line from Arozarena's "Amalia": "y soy su espejo en el remolino de un mar de mieles" (and I am her mirror in the whirl of the sea of molasses). (*Canción negra sin color y otros poemas*, 47).

61. Arozarena, "Liturgia etiópica," in his *Canción negra sin color*, 33.

62. Arozarena, "Amalia," in his *Canción negra sin color*, 46.

63. Guillén, "Secuestro de la mujer de Antonio," in his *Obra poética*, 1:129.

64. Manuel de Cabral, "Tropico suelto," in Morales, ed., *Poesía afroantillana y negrista*, 220.

65. See Sedgwick, *Between Men*, 49.

66. Evaristo Ribera Chevremont, "Morena," in his *Antología poética, 1924–1950* (1957), n.p.

67. Palés Matos, *Poesía completa y prosa selecta*, 1:197.

68. Palés Matos, "Mulata-Antilla," in his *Tuntún de pasa y grifería: Poemas afroantillanos*, 107.

69. Ibid., 108.

70. Ibid., 108–13; Frederick Habibe, *El compromiso en la poesía afroantillana de Cuba y Puerto Rico*, 115.

71. Palés Matos, "Majestad negra," in his *Tuntún de pasa y grifería*,

57. The translation is Aníbal González Pérez's ("Ballad of the Two Poets: Nicolás Guillén and Luis Palés Matos," 289).

72. The lines I have in mind here are: "aquí molerán tus ancas / la zafra de tu sudor" (here your behind will grind / the harvest of your sweat) " (Guillén, "Secuestro de la mujer de Antonio," in his *Obra poética*, 1:130.

73. Moreno Fraginals, "Aportes culturales y deculturación," in Fraginals, ed., *Africa en América Latina*, 21. See also Pedrozo's "Hermano negro" (Black brother): "¿No somos más que rumbas, lujurias negras y comparsas? / ¿No somos más que mueca y color, / mueca y color?" (Aren't we more than rumbas, black promiscuity, and carnivals? / Aren't we more than grimace and color, / grimace and color?) (*Nosotros*, n.p.).

74. González Pérez, "Ballad of the Two Poets," 288–89.

75. Felipe Pichardo Moya, "Filosofía del bronce," in Morales, ed., *Poesía afroantillana y negrista*, 325–26.

76. Ibid., 327.

77. See Arenas, *Graveyard of the Angels*, 63–65.

Select Bibliography

Acosta, Agustín. *La zafra: Poema de combate*. Havana: Editorial Minerva, 1926.

Ades, Dawn, et al. *Art In Latin America: The Modern Era, 1820–1980*. New Haven, Conn.: Yale Univ. Press, 1989.

Aguilar, Luis E. *Cuba 1933: Prologue to Revolution*. Ithaca, N.Y.: Cornell Univ. Press, 1972.

Anderson, Benedict. *Imagined Communities: Reflections on the Origin and Spread of Nationalism*, 2d ed., rev. and extended. London: Verso, 1991.

Andrews, William. *To Tell a Free Story: The First Century of Afro-American Autobiography, 1760–1865*. Urbana: Univ. of Illinois Press, 1986.

Anzaldúa, Gloria. *Borderlands/La Frontera: The New Mestiza*. San Francisco, Calif.: Spinsters/Aunt Lute Book Company, 1987.

Arenas, Reinaldo. *Graveyard of the Angels*. Trans. Alfred J. MacAdam. New York: Avon Books, 1987.

Arnold, A. James. "Caribbean Literature/Comparative Literature." In *Mélanges offerts a Albert Gérard. Semper Aliquid Novi. Littérature comparée et littératures d'Afrique*, ed. Janos Riesz and Alain Richard, 39–46. Tübingen: Gunter Narr Verlag, 1990.

Arozarena, Marcelino. *Canción negra sin color y otros poemas*. Havana: Contemporáneos, 1966.

Arrom, José Juan. *Certidumbre de América: Estudios de letras, folklore, y cultura*. 1954; rpt. Havana: Editorial Letras Cubanas, 1980.

———. *Historia de la literatura dramática cubana*. New Haven, Conn.: Yale Univ. Press, 1942.

———. "La poesía afrocubana." *Revista Iberoamericana* 4 (1942): 379–411.

Artel, Jorge. *Antología poética*. Bogotá: Ediciones Ecoe, 1979.

Augier, Angel. *Nicolás Guillén: Notas para un estudio biográfico-crítico*. Santa Clara, Cuba: Universidad Central de las Villas, 1962–64.

Bachiller y Morales, Antonio. "Plácido." *Revista Cubana* 2 (1885): 547–61.

Baker, Houston A., Jr. *Modernism and the Harlem Renaissance*. Chicago: Univ. of Chicago Press, 1987.

Ballagas, Emilio, *Cuaderno de poesía negra*. Santa Clara, Cuba: Imprenta La Nueva, 1934.

———. "La poesía afrocubana." *Revista de la Biblioteca Nacional de Cuba*, 2d ser., 2 (1951): 6–18.

———. "Situación de la poesía afroamericana." *Revista Cubana* 21 (1946): 5–60.

———. *Antología de la poesía negra hispano americana*. Madrid: Bolaños y Aguilar, 1935.

———. ed. *Mapa de la poesía negra americana*. Buenos Aires: Editorial Pleamar, 1946.

Balutansky, Kathleen M. "Naming Caribbean Women Writers: A Review Essay." *Callaloo* 13 (1990): 539–50.

Banta, Martha. *Imaging American Women: Idea and Ideals in Cultural History*. New York: Columbia Univ. Press, 1987.

Bar-Lewaw, Itzhak. *Plácido: Vida y obra*. Mexico: Ediciones Botas, 1960.

Barnet, Miguel. ed. *The Autobiography of a Runaway Slave*, trans. Jocasta Innes. 1968; rpt. New York: Vintage Books, 1973.

———. *Biografía de un cimarrón*. 1966; rpt. Madrid: Ediciones Alfaguara S.A., 1984.

Barreda, Pedro. *The Black Protagonist in the Cuban Novel*. Amherst: Univ. of Massachusetts Press, 1979.

Barthes, Roland. "Encore le corps." *Critique* (1982): 423–42.

———. *Mythologies*. Trans. Annette Lavers. New York: Hill & Wang, 1979.

Benítez Rojo, Antonio. "Azúcar/poder/literatura." *Cuadernos Hispanoamericanos* (1988): 195–215, 451–52.

———. *La isla que se repite: El Caribe y la perspectiva posmoderna*. Hanover, N.H.: Ediciones del Norte, 1989.

———. "Nicolás Guillén and Sugar." *Callaloo* 10 (1987): 329–51.

———. *The Repeating Island: The Caribbean and the Postmodern Perspective*. Trans. James Maraniss. Durham, N.C.: Duke Univ. Press, 1992.

Benjamin, Jules R. *The United States and the Origins of the Cuban Revolution: An Empire of Liberty in an Age of National Liberation*. Princeton, N.J.: Princeton Univ. Press, 1990.

Berger, John. *Ways of Seeing*. London: BBC and Penguin, 1972.

Berzon, Judith R. *Neither White nor Black: The Mulatto Character in American Fiction.* New York: New York Univ. Press, 1978.

Bhabha, Homi K., ed. *Nation and Narration.* London: Routledge, 1990.

―――. "The Other Question." *Screen* 24 (1983): 18–36.

Blanco, Tomás. "Escorzos de un poeta antillano (Luis Palés Matos)." *Revista Bimestre Cubana* 42 (1938): 221–40.

Blomberg, Hector Pedro. "La negra y la mulata en la poesía americana." *Atenea* 80 (1945): 4–21.

Boti, Regino E. "La poesía cubana de Nicolás Guillén." *Revista Bimestre Cubana* 29 (1932): 343–53.

Boulware, Kay. "Women and Nature in *negrismo.*" *Studies in Afro-Hispanic Literature* 1 (1977): 16–25.

Brathwaite, Edward Kamau. "The African Presence in Caribbean Literature." *Dedalus* 103 (1975): 73–109.

―――. *Contradictory Omens: Cultural Diversity and Integration in the Caribbean.* Mona: Savacou Publications, 1974.

Brown, Paul. "'This thing of darkness I acknowledge mine': *The Tempest* and the Discourse of Colonialism." In *Political Shakespeare: New Essays in Cultural Materialism,* ed. Jonathan Dollimore and Alan Sinfield, pp. 48–71. London: Manchester Univ. Press, 1985.

Bueno, Salvador. "La canción del bongó: Sobre la cultura mulata de Cuba." *Cuadernos Americanos* 106 (1976): 89–106.

―――. *Historia de la literatura cubana.* Havana: Editorial del Ministerio de Educación, 1968.

―――. *Las ideas literarias de Domingo Del Monte.* Havana: UNESCO, 1954.

―――. *El negro en la novela hispanoamericana.* Havana: Editorial Letras Cubanas, 1986.

Bush, Clive. *The Dream of Reason: American Consciousness and Cultural Achievement from Independence to the Civil War.* London: Edward Arnold, 1977.

Calcagno, Francisco, ed. *Poetas de color.* Havana: Imprenta Mercantil de los Herederos de Santiago, 1887.

Camín, Alfonso. *Maracás y otros poemas.* Mexico: Impresora Azteca, 1952.

Carby, Hazel V. "The Multicultural Wars." *Radical History Review* 54 (1992): 7–18.

―――. *Reconstructing Womanhood: The Emergence of the Afro-American Woman Novelist.* New York: Oxford Univ. Press, 1987.

Carpentier, Alejo. *¡Ecue Yamba-O!* 1933; rpt. Barcelona: Editorial Bruguera, 1979.

———. *La música en Cuba.* Mexico: Fondo de Cultura Económica, 1946.

———. *Obras completas.* Mexico: Siglo Veintiuno, 1983.

———. *Los pasos perdidos.* 1953; rpt. Madrid: Catedra, Letras Hispánicas, 1985.

———. *The Lost Steps.* Trans. Harriet de Onís. 1956; rpt. New York: Knopf, 1977.

Carruthers, Ben Frederic. "The Life, Work, and Death of Plácido." Pd.D. dissertation, University of Illinois, 1941.

Cartey, Wilfred. *Black Images.* New York: Teachers College Press, Columbia University, 1970.

Casals, Jorge. *Plácido como poeta cubano.* Havana: Publicaciones del Ministerio de Educación, 1944.

Castellanos, Israel. "La briba hampona." *Revista Bimestre Cubana* 9 (1914): 94–104, 183–98, 253–59.

———. "El tipo brujo (Acotación de etnología criminal cubana)." *Revista Bimestre Cubana* 9 (1914): 328–44.

———, trans. "Antropología y patología comparada de los negros esclavos," by Henri Dumont. *Revista Bimestre Cubana* 10 (1915–16): 161–71, 263–74, 344–53, 407–20, and 11, 15–30, 78–90.

Castellanos, Jorge. *Plácido: Poeta social y político.* Miami: Ediciones Universal, 1984.

Cendrars, Blaise, ed. *Anthologie nègre* (1921), rev. ed. Paris: Editions Buchet/Chastel, 1979.

Cobb, Martha K. *Harlem, Haiti, and Havana: A Comparative Critical Study of Langston Hughes, Jacques Roumain, and Nicolás Guillén.* Washington, D.C.: Three Continents, 1979.

Coleman, Ben. "Black Themes in the Literature of the Caribbean." *The Rican: A Journal of Contemporary Puerto Rican Thought* 3 (1973): 48–54.

Conte, Rafael, and José M. Capmany. *Guerra de razas: Negros contra blancos en Cuba.* Havana: Imprenta Militar de Antonio Pérez, 1912.

Coulthard, Gabriel R. *Race and Colour in Caribbean Literature.* New York: Oxford Univ. Press, 1962

Cruz, Mary. *Creto Gangá.* Havana: Contemporáneo, 1974.

Cudjoe, Selwyn R., ed. *Caribbean Women Writers: Essays from the First International Conference.* Wellesley, Mass.: Calaloux Publications, 1990.

Cullen, Countee, ed. *Caroling Dusk: An Anthology of Verse by Negro Poets.* New York: Harper and Brothers, 1927.

Cunningham, Lucía Guerra, ed. *Splintering Darkness: Latin American*

Women Writers in Search of Themselves. Pittsburgh, Pa.: Latin American Literary Review Press, 1990.

Cyrus, Stanley, ed. *El cuento negrista sudamericano: Antología.* Quito: Editorial Casa de la Cultural Ecuatoriana, 1973.

Davies, Carole Boyce, and Elaine Savory Fido, eds. *Out of the Kumbla: Caribbean Women and Literature.* Trenton, N.J.: Africa World Press, 1990.

Dearborn, Mary. *Pocahontas's Daughters: Gender and Ethnicity in American Culture.* New York: Oxford, 1986.

De Certeau, Michel. *Heterologies: Discourse on the Other.* Minneapolis: Univ. of Minnesota Press, 1986.

DeCosta, Miriam, ed. *Blacks in Hispanic Literature. Critical Essays.* Port Washington, N.Y.: Kennikat, 1977.

De Jesús Márquez, José. *Plácido y los conspiradores de 1844.* Havana, 1984.

De Juan, Adelaida. *Pintura cubana: Temas y variaciones.* Havana: UN-EAC, 1978.

———. *Pintura cubana: Temas y variaciones,* rev. ed. Mexico: Universidad Nacional Autónoma de México, 1980.

———. *Pintura y grabado colonial cubano.* Havana: Instituto Cubano del Libro, 1974.

De la Concepción Valdés, Gabriel (Plácido). *Plácido, poesías completas,* ed. Sebastián Alfredo de Morales. Havana: La Primera del Papel, 1886.

———. *Poesías de Plácido,* ed. F. J. Vingut. 3d ed., 2 vols. New York: Lockwood & Son, 1857.

———. *Poesías escogidas: Gabriel de la Concepción Valdés (Plácido),* ed. Salvador Arias. Havana: Editorial Arte y Literatura, 1977.

De Lauretis, Teresa. "Eccentric Subjects: Feminist Theory and Historical Consciousness." *Feminist Studies* 16 (1990): 115–51.

———. *Technologies of Gender: Essays on Theory, Film, and Fiction.* Bloomington: Indiana Univ. Press, 1987.

Depestre, René. *Buenas días y adiós a la negritud.* Havana: Casa de las Américas, 1986.

Dixon, Melvin. "Rivers Remembering Their Source: Comparative Studies in Black Literary History—Langston Hughes, Jacques Roumain, and Negritude." In *Afro-American Literature: The Reconstruction of Instruction,* ed. Dexter Fisher and Robert B. Stepto, 25–43. New York: Modern Language Association, 1979.

Duvalier, Vauquelin. "La poesía negroide de Cuba." *Atenea* 145(1937): 28–36.

Elfenbein, Anna Shannon. *Women on the Color Line: Evolving Stereo-*

types and the Writing of George Washington Cable, Grace King, Kate Chopin. Charlottesville: Univ. Press of Virginia, 1989.

Ellison, Julie. *Delicate Subjects: Romanticism, Gender, and the Ethics of Understanding.* Ithaca, N.Y.: Cornell Univ. Press, 1990.

Fermoselle-López, Rafael. "Black Politics in Cuba: The Race War of 1912." Ph.D. dissertation, American University, 1972. This dissertation was published as *Política y Color en Cuba.* Montevideo: Ediciones Geminis, 1974.

Fernández de Castro, José A. "El aporte negro de las letras de Cuba en el siglo XIX." *Revista Bimestre Cubana* 38 (1936): 46–66.

———. "La literatura negra actual en Cuba (1902–1934): Datos para un estudio." *Estudios Afrocubanos* 4 (1940): 3–22.

Fernández de la Vega, Oscar, and Alberto Pamies. *Iniciación a la poesía afroamericana.* Miami: Ediciones Universal, 1973.

Fernández Retamar, Roberto. *Caliban.* 1971; rpt. Minneapolis: Univ. of Minnesota Press, 1991.

———. *La poesía contemporánea en Cuba, 1927–1953.* Havana: Orígenes, 1954.

Forbes, Jack D. *Black Africans and Native Americans: Color, Race, and Caste in the Evolution of Red-Black Peoples.* New York: Basil Blackwell, 1988.

Foucault, Michel. *Discipline and Punish: The Birth of the Prison.* New York: Random House/Vintage, 1979.

———. *The History of Sexuality,* vol. 1. New York: Random House / Vintage, 1990.

Franco, Jean. *Plotting Women: Gender and Representation in Mexico.* New York: Columbia Univ. Press, 1989.

———. "Trends and Priorities for Research in Latin American Literature." *Ideologies and Literature* 16 (1983): 107–20.

Franco, José Luciano, ed. *Autobiografía, cartas, y versos de Juan Fco. Manzano.* Havana: Municipio de La Habana, 1937.

Fredrickson, George M. *The Black Image in the White Mind: The Debate on Afro-American Character and Destiny, 1817–1914.* New York : Harper and Row, 1971.

Friol, Roberto, *Suite para Juan Francisco Manzano.* Havana: Editorial Arte y Literatura, 1977.

Froula, Christine. "The Daughter's Seduction: Sexual Violence and Literary History." *Signs* 11 (1986): 621–44.

Galan, Natalio. *Cuba y sus sones.* Valencia: Pre-Textos/Música,1983.

Garfield, Evelyn Picon. *Women's Voices from Latin America: Interviews with Six Contemporary Authors.* Detroit: Wayne State Univ. Press, 1985.

Garófala Mesa, García. *Plácido, poeta y mártir.* Mexico, Ediciones Botas, 1938.

Gates, Henry Louis Jr., "'Authenticity,' or the Lesson of Little Tree." *New York Times Book Review,* November 24, 1991.

Gilbert, Sandra M., and Susan Gubar. *The Madwoman in the Attic: The Woman Writer and the Nineteenth-Century Literary Imagination.* New Haven, Conn.: Yale Univ. Press, 1979.

Gilman, Sander L. "Black Bodies, White Bodies: Toward an Iconography of Female Sexuality in Late Nineteenth-Century Art, Medicine, and Literature." *Critical Inquiry* 12 (1985): 204–42. Rpt. in his *Difference and Pathology: Stereotypes of Sexuality, Race, and Madness.* Ithaca, N.Y.: Cornell Univ. Press, 1985.

Glissant, Edouard. *Caribbean Discourse: Selected Essays.* Trans. J. Michael Dash. Charlottesville: Univ. Press of Virginia, 1989.

Gnutzman, Rita. "La evolución de un tema: El negro en la obra de Alejo Carpentier." *Cuadernos Americanos* 3, no. 14 (1989): 117–39.

Gómez, Zoila. *Amadeo Roldán.* Havana: Editorial Arte y Literatura, 1977.

González, José Luis, and Mónica Mansour, eds. *Poesía negra de América.* Mexico: Ediciones Era, 1976.

González Contreras, Gilberto. "La poesía negra." *Revista Bimestre Cubana* 37 (1936): 40–45.

González Echevarria, Roberto. *Alejo Carpentier: The Pilgrim at Home.* Ithaca, N.Y.: Cornell Univ. Press, 1977.

———. "Guillén as Baroque: Meaning in *Motivos de son.*" *Callaloo* 10 (1987): 302–17.

———. "Literature of the Hispanic Caribbean." *Latin American Literary Review* 8 (1978): 1–20.

———. *The Voice of the Masters: Writing and Authority in Modern Latin American Literature.* Austin: Univ. of Texas Press, 1985.

———. "Where the Singers Come From: Fragments." *New England Review and Bread Loaf Quarterly* 7 (1985): 566–75.

González Pérez, Armando. *Poesía afrocubana última.* Milwaukee: Center for Latin America, University of Wisconsin, 1975.

González Pérez, Hanibal. "Ballad of the Two Poets: Nicolás Guillén and Luis Palés Matos." *Callaloo* 10 (1987): 285–301.

Guarachas cubanas: Curiosa recopilación desde las más antiguas hasta las más modernas, 2d ed. Havana: Librería "La Principal," 1882.

Guerra, Ramiro. *Azúcar y población en las Antillas* (1927), 3d ed. 1944; rpt. Havana: Editorial de Ciencias Sociales, 1970.

Guillén, Nicolás. "Conversación con Langston Hughes." *El Diario de la Marina,* March 9, 1930.

———. *The Daily Daily.* Trans. Vera M. Kutzinski. Los Angeles: Univ. of California Press, 1989.

———. *Man-Making Words: Selected Poems of Nicolás Guillén.* Ed. and trans. Robert Márquez and David Arthur MacMurray. Amherst: Univ. of Massachusetts Press, 1972.

———. *Motivos de son: Música de Amadeo Roldán, Alejandro Gracía Caturla, Eliseo Grenet, Emilio Grenet.* Edición Especial 50 Aniversario. Havana: Editorial Letras Cubanas, 1980.

———. *Obra poética: 1920–1972,* 2 vols. Ed. Angel Augier. Havana: Editorial Arte y Literatura, 1974.

Guirao, Ramón, ed. *Orbita de la poesía afrocubana, 1928–37 (Antología).* Havana: Ucar, García y Cía, 1938.

———. "Poetas negros y mestizos de la época esclavista." *Bohemia* 26 (1943): 43–44, 123–24.

Habibe, Fredrick Hendrick. *El compromiso en la poesía afroantillana de Cuba y Puerto Rico.* Curaçao, 1985.

Hall, Stuart. "The Whites of Their Eyes: Racist Ideologies and the Media." In *Silver Linings: Some Strategies for the Eighties,* ed. George Bridges and Rosalind Brunts. London: Lawrence and Wishart, 1981.

———, and Donald James, eds. *Politics and Ideology: A Reader.* Philadelphia, Pa.: Open University Press, 1985.

Hampton, Janet Jones. "The Image of the Black Woman in the Spanish-American Novel: A Study of Characterization in Select Spanish-American Novels." Ph.D. dissertation, Catholic University of America, 1985.

Harris, Wilson. *The Womb of Space: The Cross-Cultural Imagination.* Westport, Conn.: Greenwood Press, 1983.

Herrera McElroy, Onyria. "Martín Morúa Delgado, precursor del afrocubanismo." *Afro-Hispanic Review* 2 (1983): 19–24.

Horrego Estuch, Leopoldo. *Martín Morúa Delgado, vida y mensaje.* Havana: Editorial Sánchez, 1957.

———. *Plácido, el poeta infortunado.* Havana, 1960. Rev. ed.

Hughes, Langston, and Ben Frederic Carruthers, eds. and trans. *Cuba Libre: Poems by Nicolás Guillén.* Los Angeles, Calif.: Ward Ritchie Press, 1948.

Hull, Gloria T. *Color, Sex, and Poetry; Three Women Writers of the Harlem Renaissance.* Bloomington: Indiana Univ. Press, 1987.

Instituto de Literatura y Lingüística de la Academía de Ciencias de Cuba, ed. *Perfil histórico de las letras cubanas.* Havana: Editorial Letras Cubanas, 1983.

Jackson, Richard L. *The Black Image in Latin American Literature.* Albuquerque: Univ. of New Mexico Press, 1976.

———. *Black Literature and Humanism in Latin America.* Athens: Univ. of Georgia Press, 1989.

———. *Black Writers in Latin America.* Albuquerque: Univ. of New Mexico Press, 1979.

———. "Literary Blackness and Literary Americanism: Toward an Afro Model for Latin American Literature." *Afro-Hispanic Review* 1 (1982): 5–11.

———. "'Mestizaje' vs. Black Identity: The Color Crisis in Latin America." *Black World* 24, no. 9 (1975): 4–21.

———. "Racial Identity and the Terminology of Literary Blackness in Spanish America." *Revista Chicano-Riqueña* 5 (1978): 43–48.

Jackson, Shirley M. *La novela negrista en Hispanoamérica.* Madrid: Editorial Pliegos, 1986.

Johnson, James Weldon. *The Book of American Negro Poetry.* 1922 and rev. ed. 1931; rpt. New York: Harcourt Brace Jovanovich, 1969.

Koestenbaum, Wayne. *Double Talk: The Erotics of Male Literary Collaboration.* New York: Routledge, 1989.

Kristeva, Julia. *The Power and the Horror.* New York: Columbia Univ. Press, 1982.

Kubayanda, J. Benukuru. "The Linguistic Core of Afro-Hispanic Poetry." *Afro-Hispanic Review* 1 (1982): 21–26.

Kutzinski, Vera M. *Against the American Grain: Myth and History in William Carlos Williams, Jay Wright, and Nicolás Guillén.* Baltimore: Johns Hopkins Univ. Press, 1987.

Latino, Simón. *Los mejores versos de la poesía negra.* Buenos Aires: Cuadernos de Poesía, no. 23, 1963.

Lewis, Marvin A. *Afro-Hispanic Poetry, 1940–1980: From Slavery to Negritud" in South American Verse.* Columbia: Univ. of Missouri Press, 1983.

Locke, Alain, ed. *The New Negro.* 1925; rpt. New York: Atheneum, 1977.

Luis, William. *Literary Bondage: Slavery in Cuban Narrative.* Austin: Univ. of Texas Press, 1990.

———, ed. *Voices from Under: Black Narrative in Latin America and the Caribbean.* Westport, Conn.: Greenwood Press, 1984.

MacCormack, Carol P., and Marilyn Strathern, eds. *Nature, Culture, and Gender.* Cambridge: Cambridge Univ. Press, 1980.

Madden, Richard R., ed. *Poems by a Slave in the Island of Cuba, Recently Liberated; Translated from the Spanish by R. R. Madden,*

M.D. with the History of the Early Life of the Negro Poet, Written by Himself . . . London: Thomas Ward and Co., 1840.

Magnarelli, Sharon. *The Lost Rib: Female Characters in the Spanish-American Novel.* Bucknell, Pa.: Bucknell Univ. Press, 1985.

Mansour, Mónica. *La poesía negrista.* Mexico: Ediciones Era,1973.

Mañach, Jorge. "La crisis de la alta cultura en Cuba." *Revista Bimestre Cubana* 20 (1925): 129–63.

Marrero, Leví, ed. *Los ingenios de Cuba.* Coral Gables, Fla.: La Moderna Poesía Inc./Colección CUBA, 1984.

Martí, José. *The America of José Martí: Selected Writings of José Martí.* Ed. and trans. Juan De Onís. New York: Minerva Press, 1954.

———. *Cuba.* Ed. Gonzalo de Quesada. Havana: Imprenta y Papelería de Rambla, Bouza, y Ca., 1919.

———. *Nuestra América.* Ed. Gonzalo de Quesada. Havana: Imprenta y Papelería de Rambla y Bouza, 1909.

Martínez-Alier, Verena. *Marriage, Class, and Colour in Nineteenth-Century Cuba: A Study of Racial Attitudes and Sexual Values in a Slave Society.* Ann Arbor: Univ. of Michigan Press, 1989.

Miller, Beth, ed. *Women in Hispanic Literature: Icon and Fallen Idols.* Berkeley: Univ. of California Press, 1983.

Mintz, Sidney W. *Caribbean Transformations.* Baltimore: Johns Hopkins Univ. Press, 1974.

———. *Sweetness and Power: The Place of Sugar in Modern History.* New York: Viking Penguin, 1986.

Michie, Helena. *The Flesh Made Word: Female Figures and Women's Bodies.* New York: Oxford Univ. Press, 1987.

Molloy, Sylvia. "From Serf to Self: The Autobiography of Juan Francisco Manzano." *MLN* 104 (1989): 393–417.

Morales, Jorge Luis, ed. *Poesía afroantillana y negrista (Puerto Rico, República Domínica, Cuba),* rev. ed. Río Piedras: Editorial Universitara, Universidad de Puerto Rico, 1981.

Morales y Morales, Vidal. *Iniciadores y primeros martires de la Revolución cubana.* Havana: Imprenta Avisador Comercial, 1901.

Mordecai, Pamela, and Betty Wilson, eds. *Her True-True Name: An Anthology of Women's Writing from the Caribbean.* Portsmouth: Heinemann Educational Books, 1990.

Morejón, Nancy, *Nación y mestizaje en Nicolás Guillén.* Havana: UNEAC, 1982.

Moreno Fraginals, Manuel. *El ingenio: Complejo económico social cubano del azúcar,* 3 vols. Havana: Editorial de Ciencias Sociales, 1978.

————, ed. *Africa en América Latina*. Mexico: Siglo Veintiuno y UN-ESCO, 1977.

————. ed. *Africa in Latin America: Essays on History, Culture, and Socialization*. New York and Paris: Holmes and Meier/UNESCO, 1984.

Morrison, Toni. *Playing in the Dark: Whiteness and the Literary Imagination*. Cambridge, Mass.: Harvard Univ. Press, 1992.

Morúa Delgado, Martín. "Las novelas del Sr. Villaverde" (1891), in *Obras completas*, vol. 5: *Impresiones literarias y otras paginas*, 17–51. Havana: Edición de la Comisión Nacional del Centenario de Martín Morúa Delgado, 1959.

————. *Sofía*. 1891; rpt. Havana: Instituto Cubano del Libro, 1972. Muguercia Muguercia, Alberto. "Teodora Ginés ¿mito o realidad histórica?" *Revista de la Biblioteca Nacional José Martí* 8 (September-December 1971): 53–85.

Mullen, Edward J., ed. *The Life and Poems of a Cuban Slave: Juan Francisco Monzano, 1797–1854*. Hamden, Conn.: Archon Books, 1981.

Netchinsky, Jill Ann. "Engendering a Cuban Literature: Nineteenth-Century Antislavery Narrative (Manzano, Suárez y Romero, Gómez de Avellandea, A. Zambrana)." Ph.D. dissertation, Yale Univ., 1985.

Newman, Karen. "And Wash the Ethiop White": Femininity and the Monstrous in *Othello*." In *Shakespeare Reproduced: The Text in History and Ideology*, ed. Jean E. Howard and Marion F. O'Connor, 143–61. New York: Methuen, 1987.

Noble, Enrique, ed. *Literatura afro-hispanoamericana: poesía y prosa de ficción*. Lexington, Mass.: Xerox Publishing, 1973.

Núñez Jiménez, Antonio. *Cuba en las marquillas cigarreras del siglo XIX*. Havana: Ediciones turísticas de Cuba, 1985.

————. ed. *Marquillas cigarreras cubanas*. Havana: Ediciones Tabapress, 1989.

Ortiz, Fernando. *La antigua fiesta afrocubana del "Día de Reyes."* 1920; rpt. Havana: Ministerio de Relaciones Exteriores Departamento de Asuntos culturales, 1960.

————. *Contrapunteo cubano del tabaco y el azúcar*. Havana: Jesús Montero, 1940.

————. *Cuban Counterpoint: Tobacco and Sugar*, trans. Harriet de Onís. New York: Vintage, 1970.

————. "Dos 'diablitos' de Landaluze." *Bohemia* 45, no. 44 (1 November 1953).

————. *Ensayos etnográficos*. Ed. Miguel Barnet and Angel Fernández. Havana: Editorial de Ciencias Sociales, 1984.

————. *Hampa afro-cubana: Los negros brujos (Apuntes para un estudio de etnología criminal)*. 1906; rpt. Miami: Edicional Universal, 1973.

————. "Más acerca de la poesía mulata: Escorzos para su estudio." *Revista Bimestre Cubana* 37 (1936): 23–39, 218–27, 439–43.

————. "La reforma pentitenciara en Cuba." *Revista Bimestre Cubana* 6 (1911): 440–58.

————. Review of *Black Folk* by W. E. B. Du Bois. *Revista Bimestre Cubana* 44 (1939): 318–20.

————. "Los últimos versos mulatos." *Revista Bimestre Cubana* 35 (1935): 321–36.

Ostendorf, Berndt. *Black Literature in White America*. Sussex,N.J.: The Harvester Press/Barnes and Noble, 1982.

Palés Matos, Luis. *Poesía completa y prosa selecta*. Ed. Margot Arce de Vásquez. Carácas: Bibliotéca Ayacucho, 1978.

————. *Tuntún de pasa y grifería: Poemas afroantillanos*. San Juan: Bibliotéca de Autores Puertorriqueños, 1937.

Paquette, Robert L. *Sugar Is Made with Blood: The Conspiracy of La Escalera and the Conflict between Empires over Slavery in Cuba*. Middletown, Conn.: Wesleyan Univ. Press, 1988.

Paz, Octavio. *The Labyrinth of Solitude: Life and Thought in Mexico*. Trans. Lysander Kemp. 1959; rpt. New York: Grove Press, 1978.

Pedrozo, Regino. *Nosotros*. Havana: Editorial Tropico, 1933.

Percival, MacIver. *The Fan Book*. New York: Frederick A. Stokes Co., 1921.

Pereda Valdes, Ildefonso. *La guitarra de los negros*. Montevideo: Ricordi 1926. Reviewed in *Revista Bimestre Cubana* 24, no. 5 (1929): 795.

————. *Lo negro y lo mulato en la poesía cubana*. Montevideo: Ediciones Ciudadela, 1970.

————. *Raza negra*. Montevideo: n.p., 1929.

————, ed. *Antología de la poesía negra americana*. Santiago de Chile: Ediciones Ercilla, 1936.

Pereira, Joseph R. "The Black Presence in Cuban Theatre." *Afro-Hispanic Review* 2 (1983): 13–18.

Perera, Hilda. *Idapo: El sincretismo en los cuentos negros de Lydia Cabrera*. Miami: Ediciones Universal, 1971.

Pérez, Louis A., Jr. *Cuba under the Platt Amendment, 1902–1934*. Pittsburgh, Pa.: Univ. of Pittsburgh Press, 1986.

Pérez Firmat, Gustavo. *The Cuban Condition: Translation and Identity in Modern Cuba*. Cambridge: Cambridge University Press, 1990.

————, ed. *Do the Americas Have a Common Literature?* Durham, N.C.: Duke Univ. Press, 1990.

Phaf, Ineke. "Caribbean Imagination and Nation Building in Antillean and Surinamese Literature." *Callaloo* 11 (1988): 148–72.

Plácido. *See* De la Concepción Valdés, Gabriel

Portell Vilá, Herminio. "Conflictos de población y de razas en los Estados Unidos: Resultantes sociales y problemas del futuro." *Revista Bimestre Cubana* 42 (1938): 5–23.

———. "La población negra norteamericana como factor de la vida nacional." *Revista Bimestre Cubana* 40 (1937): 236–55.

Portuondo, Aleyda T. *Vigencia política y literaria de Martín Morúa Delgado (un ensayo sobre el gran negro cubano).* Miami: Ediciones Universal, 1978.

Portuondo, José Antonio. "Miseria y soledad de Plácido, el mulato." In *Capítulos de literatura cubana,* 191–203. Havana: Editorial Letras Cubanas, 1981.

Pryor Rice, Argyll. *Emilio Ballagas: Poeta y poesía.* Mexico, Ediciones de Andrés, 1967.

Ramchand, Kenneth. "West Indian Literary History: Literariness, Orality, and Periodization." *Callaloo* 11 (1988): 95–110.

Rampersad, Arnold. *The Life of Langston Hughes,* vol. 1, *I, Too, Sing America.* New York: Oxford Univ. Press, 1986.

Ribera Chevremont, Evaristo. *Antología poética, 1924–1950.* Río Piedras: Universidad de Puerto Rico, 1957.

Rich, Adrienne. "Disloyal to Civilization: Feminism, Racism, Gynephobia." In her *On Lies, Secrets, and Silence: Selected Prose, 1966–1978,* 275–310. New York: W. W. Norton, 1979. 275–310.

Rodríguez, Ilena. "Romanticismo literario y liberalismo reformista: El grupo de Domingo Del Monte." *Caribbean Studies* 20 (1980): 35–56.

Rodríguez Monegal, Emir. "The Metamorphoses of Caliban." *Diacritics* 7 (1977): 78–83.

Rosaldo, Michelle Zimbalist, and Louise Lamphere, eds. *Woman, Culture, and Society.* Stanford, Calif.: Stanford Univ. Press, 1974.

Ruiz del Vizo, Hortensia, ed. *Black Poetry of the Americas,* 2 vols. Miami: Ediciones Universal, 1972.

———, ed. *Poesía negra del Caribe y otra areas.* Miami: Ediciones Universal, 1972.

Saco, José Antonio. *Historia de la esclavitud de la raza africana en el Nuevo Mundo,* 4 vols. 1879; rpt. Havana: Colección de Libros Cubanos, 1938.

Said, Edward. *Orientalism.* New York: Random House, 1979.

Salazar, Adolfo. "El movimiento africanista en la música de arte cubana." *Estudios Afrocubanos* 2, no. 1 (1938): 3–18

Saldívar, José David. *The Dialectics of Our America: Genealogy, Cultural Critique, and Literary History*. Durham, N.C.: Duke Univ. Press, 1991.

Salper, Roberta L. "Gender and Ideology in Caribbean Narratives." *Critical Studies* 3 (1991): 167–87.

Sánchez, Marta E. "Caliban: The New Latin American Protagonist of *The Tempest*." *Diacritics* 6 (1976): 54–61.

Sánchez, Reinaldo, and José A. Madrigal, eds. *Homenaje a Lydia Cabrera*. Barcelona: Ediciones Universal, 1977.

Sánchez de Fuentes, Eduardo. *Influencia de los ritmos africanos en nuestro cancionero (Conferencia)*. Havana: Imprenta El Siglo XX, 1927.

Sanz y Diaz, José, ed. *Lira negra: Selecciones afroamericanas y españolas*. 1945; rpt. Madrid: Aguilar, 1962.

Schorr, Naomi. *Reading in Detail: Aesthetics and the Feminine*. New York and London: Routledge, 1989.

Schulman, Ivan, ed. *Autobiografía de un esclavo: Introducción, notas, y actualización del texto*. Madrid: Guadarrama, 1975.

Sedgwick, Eve Kosofsky. *Between Men: English Literature and Male Homosocial Desire*. New York: Columbia Univ. Press, 1985.

Smart, Ian Isidore. *Central American Writers of West Indian Origin: A New Hispanic Literature*. Washington, D.C.: Three Continents Press, 1984.

———. *Nicolás Guillén: The Caribbean's Popular Poet*. Columbia: Univ. of Missouri Press, 1990.

Smith, Paul Julian. *The Body Hispanic: Gender and Sexuality in Spanish and Spanish American Literature*. Oxford: Clarendon Press, 1989.

Sollors, Werner. "'Never Was Born': The Mulatto, an American Tragedy?" *Massachusetts Review* 27 (1986): 293–316.

Sommer, Doris. *Foundational Fictions: The National Romances of Latin America*. Berkeley: Univ. of California Press, 1991.

Spillers, Hortense J. "Mama's Baby, Papa's Maybe: An American Grammar Book." *Diacritics* 17 (1987): 65–81.

———. "Notes on an Alternative Model—Neither/Nor." In *The Difference Within: Feminism and Critical Theory*, ed. Elizabeth Meese and Alice Parker, 165–87. Amsterdam: John Benjamins, 1988.

Stimson, Frederick S. *Cuba's Romantic Poet: The Story of Plácido*. Chapel Hill: Univ. of North Carolina Press, 1964.

———, and Humberto E. Robles, eds. *Los poemas más representativos de Plácido*. Chapel Hill, N.C.: Estudios de Hispanófila, 1976.

Suleiman, Susan Rubin, ed. *The Female Body in Western Culture: Contemporary Perspectives.* Cambridge, Mass.: Harvard University Press, 1985.

Toll, Robert C. *Blacking Up: The Minstrel Show in Nineteenth-Century America.* New York: Oxford Univ. Press, 1974.

Urfé, Odilio. "Factores que integran la música cubana." *Islas* 2 (September-December 1959): 7–21

Uzanne, Octavio. *The Fan.* London: J. C. Nimmo and Bain, 1884.

Valdés Cruz, Rosa E., ed. *La poesía negroide en América.* New York: Las Américas, 1970.

Venture Young, Ann. "Black Women in Hispanic American Poetry: Glorification, Deification, and Humanization." *Afro-Hispanic Review* 1 (1982): 23–28.

———. *The Image of Black Women in Twentieth Century South American Poetry.* Washington, D.C.: Three Continents Press, 1987.

Villaverde, Cirilo. "Cecilia Valdés." *La Siempreviva* 2 (1839): 75–87, 242–54.

———. *Cecilia Valdés, o la loma del Angel: Novela de costumbres cubanas.* 1882; rpt. Havana: Consejo Nacional de Cultura, 1964.

———. *Cecilia Valdés, or Angel's Hill: A Novel of Cuban Customs by Cirilo Villaverde.* Trans. Sydney Gest. New York: Vantage Press, 1962.

Virgillo, Carmelo, and Naomi Linstrom, eds. *Woman as Myth and Metaphor in Latin American Literature.* Columbus: Univ. of Ohio Press, 1985.

Vizcarrondo, Fortunato. *Dinga y Mandinga (poemas).* 1942; rpt. San Juan: Instituto de Cultura Puertorriqueña, 1982.

Wagner, Roy. *The Invention of Culture,* rev. ed. Chicago: Univ. of Chicago Press, 1981.

Warner, Michael. "Homo-Narcissism; or, Heterosexuality." In *Engendering Men: The Question of Male Feminist Criticism,* ed. Joseph A. Boon and Michael Cadden, 190–206. New York: Routledge, 1990.

Wiegman, Robyn. "Economies of the Body: Gendered Sites in *Robinson Crusoe* and *Roxanna.*" *Criticism* 31 (1989): 33–51.

Williams, Claudette May. "Images of Black and Mulatto Women in Spanish Caribbean Poetry: Discourse and Ideology." Ph.D. dissertation, Stanford Univ., 1986.

Williamson, Joel. *The Crucible of Race: Black-White Relations in the American South since Emancipation.* New York: Oxford Univ. Press, 1984.

Zaldívar, Gladys B., and Rosa Martínez de Cabrera, eds. *Homenaje a Gertrudis Gómez de Avellaneda: Memorias del simposio en el centenario de su muerte.* Miami: Ediciones Universal, 1981.

Zambrana, Antonio. *El negro Francisco.* 1875; Havana: P. Fernández y Cía, 1953.

Index

New World Studies

New World Studies publishes interdisciplinary research that seeks to redefine the cultural map of the Americas and to propose particularly stimulating points of departure for an emerging field. Encompassing the Caribbean as well as continental North, Central, and South America, the series books examine cultural processes within the hemisphere, taking into account the economic, demographic, and historical phenomena that shape them. Given the increasing diversity and richness of the linguistic and cultural traditions in the Americas, the need for research that privileges neither the English-speaking United States nor Spanish-speaking Latin America has never been greater. The series is designed to bring the best of this new research into an identifiable forum and to channel its results to the rapidly evolving audience for cultural studies.

SERIES EDITOR: A. James Arnold (University of Virginia).
ASSOCIATE EDITORS: J. Michael Dash (University of the West Indies, Mona), David T. Haberly (University of Virginia), and Roberto Márquez (Mt. Holyoke College). Consulting Editors: Antonio Benítez-Rojo (Amherst College), Joan Dayan (University of Arizona), Dell H. Hymes (University of Virginia), Vera M. Kutzinski (Yale University), Candace Slater (University of California, Berkeley), and Iris Zavala (University of Utrecht).